TABLE OF CONTENTS

THE FUTURE OF WAR

NIJHOFF LAW SPECIALS

VOLUME 46

The titles published in this series are listed at the end of this volume.

Foundation of War Studies

The Future of War

Edited by
Gwyn Prins & Hylke Tromp

KLUWER LAW INTERNATIONAL
THE HAGUE / BOSTON / LONDON

A C.I.P. Catalogue record for this book is available from the Library of Congress.

ISBN 90-411-1399-1 ✓

Published by Kluwer Law International,
P.O. Box 85889, 2508 CN The Hague, The Netherlands.

Sold and distributed in North, Central and South America
by Kluwer Law International,
675 Massachusetts Avenue, Cambridge, MA 02139, U.S.A.

In all other countries, sold and distributed
by Kluwer Law International,
P.O. Box 85889, 2508 CN The Hague, The Netherlands.

Layout and camera-ready copy:
Anne-Marie Krens, Tekstbeeld – Oegstgeest – The Netherlands

Printed on acid-free paper

Printed in the Netherlands.

LIST OF CONTRIBUTORS

MOHAMMED AYOOB is University Distinguished Professor of International Relations, Michigan State University. A specialist on conflict and security in the Third World, his publications include conceptual essays as well as case studies covering South Asia, South-east Asia, the Gulf and the Middle East. A recipient of grants and fellowships from the Ford, Rockefeller, and MacArthur Foundations, the Institute for South-east Asian Studies, Singapore, and the East-West Center, Hawaii, he has authored and co-authored many books and approximately 70 research papers. His latest book is *The Third World Security Predicament: State Making, Regional Conflict, and the International System* (1995).

CHRISTOPH BERTRAM has been since 1998 the Director of the Foundation 'Wissenschaft & Politik', Ebenhausen, Germany, a research center on international affairs which advises the German government and parliament. Between 1974 and 1982 he served as the Director of the International Institute for Strategic Studies in London. In 1982 he became Senior Editor of *Die Zeit* in Hamburg. His publications include *Europe in the Balance – Securing the Peace that won in the Cold War* (1995).

CARL BILDT served as Prime Minister of Sweden from 1991 until late 1994, and has been a member of parliament since 1979. In 1995, he was appointed as the European Union's Special Representative to Former Yugoslavia and Co-Chairman of the International Conference on Former Yugoslavia. He also served as Co-Chairman of the Dayton peace talks in November 1995. He is the author of *Peace Journey* (1997).

JUTTA BIRMELE received her law degree from the Free University of Berlin, took an MA in German literature at California State University, San Francisco, and a PHD in history at The Claremont Graduate University. She is a Professor of German Studies at California State University, Long Beach.

MARTIN VAN CREVELD is Professor of History at the Hebrew University of Jerusalem and is a well-known expert on military history and strategy. He is the author of *Supplying War* (1977), *Command in War* (1985), *Technology and War* (1989) and *The Transformation of War* (1991).

FRANCIS MADING DENG is Director of the Harvard Negotiation Project, Williston Professor of Law *Emeritus* at the Harvard Law School and founder and Senior Advisor to the non-profit Conflict Management Group. He has served as Human Rights Officer in the United Nations Secretariat and as the Sudan's Ambassador to Canada, the Scandinavian countries and the United States. As a scholar, he was attached to organizations such as the Woodrow Wilson International Center in Washington, DC, to the US Institute for Peace and to the Brookings Institution. His recent publications include *Sovereignty as Responsibility: Conflict Management in Africa* (1996) *and African Reckoning: A Quest for Good Governace* (co-authored with Terrence Lyons, 1998).

PETER VAN DEN DUNGEN has been Lecturer in Peace Studies at the University of Bradford since 1976 and has published widely in the area of peace history and peace research, amongst others on *The Making of Peace: Jean de Bloch and the First Hague Peace Conference* (1983).

LAWRENCE FREEDMAN has been Professor of War Studies at King's College, London since 1982. His publications include *The Evolution of Nuclear Strategy* (1989), *Signals of War* (with Virginia Gamba-Stonehouse, 1991), *Britain and the Falklands War* (with Michael Clarke, 1991) and *The Gulf Conflict 1990-91* (with Efraim Karsh, 1993).

PIERRE HASSNER is Senior Research Associate at the Centre d'Etudes et de Recherches Internationales (CERI) in Paris and Visiting Professor at Johns Hopkins University European Center, Bologna, and the Committee on Social Thought, Chicago University. He is author most recently of *Violence and Peace* (1997).

KLAUS-PETER KLAIBER studied law, economics and history in Tübingen, Mainz and Geneva before he joined the German Foreign Service. He is now the NATO Assistant Secretary-General for Political Affairs.

JOHN KEEGAN has been the Defence Editor of the London *Daily Telegraph* since 1986, and gave the Reith Lectures on 'War in Our World' for the BBC in 1998. From 1960 to 1986 he was the Senior Lecturer in Military History at the Royal Military Academy Sandhurst. He has been a Fellow of Princeton University and Delmas Distinguished Professor of History at Vassar. He is the author of many books on military history including *The Face of Battle* (1976), *The History of Warfare* (1993) and *The First World War* (1998).

EDWARD LUTTWAK is Senior Fellow at the Center for Strategic and International Studies in Washington DC. He has served as consultant to the US National Security Council, the White House Chief of Staff, the State Department, the Department of Defense, and several foreign governments. He is the author of *Coup d'Etat* (1967), *Strategy: The Logic of War and Peace* (1985), and *On the Meaning of Victory* (1986), amongst other books.

GWYN PRINS was for 20 years a Fellow and Director of Studies in History at Emmanuel College, Cambridge. He was Founder and Director of the Global Security Programme at the University of Cambridge from 1989. He is now Senior Research Fellow at the Royal Institute of International Affairs (Chatham House, London), the first Visiting Senior Fellow at the Defence Evaluation and Research Agency (Farnborough, UK), and Senior Fellow in the Office of the Special Advisor to the Secretary-General of NATO (Brussels).

MICHAEL ROSE served in the Middle and Far East, Northern Ireland, the Falkland Islands and Bosnia. Since leaving the British army, he has lectured extensively on peacekeeping and leadership. He is the author of *Fighting for Peace* (1998).

HYLKE TROMP is Professor of International Security and Director of the Foundation for War Studies at the University of Groningen, The Netherlands.

ANDRZEJ WERNER taught political science at the University of Warsaw before working at the Ministry of Foreign Trade from 1960-1977. In 1981 he joined the International Peace Movement and became an independent peace researcher.

Among his publications are *Jan Bloch (1836-1902): Forgotten Pacifist and Entrepreneur* (1986) and *Jan Bloch – Railroad King and Pacifist* (1986).

HIS ROYAL HIGHNESS WILLEM-ALEXANDER, PRINCE OF THE NETHERLANDS, PRINCE OF ORANGE-NASSAU, studied history at Leiden University and graduated in 1993. The Prince of Orange performed his military service in the Royal Netherlands Navy from August 1985 to January 1987. He holds officer's rank in the three armed services. The Prince is particulary interested in water management, and attends international conferences and symposia on this subject. He is an honorary member of the World Commission on Water for the 21st Century and patron of the Global Water Partnership.

FOREWORD

by

PETER KOOIJMANS

On the eve of the 20th century a Polish banker and industrialist, Jan Bloch, wrote a voluminous treatise, entitled the *Future of War,* in which he contended that war, carried on under modern conditions, had become impossible or, rather, self-destructive.

Also on the eve of the 20th century an inter-governmental conference, dedicated to the problems of the avoidance of war and the future of peace, took place in The Hague. This conference had been convened on the initiative of the Czar of All Russians, whose advisor Jan Bloch was. The future of peace turned out to be less certain than that of war and the events of the first half of the 20th century put Bloch in the right.

On the eve of the 21st century, this 1899 Peace Conference was commemorated in the Peace Palace in The Hague. At the same time, armed activities were carried on under the most modern conditions by an alliance of 19 sovereign states against the territory of a relatively small state in south-east Europe. *Plus ça change, plus c'est la même chose?* Certainly not, for the connotations of the terms 'war' and 'peace' have radically changed in the course of the last 100 years.

At the end of the 19th century, 'war' stood for 'a state of belligerency between two or more states', which usually was followed by the conclusion of a peace-treaty, leading to an end of hostilities and a disengagement of military forces. Such wars and such peace agreements have largely, though not completely, disappeared in the second half of the 20th century.

The wars of the end of the 20th century are mostly armed conflicts finding their origin in situations *within* a state. They are no longer fought by armies on battlefields but, often by irregular militias, in the streets of cities and the fields around villages and hamlets. As a consequence, the number of civilian war casualties has risen from 15 per cent at the beginning of the century to 90 percent at its end.

With the meaning of the term 'war' the meaning of the term 'peace' has changed. As the High Commissioner for Refugees, Ms Sadako Ogata, once said 'Wars that change in character must necessarily lead to peace of a different kind'. The peace treaties which terminated the inter-state wars of the past initiated a period of absence of violence and force, even when they sometimes already contained the seeds of a new war. Modern peace agreements, like the Dayton Agreement, important though they may be, are only elements in an on-going struggle. Peace no longer is concluded or restored. After an internal war it has to be built; peace-building has become an important term in UN-jargon.

What does peace mean in the war-torn country of Bosnia, in the war-stricken areas of Sierra Leone, in the looted and pillaged cities and villages of Kosovo, even if a 'peace' agreement has been hammered out?

On the eve of the 21st century, it seemed useful to organize a conference in order to take stock of the developments and trends of the last century and to cast a cautious glance at what we may expect in the next century. The Foundation for War Studies took the initiative to organize such a conference and chose as venue St Petersburg, the city where Bloch published his work and Czar Nicholas issued his Imperial Rescript leading to The Hague Peace Conference. Were the lessons of 1899 learned and what are the lessons of 1999? The reader may find some – often tentative – answers in the present book.

PART I

INTRODUCTION

1

EDITORS' INTRODUCTION

Gwyn Prins & Hylke Tromp

The 20th century ended as it began, besieged by nagging questions and beset by the threat of violence. Few living 100 years ago foresaw so systematically and with such precision the likely nature of the next great war as did Jan Bloch, or anticipated its unavoidability, despite all reason. The six volumes of his *Future of War* documented his belief that 'the dimensions of modern armaments and the organisation of society have rendered its prosecution an economic impossibility.' Reason, he believed, would show why war had now acquired a nature that would reliably frustrate any political ambitions for which war might be undertaken. But as his conversation with the journalist William Stead (which follows this Introduction) reveals, Bloch did not count blindly upon the power of rational argument to prevail. 'If any attempt were made to demonstrate the inaccuracy of my assertions by putting the matter to a test on a great scale', he continued, 'we should find the inevitable result in a catastrophe which would destroy all existing political organisations.' And so it was, and largely did.

Bloch explained to Stead that he believed that, terrible though its destructiveness would be, the future war would be resolved not on the battlefield, but through the economic and social disintegration of the societies making war. He anticipated the protracted bloodletting of positional trench warfare. It was inexorably prescribed, in Bloch's opinion, by the revolutionary improvement in all forms of guns and artillery which he had minutely studied and which conferred decisive advantage to the defence. But the unprecedented and unrelieved killing, in which he guessed that the lingering wounded would envy the instantly dead, would not end the war. Bloch believed that war like this would atomise civil society and thus prepare the way for revolution. He was right in both the short and the long terms. In the case of the Russian Empire, within which Poland was at that time included, he was right in the short term. He was right, too, for the Ottoman and Austro-Hungarian empires, which also imploded under the shock of the Great War. The French and British empires sustained suf-

3

G. Prins and H. Tromp (eds.), The Future of War, 3-17.
© 2000 *Kluwer Law International. Printed in the Netherlands.*

ficiently deep and pervasive social and economic damage that, by mid-century, the generals of the Great War had, pre-emptively, done for them too. And, of course, the manner in which Wilhelmine Germany was smashed, before and at Versailles, provided ample rubble with which to lay a pathway to Poland, *via* Czechoslovakia and the Rhineland. It was a pathway along which, once recovered in body but endlessly brooding in mind, a gassed runner from the trenches near Croonart's Wood in the Ypres Salient, Corporal Schickelgrüber, could march to power as leader of a Third Reich.

Strangely, by century's end, the shadows cast over its beginning by the Great War of 1914-18 have not fled with the passage of time. If anything, they have darkened. As the experience of the Great War slips out of living human memory, great insistent questions about it loom the moreso. How could it have been that Bloch was so grimly correct in both parts of the prediction quoted above: that it might be as it was and that it would be nevertheless? What spirit, what vision was it that carried so many millions of people voluntarily into the fratricidal European civil war, which has occupied the continent for almost half the time since Bloch made his predictions? How confident may we be that we have now found that reliable preventative of and substitute for war, which statesmen sought but which eluded them in The Hague Conference of 1899, convened by Tsar Nicholas and Queen Wilhelmina of The Netherlands very largely under the influence of Bloch's analysis (as Dr van den Dungen demonstrates)? The Imperial Rescript of 1898, also reproduced in this introductory section, is as lucid a political distillation of Bloch's insight as one might hope to see; astonishingly so; and the great peace conferences did take place; and yet still the war came.

Questions about the war that came, and the value of reassessing the role of Jan Bloch in his own time, are not only of antiquarian interest. At the end of the 20th century, collectively, anxiously we peer into the coming millennium unsure whether to believe that the cohering, wealth-creating, sovereignty-surpassing, life-enhancing qualities of what is confusingly called the 'post-modern' world outweigh the many disintegrating and disintegrative forces which equally can be foreseen. In its sense of uncertainty, the cultural tone of the 20th *fin de siècle* resonates with that of the 19th. Therefore, in the final contribution to this introductory section, His Royal Highness, Prince Willem-Alexander, the Prince of Orange, great-grandson of the Queen who, with Tsar Nicholas, convened The Hague Peace Conference 100 years ago, captures the implication of these reverberations, and raises key questions which transpose his mission and his questions and locate Jan Bloch in the late 20th century's context.

Unlike the other chapters of this book, the Prince's speech is reproduced as he gave it in the Theatre of The Hermitage in St Petersburg. It was on the occasion of a conference, conceived by Hylke Tromp, and convened in February 1999 to grip a double purpose. The first, the Prince explains, is that of assessing Jan Bloch's thought and contributions in the context of his own times – the Great War which he predicted, which reason said should therefore have been prevented, which came nonetheless and which produced the social consequences that he also foresaw. The second places Jan Bloch in the context of our time: looking back across the experience of war in the 20th century, and looking forward with that knowledge, but now ten years after the 1989 revolutions, revolutions which picked up and readdressed, and in some parts resolved much of the unfinished business left in the square outside the Winter Palace at St Petersburg, in the Hall of Mirrors at Versailles and, later, in the flames of the Reichstag.

The conference was convened in the belief that there is profit to be drawn at the symbolic moment of centenary, and this one, coinciding as it does with so many endings and beginnings in world politics, more than most. Most, but not all of the chapters in this book, had their origins in papers delivered in St Petersburg. As editors, we have sought to structure the collection as faithfully as we could around the three central pivots of consideration which emerged in St Petersburg, both in the discussions that followed papers delivered in the glowing adamantine splendour of the Great Hall of the Marble Palace, as well as in the associated seminar discussions.

The first of the tasks indicated by the Prince of Orange is undertaken in Section I. Bloch's work deserves to be better known in its centenary year. So, too, the range of his influence among contemporaries internationally, and the detailed historical case which shows just how much The Hague Peace Conferences owed to him. This last point is documented conclusively in his chapter by Dr van den Dungen.

Few scholars during this century have had such an extensive opportunity to shape and influence an important diplomatic process. Who was the man who undertook this work and who achieved this end? Dr Werner's chapter provides a brief biography of Bloch, which demonstrates how his earlier work as an engineer, a railway entrepreneur and a banker, as well as his sensitivities as a Pole and a Jew within the Russian Empire, all converged to serve in his great, self-chosen and self-financed research project. It was a less public act of philanthropy than those of John D. Rockefeller and Andrew Carnegie, but far more personally demanding on the mind, emotions and energies of the donor than anything that might occur at one remove. Dr Birmele's chapter completes this first Section by documenting Bloch's influence among the small but articulate community of German intellectuals opposed to the self-conscious German national drive towards war. It is a drive which some have queried recently, but the evidence for it is embodied in the work of Fritz Fischer, first published in 1961 in *Griff nach der Weltmacht* and further elaborated by his students. The Fischer Thesis has not been disproved in any fundamental respect in the 40 years since it was published.[1]

Bloch's conversation with Stead reveals how an acute awareness of transformation was central to his thinking and reasoning. As an engineer, he began with transformations derived from practical facts. For example, a reduction in the calibre of weapons associated with improved propellents and finer engineering tolerances, gave longer flat trajectory range. That in turn improved the accuracy and lethality of fire. It also increased the number of rounds that an individual soldier could carry, hence influencing his rate of fire and his amount of fire. This form of analysis and deduction support the case for seeing Bloch as one of the first exponents of Operational Analysis. However, he was more than that.

Bloch proceeded on, through consideration of other engineering transformations (like the introduction of smokeless powder, better rangefinding and faster gunlaying computation) to transformation in the leading sectors of late 19th

---

1   The most noticed recent example of counterfactual revisionism is to be found in N. Ferguson, *The Pity of War* (1999). In a nutshell, he argues there that if only the British had kept off the continent, Hitler could have gone on painting poorish watercolours, Tsar Nicholas could have grown old with his family, and Europe could have become the EU a generation earlier. That (not Wilfred Owen's pity) was the pity of the war. In all the flurry of discussion that this arresting iconoclasm has engendered, the case for not following Ferguson, this modern Don Quixote, in an onslaught on windmills (his image) has been nowhere better or more kindly put than by P. Kennedy, 'In the shadow of the Great War', XLVI *New York Review of Books*, no. 13, 12 August 1999, pp. 36-9. Kennedy muses sensibly that the problem with counterfactual history is that it is a diverting game for dons at play, which makes it difficult to know if they really mean it to be taken seriously.

century industry and the likely effect of economic transformation on social cohesion and the political and institutional expression of civil society. These last two concerns have a powerful contemporary ring. For both these reasons, as editors, we have sought to follow Bloch precisely. The structure of the book emphasises the centrality of the phenomenon of transformation in each of the second and third sections, because it is, as well, the common concern of all the authors.

Section II turns about to face the future and to examine the second of the tasks signalled by the Prince of Orange. In common with thoughtful contemporaries (including, most systematically, those whom he most detested among the socialist and communist opponents of the Russian imperial regime), Bloch distinguished in his mind between first and second order issues: between underlying, driving trends in society and economy and their specific emanations in the technology and diplomacy of war. What made war impossible on any rational calculation was precisely the vulnerability of economic and social fabric to its hugely lengthened and strengthened claws, to rip them asunder. Yet, as Bloch also, sadly, realised, there were things within that social and economic fabric, which tended towards the great experiment about his hypotheses, which he so feared and the outcome of which he also, so accurately, predicted. Ours is now an analogous moment. Therefore, in the second section, the four authors focus upon transformation in the first order questions of economy and society.

Carl Bildt opens consideration of transformation in the international order by recollecting that grim pattern, which Bloch feared and foresaw, whereby 'great wars produce great efforts to make peace' (in Bildt's phrase). 'When will they ever learn?', plaintively enquired Marlene Dietrich in the refrain to one of the century's most celebrated anti-war songs. In Carl Bildt's opinion, as also but more enthusiastically Christoph Bertram's, it looks as if the punishing lessons of the First and Second World Wars have been finally learned, and that major war of the sort that broke out in 1914 may indeed have been rendered obsolete. This is not to say that war has been abolished. Bloch observed to Stead that his focus was not upon 'such frontier brawls, or punitive operations such as you in England, for instance, are perpetually engaging in on the frontiers of your extended empire ...'. In other words, war goes on, in Bildt's terms, in Kosovo, and such-like places. These conflicts, Bildt suspects, may increase in frequency in 'the wide arch of instability stretching from Agadir on the Atlantic Ocean to Astrakan on the Caspian Sea'; and, given his long and distinguished experience in ameliorating such conflicts, Carl Bildt is better placed than most to take such a view.

Why this distinction between zones of war and peace? In common with Bertram, he believes that a protective shield of international institution has now been put in place. While less confident about the aspect built into the United Nations, he shares Bertram's enthusiasm for the war protecting qualities of European union. Bildt's enthusiasm is narrower than Bertram's: he focuses more upon the more traditionally military and diplomatic aspects of the European project. Bertram's scope is more expansive. He offers an enthusiastic and optimistic view of how Europe has become a zone of peace. He shares with the British diplomat, Robert Cooper,[2] the belief that Europe is now overwhelmingly a territory of 'post-modern' states. Such states, Cooper suggests and Bertram agrees, no longer live within the old balance of power state system; and war between them is simply no longer conceivable. What has happened, in short, Christoph Bertram suggests, is that 200 years after its original articulation, Immanuel Kant's hopes for a system that provides perpetual peace is being realised, and realised not through the maintenance of the balance of terror, where, in Winston Churchill's famous phrase (quoted in the later chapter by Professor Martin van Creveld who does espouse this view) 'Safety is the sturdy child of terror': Bertram sees this safety in the post-modern world growing from positive roots, from 'the centrality of common, resilient institutions for the maintenance of peace', of which the European Union is the world's supreme example, in his view.

The chapters by Bildt and Bertram thus introduce two themes, which run through the rest of this collection. On one, there is general agreement; on the other, there is not. The first is the general assent, which is to be found among the authors regardless of their interpretative viewpoints, that ours is a world now riven in quite fundamental ways and that one of those ways is between zones where war lives on and where it is now, to all intents and purposes, dead. Once again, the *limetani* stand guard: the border guards of the later Roman Empire seem to have returned, and are to be seen where once they stood centuries ago: at the Danube bend; along the plains of the northern Marches; facing Constantinople. The places, the images which they conjure up, are redolent of memories of empire: and this is a strange thing, part of the circumstance

---

2   R. Cooper, *The Post-Modern State and the World Order* (London, Demos, 1996).

which keeps Bloch's War so squarely before our eyes. For the very empires
that were torn down and shattered by the forces of the Great War which opened
the European civil war, seem now to glow spectrally across the end-of-century
map of Europe. The borderlands where the Austro-Hungarian meets the Ottoman
Empire; those that were in such vicious and continuous contention between
the continental superpowers of Russia (in Soviet guise, temporarily) and
Germany throughout the European civil war are again before our eyes. It is
a truism – but nonetheless miserably true – that the century opened with western
Europeans struggling to identify and pronounce Bosnia-Herzegovina and has
ended in just the same way. On this new post-imperial empire the authors seem
to be agreed. On what has maintained peace within its walls fundamental disagreement remains. Those disagreements form a principal focus of Section III(a)
below, and rotate around the argument most explicitly of Martin van Creveld
and, tangentially, of Edward Luttwak.

Section II has as its focus the issue of sovereignty and its consequences. All
four of the authors perceive sovereignty as being both powerful and deeply
ambivalent in the manner in which it is exercised and applied, depending upon
context. Within the new Holy Roman Empire, the transcendence of sovereignty
gives force to Christoph Bertram's hopes. Gazing outside, at Africa, Professor
Francis Deng observes 'dysfunctional systems of statehood and governance'.
Yet, his subtle and humane argument is not one which seeks simply to externalise blame. Rather, he would have us see the degree to which internalised
cultural damage, through the inappropriate slamming down upon the continent
of the grid iron of the colonial states, has marked and importantly disabled
Africans, in ways in which that injury is now become organic. His call is, therefore, for the robust installation within the existing African state structure, with
all of its admitted inadequacies and contortions, of common principles of human
right and cultural liberalism. Bertram asks whether the European experience
can be exported elsewhere, and Francis Deng answers that 'ultimately what
Africa needs is a comprehensive policy framework, stipulating principles of
state responsibility and accountability, with enforcement mechanisms, as a basis
for addressing realistically the continent's problems at the national and regional
levels and in partnership with the international community'.

Professor Mohammed Ayoob is struck by the brutal irony within the dualism
of sovereignty's power. Sovereignty made the late 19th century world, but 'this
process of state making has also created its obverse phenomenon, namely, state
breaking'. His essay ensures that this dialectic is firmly before our eyes, and

that it serves to temper any excessive enthusiasm for the belief that Europe's experience of war in the 20th century has created an institutional prophylactic, which can, with any ease, be readily exported. Cultural differences, both Deng and Ayoob point out, are not only present, but essential to human fulfilment: for without a sense of identity and position, any of us feels adrift, and all the more so in those circumstances beyond the zone of the 'post-modern' states (in Robert Cooper's term) where the organic and autonomous protections of the Rights of Man are fragile or controversial. Furthermore, Ayoob reminds us, amid all the enthusiasm for the notion that war *among* the post-modern states has become impossible at last, one should not forget that 'this framework does not apply to relations between the industrialised world and the third world'. He ends this section on a chilling note, when he observes that the very disproportion in military competence between the technologically sophisticated (pre-eminently the United States), who benefit from the so-called 'revolution in military affairs', and the less sophisticated, but nonetheless technologically competent, modern states of the South, leads to a situation where 'the attraction of weapons of mass destruction however rudimentary in character can be expected to grow in a number of capitals in the Third World'. War is a hydra-headed creature and Ayoob warns us against the complacent assumption that all its most deadly potentials have been neutralised. He doubts it.

Jan Bloch's industrious researches and his political influence, which helped so powerfully to promote The Hague Peace Conference of 1899, were predicated upon the premise that war had become impossible in any rational sense. Yet war came, and when it came it was not, as it seemed to many at the time, a war to end all wars. The Great War may have seemed that way, and, as Carl Bildt observed in his chapter, the shock which it administered jolted the international body politic into renewed efforts to create a non-violent institution for the resolution of conflict (in this case the League of Nations). The Great War – the war so terrible that it might reasonably be hoped in its horror to end all wars – turned out to be the first phase (the first hot phase) of a European civil war, which in hot and cold form gripped the continent for much of the century. So, with the benefit of a further 100 years hindsight – if benefit that be – are we closer to being able to say what sort of war the Great War was and where it stands in the longer history of war? That, at least, is prerequisite in providing a benchmark against which can be made judgments about what we may expect of warfare in the next century.

The first three chapters of Section III offer three contrasting views of this large question at the largest scale. John Keegan accepts the challenge to place Bloch's war in context and to predict the future dynamic of warfare as we and our children may expect to experience it. Bloch's war – the Great War – was, in Keegan's opinion, the beginning of a monumental and fratricidal parenthesis. Whereas war in its earliest forms had been over the control of resources, 'a predatory activity by "have-nots" against "haves"', the invention of gunpowder turned the tables. 'Gunpowder equipped the civilised "haves" to be the victors over the savage "have-nots"'. Western mastery of gunpowder, linked to the European conquest of the oceans, meant that, equipped with guns and sails, the European 'haves' were in a position, from the 1530s until Bloch's time, to enlarge their power, through empire, most especially after Wellington had ended Napoleon's bid for continental mastery at Waterloo in 1815, which shock served, in the manner Bildt describes for the next century, to galvanise the Concert of Europe after the Congress of Vienna, to police Europe. This it did successfully until the Prusso-Austrian and Franco-Prussian wars returned war to the continent.

The European civil war of the 20th century was, in Keegan's terms, 'a climactic struggle of "haves" against "haves"', and it resulted in 1945 in there being no European victors: 'only a collection of impoverished neighbours in a once great continent'. The European civil war had been ended by intervention – twice – by the one gunpowder nation outside Europe which, having emerged from its own mid-century civil war, had acquired both the economic and military strength to be able to make the difference when America came to Europe. Nor did the Americans do it alone. It was the double pincer of the titanic battles of the Red Army to the East, closing with the American intervention to the West, which both ended the European civil war and laid the basis for the superpower Cold War which followed. But this was not war in the active sense. War had gone elsewhere.

War, argues Keegan, 'once a struggle over riches, or the proud vocation of peoples rich themselves, is now the calling of the wretched of the earth. This is the pitiful conclusion to a human activity 5,000 years old'. His chapter ends with a heart-felt plea that the wealthy should do their part in ending the obscenity of modern war in the poor world by cutting off the supply of arms which come, ultimately, from the rich. In this conclusion, Keegan stands miles apart from the view expressed by Edward Luttwak in the second chapter in this section.

War, argues Luttwak, has only one purpose, which is to bring peace. And the peace created by war, 'unlike the peace created by artificial treaties and other arrangements imposed by other countries, is a solid peace'. Luttwak's case is that, within the paradoxical logic of all things to do with war, the attempt to interfere and stop war by ceasefire or by armistice, and latterly in the post-Cold War world through intervention and peace-keeping, is precisely counterproductive of the purpose for which it is said to be undertaken. His chapter is, therefore, fundamentally at variance with the assumptions and dependent logic found in Section II, which seeks to substitute for or to prevent war by other international institutions – the modern extension of Bloch's own idea. Luttwak reserves his most withering criticism for those non-governmental organisations that seek to alleviate the effects of war by intervening in zones of conflict. 'They arrive at conflicts like flies on sugar and their impact is overall highly negative. They feed conflicts indirectly....' Luttwak's plea is that, as we face our new century and millennium, we do not fall into the trap of anachronistic thought. He argues that, during the era of nuclear confrontation between superpowers, the importance of averting confrontations that might lead to nuclear exchange was overwhelming. Hence, regimes of arms control, of armistice and cease fire, were quite appropriate. But not so now. War, he argues, is like fire: both burn and in burning can cleanse and resolve situations. What must be avoided at all costs, Luttwak argues, is the creation of circumstances which promise to make wars endless, as they have become, in his view, in the Balkans as a result of the systematic mismanagement of external interventions there.

Luttwak's Phillippic against prevailing views on the prevention of war stands in the middle of this collection, as it did in the St Petersburg conference, as a reference point to which others returned, most particularly in the contribution of Klaus-Peter Klaiber, the Under-Secretary General for Political Affairs of NATO, in the final chapter.

Professor van Creveld offers a third contrasting view of the large scale. Like others, he accepts that there will be a continuing need to deal in future with the 'frontier brawls or punative operations', which Bloch excluded from consideration within his main thesis. But it is about the main thesis that van Creveld worries. In contrast to most others in the collection, notably Carl Bildt and Christoph Bertram, Martin van Creveld has little confidence in positive incentives to maintain permanent peace. He is suspicious of, and fearful of a world in which the power of states is compromised, yet understands and accepts that this compromising is in part an inevitable consequence of globalisation in the modern world. But, of the basic reason for peace since the end of the European civil war, he has no doubt: 'Nuclear weapons are the real cause of whatever peace this planet of ours enjoys'. He relies on this power for reasons which, in his view, cause him to dissociate himself from Bloch. Bloch, he believes, looked to a change in the balance between reason and emotion in the human soul and this van Creveld neither sees nor expects. In consequence, his conclusion is that, facing the changing potentials and purposes of war in the 21st century, he holds to two prescriptions. One, in nuclear form, the Roman dictum 'If you desire peace, prepare for war'. The other – and his is rather more of Luttwak's view than others – that, if intervention is to be conducted in the wars of 'have-nots' *versus* 'have-nots' among the wretched of the earth, then let the interventions be swift and decisive.

The middle trio of chapters in Section III also contemplate the great divide between zones of war and peace. Neither the chapters by Hassner nor Prins believe that the distinctions are as stark as the geopolitical facts suggest. Hassner argues that a new dynamic of violence is to be seen: 'Violence', he argues, 'undergoes a double process of diffusion and fragmentation'. The so-called zone of peace, Hassner cannot forget, is the zone over which totalitarianism trampled triumphantly and in several guises since Bloch's time. It has left a legacy still not wholly swept away. In his chapter he explores possible ways in which that legacy may express itself both as a blurring of thresholds between forms of violence within post-modern societies and a dulling of sensitivities also. And why not? Hassner recalls the simple statistic that, in the 20th century, wars have killed 35 million victims, whereas, according to Rudolph Rummel, 150 millions have been killed by their own governments. So, Hassner soberly observes, the 20th century which followed Bloch's war was one in which political violence

> 'pitted governments against one part of the whole of their own people. The slogan with which one could best sum up the history of the 20th century is probably the turning around, both by Lenin and by Ludendorf, of Clausewitz's famous formula ("War is the continuation of politics by other means") into "politics is the continuation of war by other means"'.

Therefore, Hassner cannot easily share the enthusiasm of Bildt and Bertram for the war-preventing qualities of institution building. To Hassner they seem fragile at best, and to be too often potential victims of hijack when governments turn pathological. Where he does stand on common ground with the authors of the previous section is in his sense that the state is both made by war and makes war; so, therefore, its transcendence is an essential part of fulfilment of Bloch's dream. But the path, in Hassner's view, is a hard one: it is through a dialectic between 'the bourgeois and the barbarian, tending to replace the Hegelian one of the master and the slave'. Certainly, active violence is most often to be seen in the management of civil wars and the external imposition of order in contexts of chaos and collapsed states. But, whereas Hassner does not stand with van Creveld in his prescription for the maintenance of order through fear, he does share a broad unease, fed by the grim statistics of political violence in the 20th century, about claims to restore civility through aspiration alone.

For Hassner, as for Prins, the *locus classicus* for assessment of the success of Europeans in managing the social destructiveness of political violence is to be seen in the recent Balkan wars. Prins argues that the potentials and purposes of political violence hang suspended in a desperate dialectic over containment (and hence control) of applied force. On the one hand stands a long and dogged struggle to give substance to the principles of just war. It has been in the face of a 20th century which has witnessed the erosion of commitment to the second Augustinian principle of *ius in bello* at the same time that circumstance has made the promiscuous use of violence by totalitarian agency all the easier. Like Hassner, he cannot forget the industrialisation of genocide as governments devoured their own people in the concentration camps of the mid-century. But, with Carl Bildt, Prins recognises the laggardly dialectic: the manner in which – always after the event and never able to prevent the event – international society has sought to outlaw horrors once they have become known.

Hence, the establishment at the end of the Second World War simultaneously of two streams of legitimation for international action. The first was given primary expression in the Charter of the United Nations: to save succeeding generations from the scourge of war. The second was grounded in the fact of the Tribunal and the nature of the judgments at Nuremberg, which hammered in the stakes to which are guyed the ropes supporting the edifice of human rights. Nuremberg distinguished between war and crime and Prins is struck by the dramatic symbolism of coincidence between the two most recent events, which have imparted new impetus to the drive to create a regime of enforceable human rights, namely the mandate for the Kosovo operation (most succinctly expressed in Prime Minister Blair's Chicago speech of 22 April 1999) and the Pinochet extradition case. 'The cases of Kosovo and Pinochet show how sharp has become the 1999 restatement of the 1899 St Petersburg paradox'.

It is, Prins suggests, in the massacres of Srebrenica in July 1995 that we should locate the turning point. His chapter offers a detailed review of the loss of the so-called 'safe area', and argues that, from this nadir, has come both the will and increasingly the capacity to apply armed force, under legal constraint and political control, for new purposes. The purposes were succinctly stated by Bill Maynes, when he observed that 'the uses of force have changed in much of the world ... throughout the Cold War force was needed to deter the other side from doing bad things outside its borders. Today force is needed to compel the other side to do good things inside its borders.'[3]

One of the characteristics of Bloch's work, that is most admirable and most enduring, was his persistent resolve to ensure that the product of his scholarly analysis should be translated into politically and diplomatically active form: that ideas drawn from study of the world should act hermeneutically upon that world. Therefore, in conceiving both the St Petersburg conference and this collection, it would be strange and remiss not to seek to make that link at century's end, as Bloch did 100 years before us.

Professor Lawrence Freedman sets the context for the potentials in the application of force under the new agenda in the 'frontier brawls or punative operations' by warning of the dangers of overconfidence in technological prowess. There are (as there have been before, he reminds us) 'revolutions in military affairs'. But it would be unwise to assume that the balance is overwhelmingly in favour of those who possess the new means, most particularly, in access to and processing of information. On the one hand, the revolution in information technology means that 'the sort of information that previous commanders might have dreamt about receiving in good time will be available almost immediately', but that, equally, 'information is becoming less and less of a privileged resource as more people have more means of tapping into more forms'.

The idea that a revolution in military affairs has occurred, which gives the possessors of the means a bandolier of silver bullets, which can, with utter certainty, absolute precision and minimal risk to those applying such force, produce decisive transformations in a conflict, is not an argument that Freedman

---

3 C.W. Maynes, 'Squandered triumphed. The West botched the post-Cold War world', 78 *Foreign Affairs*, no. 1, 1999, p. 21.

advocates. In particular, he is unimpressed by those who argue for a radical new form of warfare, in which the victims are not territory or people but rather information targets in cyberspace. His paper was written and delivered before the recent war over Kosovo; but nothing that has since emerged about the relative importance of the high-level bombing campaign against Serb targets, as compared to other means of bringing influence to bear to frustrate Mr Milosevic's aim, disturbs the thrust of Freedman's argument.

Indeed, the second author in this section, General Sir Michael Rose, was a vociferous and public critic of the belief during that war that anything short of a credible threat to occupy the territory would make a difference. In his paper in this collection, he distills his lessons about command in the Balkans and articulates the principles which should underpin the art of military intervention. The salutary lesson which he draws is, in one sense, congruent with one part of Luttwak's lesson: 'At the end of the day, you do not go to war in white-painted vehicles.' If a political objective must be achieved by force then force must be applied in whatever form is required and without the imposition of impossible constraints upon the commander once the decision to use the military instrument has been made. But Rose is equally firm in his belief that his professional art is and only ever can be palliative: peace is not built through war, it is built on justice and a secure footing once war has ended. In this too, his view echoes an aspect of Luttwak's case. But Rose sees little choice, for, with President Truman, he observes that 'if you are not prepared to pay the price of peace, then you'd better be prepared to pay the price of war'.

Luttwak's argument is engaged directly by Klaiber in his concluding essay. Like Rose, he finds aspects of the case undeniable: the need for resolution; the need for firmness and decisiveness of action when it is decided to act: these are principles that it is valuable to reiterate. But where he is entirely at variance with Luttwak is in his studied refusal to include any other criteria than those of relative strength. Klaiber agrees that wars should end quickly, 'and the international community should not contribute to extending conflict. If that means not interfering, fine. *But* we cannot stand aside in the face of genocide – even if standing aside brings the war to an end more quickly. We cannot sit on our hands in the face of ethnic cleansing, or mass executions and rapes, of mass terror, of gross violations of human rights. Peace is important – *but peace must come with justice.*' Therefore, he advocates that where intervention is demanded (and he shares and accepts the view that there may be increasing calls for the use of force in this way in defence of human rights) the form be entirely practical. This is the tendency which pervades the last three chapters of the book.

2

CONVERSATIONS WITH M. BLOCH

William T. Stead

"The Future of War" is the title of M. de Bloch's voluminous cyclopaedia on the art of war, past, present, and to come. But that is a mistake. For M. Bloch's thesis is that there is no war to come, that war indeed has already become impossible.

It would really have been clearer therefore to call this translation of the sixth and concluding volume of his immense book "Is War Now Impossible?" – as in the English edition – for this title gives a much clearer idea of the contents. For M. Bloch contends in all sober seriousness that war – great war in the usual acceptation of the word – has already, by the natural and normal development of the art or science of warfare, become a physical impossibility! That is what this book was written to prove.

PREFACE

But, before reading the chapters crammed with statistics and entering upon the arguments of the great Polish economist, the reader may find it convenient to glance over, as a preliminary introduction to the book, the following free rendering of the conversations which I have had the privilege of enjoying with the author at St. Petersburg and in London.

"Utopians," said M. Bloch; "and they call us Utopians, idealists, visionaries, because we believe that the end of war is in sight? But who are the Utopians, I should like to know? What is a Utopian, using the term as an epithet of opprobrium? He is a man who lives in a dream of the impossible; but what I know and am prepared to prove is, that the real Utopians who are living in a veritable realm of phantasy are those people who believe in war. War has been possible, no doubt, but it has at last become impossible, and those who are preparing for war, and basing all their schemes of life on the expectation of war, are

19

G. Prins and H. Tromp (eds.), The Future of War, 19-58.
© 2000 Kluwer Law International. Printed in the Netherlands.

visionaries of the worst kind, for war is no longer possible." "That is good news, M. Bloch," I replied; "but is it not somewhat of a paradox? Only last year we had the Spanish-American war; the year before, the war between Turkey and Greece. Since when has war become impossible?" "Oh," replied M. Bloch, with vivacity, "I do not speak of such wars. It is not to such frontier brawls, or punitive operations such as you in England, for instance, are perpetually engaging in on the frontiers of your extended empire, that I refer when I say that war has become impossible. When soldiers and statesmen speak about the War of the Future, they do not refer to such trumpery expeditions against semi-barbarous peoples. The war of the future, the war which has become impossible, is the war that has haunted the imagination of mankind for the last thirty years, the war in which great nations armed to the teeth were to fling themselves with all their resources into a struggle for life and death. This is the war that every day becomes more and more impossible. Yes, it is in preparations against that impossible war that these so-called practical men, who are the real Utopians of our time, are wasting the resources of civilisation." "Pray explain yourself more clearly, M. Bloch." "Well," said he, "I suppose you will admit that war has practically become impossible for the minor States. It is as impossible for Denmark or for Belgium to make war to-day as it would be for you or for me to assert the right of private war, which our forefathers possessed. We cannot do it. At least, we could only try to do it, and then be summarily suppressed and punished for our temerity. That is the position of the minor States. For them war is practically forbidden by their stronger neighbours. They are in the position of the descendants of the feudal lords, whose right of levying war has vanished owing to the growth of a strong central power whose interests and authority are incompatible with the exercise of what used to be at one time an almost universal right. For the minor States, therefore, war is impossible." "Admitted," I replied. "Impossible, that is to say, without the leave and licence of the great Powers." "Precisely," said M. Bloch; "and hence, when we discuss the question of future war, we always deal with it as a war between great Powers. That is to say, primarily, the long talked-of, constantly postponed war between France and Germany for the lost provinces; and, secondly, that other war, the thought of which has gradually replaced that of the single-handed duel between France and Germany, viz. , a war between the Triplice and the Franco-Russian Alliance. It is that war which constantly preoccupies the mind of states-men and sovereigns of Europe, and it is that war which, I maintain, has become absolutely impossible." "But how impossible, M. Bloch? Do you mean morally impossible?" "No such thing," he replied. "I am dealing not with moral con-siderations, which cannot be measured, but with hard, matter-of-fact, material things, which can be estimated and measured with some approximation to absolute accuracy. I maintain that war has become impossible alike from a military, economic, and political point of view. The very development that has taken place in the mechanism of war has rendered war an impracticable operation. The dimensions of modern armaments and the organisation of society have rendered its prosecution an economic impossibility, and, finally, if any attempt were made to demonstrate the inaccuracy of my assertions by putting the matter to a test on a great scale, we should find the inevitable result in a catastrophe which would destroy all existing political organisations. Thus, the great war cannot be made, and any attempt to make it would result in suicide. Such, I believe, is the simple demonstrable fact." "But where is the demonstration?" I asked. M. Bloch turned and pointed to his encyclopaedic work upon "The Future of War," six solid volumes, each containing I do not know how many quarto pages, which stood piled one above the other. "Read that," he said. "In that book you will find the facts upon which my demonstration rests." "That is all very well," I said; "but how can you, M. Bloch, an economist and a banker, set yourself up as an authority upon military matters?" "Oh," said M. Bloch, "you have a saying that it is often the outsider that sees most; and you must remember that the conclusions arrived at by military experts are by no means inaccessible to the general student. In order to form a correct idea as to the changes that have taken place in the mechanism of war, it is quite conceivable that the bystander who is not engaged in the actual carrying out of the evolution now in progress may be better able to see the drift and tendency of things than those who are busily engaged in the actual detail of the operation. I can only say that while at first hand I have no authority whatever, and do not in any way pose as a military or naval expert, I have taken all imaginable pains in order to master the literature of warfare, especially the most recent treatises upon military operations and the handling of armies and fleets, which have been published by the leading military authorities in the modern world. After mastering what they have written, I have had opportunities of discussing personally with many officers in all countries as to the conclusions at which I have arrived, and I am glad to know that in the main there is not much difference of opinion as to the accuracy of my general conclusions as to the nature of future warfare." "But do they also agree with you," I said, "that war has become impossible?" "No," said M. Bloch, "that would be too much to expect. Otherwise Othello's occupation would be gone. But as they have admitted the facts, we can draw our own conclusions." "But I see in your book you deal with every branch of the service, armaments of all kinds, manoeuvres, questions of strategy, problems of fortification – everything, in fact, that comes into the consideration of the actual conduct of modern war. Do you mean to tell me that military men generally think you have made no mistakes?" "That would be saying too much. The book was referred by the Emperor of Russia at my request to the Minister of War, with a request that it should be subjected to examination by a council of experts. The results of that council were subsequently communicated to the Emperor in the shape of a report, which set forth that while in dealing with so very many questions it was impossible to avoid some mistakes, it was their opinion that the book was a very useful one, and that it was most desirable that it should be placed in the hands of all staff officers. They also added an expression of opinion that no book could contribute so much to the success of the Conference or to the information of those who were to take part in its deliberations. "The one question upon which strong difference of opinion existed was that concerning the use of the bayonet. I have arrived at the conclusion, based upon a very careful examination of various authorities, that the day of the bayonet is over. In the Franco-German war the total mortality of the Germans from cold steel amounted to only one per cent. The proportion on the French side was higher, but I think it can be mathematically demonstrated that, in future, war will be decided at ranges which will render the use of the bayonet impossible. General Dragomiroff, however, a veteran of the old school, cannot tolerate this slight upon his favourite weapon. In his eyes the bayonet is supreme, and it is cold steel which at the last will always be the deciding factor in the combats of peoples. He therefore strongly condemns that portion of my book; but it stands on its own merits, and the reader can form his own judgment as to the probability of the bayonet being of any practical use in future war." "General Dragomiroff's devotion to the bayonet," I remarked, "reminds me of our admirals' devotion to sails in our navy. Fifteen years ago it was quite obvious that the fighting ship of the future had no need for sails – that, indeed, sails were an encumbrance and a danger; but all the admirals of the old school attached far more importance to the smartness in furling and unfurling sail than they did to proficiency in gunnery or in any of the deciding factors in naval battles. They clung to masts and yards for years after all the younger officers in the service knew that they might as well have clung to bows and arrows; and I suppose you will find the same thing in regard to the bayonet." "Yes," said M. Bloch, "the bayonet seems to me altogether out of date. No doubt it is a deadly enough weapon, if you can get within a yard of your enemy; but the problem that I have been asking myself is whether in future combatants will ever be able to get within one hundred yards of one another, let alone one yard." "But then," I rejoined, "if that be so, wars will be much less deadly than they were before." "Yes and no," said

M. Bloch; "they will become less deadly because they have become more deadly. There is no kind of warfare so destructive of human life as that in which you have bodies of men face to face with each other, with nothing but cold steel to settle the issue. The slaughter which took place in the old wars between barbarians, or between the Romans and the barbarian tribes on their frontiers, was simply appalling. There is nothing like it in modern warfare, and this diminution of the mortality in battle has been, paradoxically enough, produced by the improved deadliness of the weapons with which men fight. They are, indeed, becoming so deadly that before long you will see they will never fight at all." "That," I replied, "was the faith of Rudyard Kipling, who wrote me a few months ago saying that he relied for the extinction of war upon the invention of a machine which would infallibly slay fifty per cent. of the combatants whenever battle was waged. 'Then,' he said, 'war would cease of itself.' The same idea was expressed by Lord Lytton in his novel of 'The Coming Race,' in which he attributed the final disappearance of war from the planet to the discovery of vril, a destructive so deadly that an army could be annihilated by the touch of a button by the finger of a child." "Yes," said M. Bloch; "that is so; but until mankind has made experience of the deadliness of its weapons there will be terrible bloodshed. For instance, at Omdurman the destruction inflicted upon the forces of the Khalifa came very near the fifty per cent. standard of Rudyard Kipling. That one experience was probably sufficient even for the Dervishes. They will never again face the fire of modern rifles. The experience which they have learned is rapidly becoming generalised throughout the armies of Christendom, and although there may be some frightful scenes of wholesale slaughter, one or two experiences of that kind will rid our military authorities of any desire to come to close quarters with their adversaries." "What a paradox it is!" I replied. "We shall end by killing nobody, because if we fought at all we should kill everybody. Then you do not anticipate increased slaughter as the result of the increased precision in weapons?" "You mistake me," said M. Bloch. "At first there will be increased slaughter – increased slaughter on so terrible a scale as to render it impossible to get troops to push the battle to a decisive issue. They will try to, thinking that they are fighting under the old conditions, and they will learn such a lesson that they will abandon the attempt for ever. Then, instead of a war fought out to the bitter end in a series of decisive battles, we shall have as a substitute a long period of continually increasing strain upon the resources of the combatants. The war, instead of being a hand-to-hand contest in which the combatants measure their physical and moral superiority, will become a kind of stalemate, in which neither army being able to get at the other, both armies will be maintained in opposition to each other, threatening each other, but never being able to deliver a final and decisive attack. It will be simply the natural evolution of the armed peace, on an aggravated scale." "Yes," said M. Bloch, "accompanied by entire dislocation of all industry and severing of all the sources of supply by which alone the community is enabled to bear the crushing burden of that armed peace. It will be a multiplication of expenditure simultaneously accompanied by a diminution of the sources by which that expenditure can be met. That is the future of war – not fighting, but famine, not the slaying of men, but the bankruptcy of nations and the break-up of the whole social organisation." "Now I begin to perceive how it is that we have as a prophet of the end of war a political economist, and not a soldier." "Yes," said M. Bloch, "it is as a political economist that I discovered the open secret which he who runs may read. The soldier by natural evolution has so perfected the mechanism of slaughter that he has practically secured his own extinction. He has made himself so costly that mankind can no longer afford to pay for his maintenance, and he has therefore transferred the sceptre of the world from those who govern its camps to those who control its markets." "But now, M. Bloch, will you condescend to particulars, and explain to me how this great evolution has been brought about?" "It is very simple," said M. Bloch. "The outward and visible sign of the end of war was the introduction of the magazine rifle. For several hundred years after the discovery of gunpowder the construction of firearms made little progress. The cannon with which you fought at Trafalgar differed comparatively little from those which you used against the Armada. For two centuries you were content to clap some powder behind a round ball in an iron tube, and fire it at your enemy. "The introduction of the needle gun and of breech-loading cannon may be said to mark the dawn of the new era, which, however, was not definitely established amongst us until the invention of the magazine rifle of very small calibre. The magazine gun may also be mentioned as an illustration of the improved deadliness of firearms; but, as your experience at Obdurman showed, the deciding factor was not the Maxim, but the magazine rifle." "Yes," I said; "as Lord Wolseley said, it was the magazine rifle which played like a deadly hose spouting leaden bullets upon the advancing enemy." "Yes," said M. Bloch, "and the possibility of firing half a dozen bullets without having to stop to reload has transformed the conditions of modern war." "Do you not exaggerate the importance of mere rapidity of fire?" I asked. "No," said M. Bloch; "rapidity of fire does not stand alone. The modern rifle is not only a much more rapid firer than its predecessors, but it has also an immensely wider range and far greater precision of fire. To these three qualities must be added yet a fourth, which completes the revolutionary nature of the new firearm, and that is the introduction of smokeless powder." "The Spanish-American campaign," I said, "illustrated the importance of smokeless powder; but how do you think the smokelessness of the new explosives will affect warfare in the future?" "In the first case," said M. Bloch, "it demolishes the screen behind which for the last 400 years human beings have fought and died. All the last great battles have been fought more or less in the dark. After the battle is joined, friends and foes have been more or less lost to sight in the clouds of dense smoke which hung heavy over the whole battlefield. Now armies will no longer fight in the dark. Every soldier in the fighting line will see with frightful distinctness the havoc which is being made in the ranks by the shot and shell of the enemy. The veil which gunpowder spread over the worst horrors of the battlefield has been withdrawn for ever. But that is not the only change. It is difficult to over-estimate the increased strain upon the nerve and morale of an army under action by the fact that men will fall killed and wounded without any visible or audible cause. In the old days the soldier saw the puff of smoke, heard the roar of the gun, and when the shell or shot ploughed its way through the ranks, he associated cause and effect, and was to a certain extent prepared for it. In the warfare of the future men will simply fall and die without either seeing or hearing anything." "Without hearing anything, M. Bloch?" "Without hearing anything, for although the smokeless powder is not noiseless, experience has proved that the report of a rifle will not carry more than nine hundred yards and volley-firing cannot be heard beyond a mile. But that brings us to the question of the increased range of the new projectiles. An army on march will suddenly become aware of the comparative proximity of the foe by seeing men drop killed and wounded, without any visible cause; and only after some time will they be able to discover that the invisible shafts of death were sped from a line of sharp-shooters lying invisible at a distance of a mile or more. There will be nothing along the whole line of the horizon to show from whence the death-dealing missiles have sped. It will simply be as if the bolt had come from the blue. Can you conceive of anything more trying to human nerves?" "But what is the range of the modern rifle?" "The modern rifle," said M. Bloch, "has a range of 3000 or 4000 metres – that is to say, from two to three miles. Of course, I do not mean to say that it will be used at such great distances. For action at long range, artillery is much more effective. But of that I will speak shortly. But you can fairly say that for one mile or a mile and a half the magazine rifle is safe to kill anything that stands between the muzzle and its mark; and therein," continued M. Bloch, "lies one of the greatest changes that have been effected in modern firearms. Just look at this table". "It will explain better than anything I can say the change that has been brought about in the last dozen years. "In the last great war, if you wished to hit a distant mark, you had to sight your rifle so as to fire high up into the air, and the ball executing a curve descended at the range at which you calculated your target stood. Between the muzzle and the target your bullet did no execution. It was soaring in the air, first rising until it reached the maximum height, and then descending it struck the target or the earth at one definite point some thousand yards distant. Contrast this with the modern weapon. There is now no need for sighting your gun so as to drop your bullet at a particular range. You aim straight at your man, and the bullet goes, as is shown in the diagram, direct to its mark. There is no climbing into the air to fall again. It simply speeds, say, five feet from the earth until it meets its mark. Anything that stands between its object and the muzzle of the rifle it passes through. Hence whereas in the old gun you hit your man only if you could drop your bullet upon the square yard of ground upon which he was standing, you now hit him so long as you train your rifle correctly on every square yard of the thousand or two thousand which may intervene between the muzzle of your gun and the end of the course of the shot. That circumstance alone, even without any increase in the rapidity of the fire, must enormously add to the deadliness of the modern firearms." "Could you give me any exact statistics as to the increased rapidity of fire?" "Certainly," said M. Bloch. "That is to say, I can give you particulars up to a comparatively recent time, but the progress of the science of firearms is so rapid that no one can say but that my statistics may be old before you print your report of this talk. The ordinary soldier will fire twelve times as many shots per minute as he was able to do in 1870, and even this is likely to be rapidly improved upon. But you may take it that what with increased rapidity of fire, greater penetrative power, and the greater precision that the gun which the soldier will carry into the battle will possess, the rifle of tomorrow will be forty times as effective as the chassepot was in the Franco-Prussian war. Even the present gun is five times as deadly." "But do not you think that with this rapid firing a soldier will spend all his ammunition and have none left?" "There, again," said M. Bloch, "the improvement in firearms has enormously increased the number of cartridges which each man can carry into action. In 1877, when we went to war with Turkey, our soldiers could only carry 84 cartridges into action. When the calibre of the rifle was reduced to 5 mm. the number which each soldier was furnished with rose to 270. With a bullet of 4 mm. he will carry 380, and when we have a rifle of 3 mm. calibre he will be able to take 575 into action, and not have to carry any more weight than that which burdened him when he carried 84, twenty years ago. At present he carries 170 of the 7.62 mm." "But we are a long way off 3 mm. calibre, are we not,

M. Bloch?" "Not so far. It is true that very many countries have not yet adopted so small a bore. Your country, for instance, has between 7½ and 8 mm. The United States have adopted one with 6; Germany is contemplating the adoption of 5; but the 3 mm. gun will probably be the gun of the future, for the increased impetus of the small bore and its advantage in lightness will compel its adoption." "You speak of the increased penetrative power of the bullet. Do you think this will add considerably to the deadliness of rifle-fire?" "Oh, immensely," said M. Bloch. "As you contract the calibre of the gun you increase the force of its projectile. For instance, a rifle with a calibre of only 6.5 mm. has 44 per cent. more penetrative power than the shot fired by an 8 mm. rifle. Then, again, in previous wars, if a man could throw himself behind a tree he felt comparatively safe, even although the bullets were hurtling all round. To-day the modern bullet will pierce a tree without any difficulty. It also finds no obstacle in earthworks such as would have turned aside the larger bullets. There is therefore less shelter, and not only is there less shelter, but the excessive rapidity with which the missile travels (for it is absurd to call the slender projectile, no thicker than a lead pencil, a ball) will add enormously to the destructive power of the shot. Usually when a bullet struck a man, it found its billet, and generally stopped where it entered; but with the new bullet this will not be the case. At a near range it will pass through successive files of infantry, but what is more serious is that should it strike a bone, it is apt to fly upwards or sideways, rending and tearing everything through which it passes. The mortality will be much greater from this source than it has been in the past." "But is this not all very much theory? Have you any facts in support of your belief that the modern bullet will be so much more deadly than its predecessor? In England quite the opposite impression prevailed, owing to the experience which we gained in Jameson's raid, when many of the combatants were shot through and seemed none the worse, even although the bullet appeared to have traversed a vital part of the body." M. Bloch replied: "I do not know about the Jameson raid. I do know what happened when the soldiers fired recently upon a crowd of riotous miners. It is true that they fired at short range, not more than thirty to eighty paces. The mob also was not advancing in loose formation, but, like most mobs, was densely packed. Only ten shots were fired, but these ten shots killed outright seven of the men and wounded twenty-five, of whom six afterwards died. Others who were slightly wounded concealed their injuries, fearing prosecution. Each shot, therefore, it is fair to estimate, must have hit at least four persons. But ignoring those unreported cases, there were thirty-two persons struck by bullets. Of these, thirteen died, a proportion of nearly 40 per cent. , which is at least double the average mortality of persons hit by rifle-bullets in previous wars. It has also been proved by experiments made by firing shots into carcases and corpses, that when the bullet strikes a bone it acts virtually as an explosive bullet, as the point expands and issues in a kind of mushroom shape. Altogether I take a very serious view of the sufferings," continued M. Bloch, "and of the injury that will be inflicted by the new weapons." "Is the improvement in the deadliness of weapons confined to small-arms? Does it equally extend to artillery firing?" "There," said M. Bloch, "you touch upon a subject which I have dealt with at much length in my book. The fact is that if the rifle has improved, artillery has much more improved. Even before the quick-firing gun was introduced into the field batteries an enormous improvement had been made. So, indeed, you can form some estimate of the evolution of the cannon when I say that the French artillery to-day is held by competent authorities to be at least one hundred and sixteen times more deadly than the batteries which went into action in 1870." "How can that be?" I asked. "They do not fire one hundred and sixteen times as fast, I presume?" "No; the increased improvement has been obtained in many ways. By the use of range-finders it is possible now to avoid much firing into space which formerly prevailed. An instrument weighing about 60 lb. will in three minutes give the range of any distance up to four miles, and even more rapid range-finders are being constructed. Then, remember, higher explosives are used; the range has been increased, and even before quick-firing guns were introduced it was possible to fire two and a half times as fast as they did previously. The effect of artillery-fire to-day is at least five times as deadly as it was, and being two or three times as fast, you may reckon that a battery of artillery is from twelve to fifteen times as potent an instrument of destruction as it was thirty years ago. Even in 1870 the German artillerists held that one battery was able absolutely to annihilate any force advancing along a line of fire estimated at fifteen paces in breadth for a distance of over four miles. "If that was so then, you can imagine how much more deadly it is now, when the range is increased and the explosive power of the shell has been enormously developed. It is estimated that if a body of 10,000 men, advancing to the attack, had to traverse a distance of a mile and a half under the fire of a single battery, they would be exposed to 1450 rounds before they crossed the zone of fire, and the bursting of the shells fired by that battery would scatter 275,000 bullets in fragments over the mile and a half across which they would have to march. In 1870 an ordinary shell when it burst broke into from nineteen to thirty pieces. To-day it bursts into 240. Shrapnel fire in 1870 only scattered thirty-seven death-dealing missiles. Now it scatters 340. A bomb weighing about 70 lb. thirty years ago would have burst into forty-two fragments. To-day, when it is charged with peroxilene, it breaks up into 1200 pieces, each of which is hurled with much greater velocity than the larger lumps which were scattered by a gunpowder explosion. It is estimated that such a bomb would effectively destroy all life within a range of 200 metres of the point of explosion. The artillery also benefits by the smokeless powder, although, as you can easily imagine, it is not without its drawbacks." "What drawbacks?" "The fact that the artillerymen can be much more easily picked off, when they are serving their guns, by sharpshooters than was possible when they were enveloped in a cloud of smoke of their own creation. It is calculated that one hundred sharp-shooters, who would be quite invisible at a range of five hundred yards, would put a battery out of action in four minutes if they could get within range of one thousand yards. At a mile's range it might take one hundred men half an hour's shooting to put a battery out of action. The most effective range for the sharp-shooter is about eight hundred paces. At this range, while concealed behind a bush or improvised earthwork, a good shot could pick off the men of any battery, or the officers, who could not avail themselves of the cover to which their men resort." "How will your modern battle begin, M. Bloch?" "Probably with attempts on outposts made by sharpshooters to feel and get into touch with each other. Cavalry will not be of much use for that purpose. A mounted man offers too good a mark to a sharp-shooter. Then when the outposts have felt each other sufficiently to give the opposing armies knowledge of the whereabouts of their antagonists, the artillery duel will commence at a range of from four to five miles. As long as the artillery is in action it will be quite sufficient to render the nearer approach of the opposing forces impossible. If they are evenly matched, they will mutually destroy each other, after inflicting immense losses before they are put out of action. Then the turn of the rifle will come. But the power of rifle-fire is so great that it will be absolutely impossible for the combatants to get to close quarters with each other. As for any advance in force, even in the loosest of formations, on a front that is swept by the enemies' fire, that is absolutely out of the question. Flank movements may be attempted, but the increased power which a magazine rifle gives to the defence will render it impossible for such movements to have the success that they formerly had. A small company can hold its own against a superior attacking force long enough to permit of the bringing up of reinforcements. To attack any position successfully, it is estimated that the attacking force ought to outnumber the assailants at least by 8 to 1. It is calculated that 100 men in a trench would be able to put out of action 336 out of 400 who attacked them, while they were crossing a fire-zone only 300 yards wide." "What do you mean by a fire-zone?" "A fire-zone is the space which is swept by the fire of the men in the trench."

"But you assume that they are entrenched, M. Bloch?" "Certainly, everybody will be entrenched in the next war. It will be a great war of entrenchments. The spade will be as indispensable to a soldier as his rifle. The first thing every man will have to do, if he cares for his life at all, will be to dig a hole in the ground, and throw up as strong an earthen rampart as he can to shield him from the hail of bullets which will fill the air. "Then," I said, "every battlefield will more or less come to be like Sebastopol, and the front of each army can only be approached by a series of trenches and parallels?" "Well, that, perhaps, is putting it too strongly," said M. Bloch, "but you have grasped the essential principle, and that is one reason why it will be impossible for the battle of the future to be fought out rapidly. All digging work is slow work, and when you must dig a trench before you can make any advance, your progress is necessarily slow. Battles will last for days and at the end it is very doubtful whether any decisive victory can be gained." "Always supposing," I said, "that the ammunition does not give out." "Ammunition will not give out. Of powder and shot there is always plenty." "I doubt that," I replied. "The weak point of all this argument as to the impossibility of war implies that the modern mechanism of war, which is quite sufficient to prevent armies coming into close contact, also possesses qualities of permanence, or rather of inexhaustibility. What seems much more probable is that with the excessive rapidity of fire, armies will empty their magazines, and the army that fires its last cartridge first will be at the mercy of the other. Then the old veteran Dragomiroff will rejoice, for the bayonet will once more come into play." M. Bloch shook his head. "I do not think that armies will run short of ammunition. All my arguments are based upon the assumption that the modern war is to be fought with modern arms. I do not take into account the possibility that there will be a reversion to the primitive weapons of an earlier day." "Well, supposing that you are right, and that ammunition does not run short, what will happen?" "I have quoted in my book," said M. Bloch, "the best description that I have ever seen of what may be expected on a modern battlefield. I will read it to you, for it seems to convey, more vividly than anything that I could say, just what we may expect: "The distance is 6000 metres from the enemy. The artillery is in position, and the command has been passed along the batteries to 'give fire.' The enemy's artillery replies. Shells tear up the soil and burst; in a short time the crew of every gun has ascertained the distance of the enemy. Then every projectile discharged bursts in the air over the heads of the enemy, raining down hundreds of fragments and bullets on his position. Men and horses are overwhelmed by this rain of lead and iron. Guns destroy one another, batteries are mutually annihilated, ammunition cases are emptied. Success will be with those whose fire does not slacken. In the midst of this fire the battalions will advance. "Now they are but 2000 metres away. Already the rifle-bullets whistle round and kill, each not only finding a victim, but penetrating files, ricocheting, and striking again. Volley succeeds volley, bullets in great handfuls, constant as hail and swift as lightning, deluge the field of battle. "The artillery having silenced the enemy is now free to deal with the enemy's battalions. On his infantry, however loosely it may be formed, the guns direct thick iron rain, and soon in the position of the enemy the earth is reddened with blood. "The firing lines will advance one after the other, battalions will march after battalions; finally the reserves will follow. Yet with all this movement in the two armies there will be a belt a thousand paces wide, separating them as by neutral territory, swept by the fire of both sides, a belt which no living being can stand for a moment. The ammunition will be almost exhausted, millions of cartridges, thousands of shells will cover the soil. But the fire will continue until the empty ammunition cases are replaced with full. "Melinite bombs will turn to dust farm-houses, villages, and hamlets, destroying everything that might be used as cover, obstacle, or refuge. "The moment will approach when half the combatants will be mowed down, dead and wounded will lie in parallel rows, separated one from the other by that belt of a thousand paces which will be swept by a cross fire of shells which no living being can pass. "The battle will continue with ferocity. But still that thousand paces unchangingly separate the foes. "Who shall have gained the victory? Neither. "This picture serves to illustrate a thought which, since the perfection of weapons, has occupied the minds of all thinking people. What will take place in a future war? Such are constrained to admit that between the combatants will always be an impassable zone of fire deadly in an equal degree to both the foes. "With such conditions, in its application to the battles of the future, the saying of Napoleon seems very questionable: 'The fate of battle is the result of one minute, of one thought, the enemies approach with different plans, the battle becomes furious; the decisive moment arrives, and a happy thought sudden as lightning decides the contest, the most insignificant reserve sometimes being the instrument of a splendid victory.' "It is much more probable that in the future both sides will claim the victory." "Pleasant pictures, certainly; and if that authority is right, you are indeed justified in believing that there will be no decisive battles in the war of the future." "There will be no war in the future," said M. Bloch; "for it has become impossible, now that it is clear that war means suicide." "But is not everything that you are saying an assumption that people will make war, and that therefore war itself is possible?" "No doubt," said M. Bloch; "the nations may endeavour to prove that I am wrong, but you will see what will happen.

Nothing will be demonstrated by the next war if it is made, in spite of warnings, but the impossibility of making war, except, of course, for the purpose of self-destruction. I do not for a moment deny that it is possible for nations to plunge themselves and their neighbours into a frightful series of catastrophes which would probably result in the overturn of all civilised and ordered government. That is, of course, possible; but when we say that war is impossible we mean that it is impossible for the modern State to carry on war under the modern conditions with any prospect of being able to carry that war to a conclusion by defeating its adversary by force of arms on the battlefield. No decisive war is possible. Neither is any war possible, as I proceed to show, that will not entail, even upon the victorious Power, the destruction of its resources and the break-up of society. War therefore has become impossible, except at the price of suicide. That would, perhaps, be a more accurate way of stating the thesis of my book." "I understand; but do you think you have proved this?" "Certainly," said M. Bloch. "So far I have only spoken about the improvements that have been wrought in two branches of the service, viz. , in the magazine rifle and the greater efficiency of artillery. Taken by themselves, they are sufficiently serious to justify grave doubt as to whether or not we have not reached a stage when the mechanism of slaughter has been so perfected as to render a decisive battle practically impossible; but these two elements are only two. They are accompanied by others which are still more formidable to those who persist in contemplating war as a practical possibility." "To what are you referring?" I asked. "Chiefly to the immensity of the modern army. The war of 1870-71 was a contest of giants, but the German armies operating in France did not exceed half a million men, whereas if war were to break out to-day, the Germans would concentrate over a million men on their front, while the French would be no whit behind them in the energy with which they would concentrate all their available fighting men on the frontier. In a war between the Triple and the Dual Alliance there would be ten millions of men under arms." "How would you make up the total of ten millions which you say would be mobilised in case of a war between the Dual and Triple Alliance?" "The figures in millions are briefly: Germany, 2,500,000; Austria, 1 3-10ths millions; Italy, 1 3-10ths millions, making a total of 5,100,000 for the Triple Alliance. France would mobilise 2½ millions, and Russia 2,800,000, making 5,300,000-10,400,000. It has yet to be proved that the human brain is capable of directing the movements and providing for the sustenance of such immense masses of human beings. The unwieldiness of the modern army has never been adequately taken into account. Remember that those millions will not be composed of veterans accustomed to act together. More than half of the German and French troops which will be confronting each other on mobilisation in case of war will be drawn from the reserves. In Russia the proportion of reserves would be only three hundred and sixty, in Italy two hundred and sixty, per thousand; but even this proportion is quite sufficient to indicate how large a mass of men, comparatively untrained, would find their place in the fighting front." "But have not great generals in the past commanded armies of millions? – Xerxes, for instance, and Tamerlane, and Attila at the head of his Huns?" "No doubt," said M. Bloch, "that is quite true; but it is one thing to direct a horde of men living in the simplest fashion, marching shoulder to shoulder in great masses, and it is an altogether different thing to manoeuvre and supply the enormously complex machine which we call a modern army. Remember, too, that in the old days men fought in masses, whereas the very essence of modern war is that you must advance in loose order and never have too big a clump of soldiers for your enemy to fire at. Hence the battle will be spread over an enormous front and every mile over which you spread your men increases the difficulties of supply, of mutual co-operation, and of combined effort." "But has not the training of officers kept pace with the extension and development of modern armaments?" "Yes," said M. Bloch, "and no. It is true, no doubt, that an effort has been made to bring up the technical training of officers to the necessary standard; but this is quite impossible in all cases. A very large proportion of the officers who will be in command in a general mobilisation would be called from the reserve, that is to say, they would be men who are not familiar with the latest developments of modern tactics, and who would find themselves suddenly called upon to deal with conditions of warfare that were almost as different from those with which they were trained to deal as the legionaries of Caesar would have been if they had been suddenly summoned to face the musketeers of Frederic the Great." "Is that not an exaggeration, M. Bloch? Do you think that the art of war has changed so much?" "Changed?" said M. Bloch; "it has been so thoroughly revolutionised in the last thirty years, that if I had a son who was preparing for a military career, I would not let him read a book on tactics or strategy that had not been written in the last fifteen years, and even then he would find that great changes had taken place within that period. It is simply appalling to contemplate the spectacle of millions of men, half of whom have been hurriedly summoned from the field, the factory, and the mine, and the whole placed under command of officers not one in a hundred of whom has ever been under fire, and half of whom have been trained in a more or less antiquated school of tactics. But even then that is not the worst. What we have to recognise is the certainty that even if all officers were most efficient when the war began, the war would not last many weeks before the majority of the officers had been killed off." "But why?" I said. "The percentage of officers killed and wounded in action was much greater even in 1870 than the proportion of privates killed and wounded. The Germans, for instance, lost two officers killed and three wounded to each private who was similarly disabled. But that was before the improved weapon came into play. In the Chilian war the proportion of officers killed was 23 per cent. and 75 per cent. wounded, whereas among the men only 13 per cent. were killed and 60 per cent. wounded." "To what do you attribute this?"I asked. "The cause is very simple. The officers are compelled to expose themselves much more than the men under their orders. They have to be up and about and moving, while the men are lying in the shelter of the trenches. This is so well recognised that every Continental army pays special attention to the training of sharp-shooters, whose word of command is that they should never waste a shot upon any one but an officer. Hence the general conviction on the part of the officers abroad that if the great war broke out they would never survive to see the conclusion of peace." "When I was in Paris, M. Bloch, that conviction did not seem to be very general on the part of the French officers." "It is different in Germany," said M. Bloch, "and in Austria-Hungary, and the French would not be long in finding it out. Again and again officers have said to me that while they would of course do their duty if they were ordered to the front, they would take their place at the head of their men knowing that they would never return. So general is this conviction that you will find very little trace of any war party among the officers in Germany. They know too well what war would mean to them. But I am not thinking so much of the fate of the individuals as the result which will inevitably follow when this massed million of men found themselves deprived of their commanders. "An army is a very highly specialised organisation. Without competent officers, accustomed to command, it degenerates into a mere mob, and of all things in the world nothing is so helpless as a mob. It can neither march, fight, manoeuvre, nor feed itself. An army without leaders is not only a mob, but it is apt to degenerate into a very cowardly mob. Remember that every man is not naturally brave. It was said long ago that a very good fighting army consisted of three sorts of soldiers: only one-third of the men in the ranks were naturally brave, another third were naturally cowards, while the last third was capable of being brave under circumstances when it was well led and kept up to its work. Take away the officers, and this middle third naturally gravitate to the cowardly contingent, with results which have been seen on many a stricken field. Hence, under modern conditions of warfare every army will tend inevitably to degenerate into such a mob. It is for those practical military men who persist in regarding war as a possibility to explain how they hope to overcome the difficulty created by the very magnitude and unwieldiness of the machine which they have created." "But do not you think, M. Bloch, that if the nations discover that their armies are too big to be used, they will only fight with such manageable armies as they can bring to the front, manoeuvre, feed, and supply with the munitions of war?"M. Bloch shook his head. "The whole drift and tendency of modern tactics," he said, "is to bring up the maximum number of men to the front in the shortest possible loss of time and to hurl them in the largest possible numbers upon the enemy's position. It is absolutely necessary, if you take the offensive, to have a superior force. It is from a military point of view an impossibility to attack a superior force with an inferior, and the effect of the improvement in modern weapons has been to still further enhance the necessity for superiority of force in attacking. There will, therefore, be no question of fighting with small armies. The largest possible force will be brought to the front, and this effort will inevitably result in the breakdown of the whole machine. "You must have the maximum ready to hand at the beginning. Remember the fighting force of an army weakens with every mile that it advances from its base. Napoleon entered Russia with 400,000 men; but although he had only fought one battle, he had only 130,000 men with him when he entered Moscow. The Germans, when they were in France, employed one-sixth of their infantry in covering their communications and defending their rear. This proportion is likely to be much increased in future wars. The opportunity for harassing the line of communications in the rear of an invading army has been enormously multiplied by the invention of smokeless powder. The *franc tireur* in the Franco-German war took his life in his hand, for the range of his gun was not very great in the first place, and in the second his whereabouts was promptly detected by the puff of smoke which showed his hiding-place. Now the whole line of communications will be exposed to dropping shots from marksmen who, from the security of thicket or hedge, will deal out sudden death without any tell-tale smoke to guide their exasperated and harassed enemy to the hiding-place. "I have now dealt," said M. Bloch, "with the difficulties in the way of modern war, arising first from the immense improvement that has been wrought in the mechanism of slaughter, and secondly with the unmanageability of the immense masses of men who will be mobilised at the outbreak of war. Let us now proceed to the third, and what to my mind constitutes far the most serious obstacle in the way of modern war – viz., the economic impossibility of waging war upon the scale on which it must be waged if it is waged at all. "The first thing to be borne in mind is that the next war will be a long war. It was the declared opinion of Moltke that the altered conditions of warfare rendered it impossible to hope that any decisive result could be arrived at before two years at the least. The Franco-German war lasted seven months, but there is no hope of any similar war being terminated so rapidly. Of course this is assuming that war is to be terminated by fighting. In reality the war of the future, if ever it takes place, will not be fighting; it will be terminated by famine." "Why should wars be so excessively prolonged?" "Because all wars will of necessity partake of the character of siege operations. When we invaded Turkey in 1877 we were detained for months behind the improvised earthworks of Plevna. If war were to break out in Europe to-day, each combatant would find itself confronted, not by an isolated and improvised Plevna, but by carefully prepared and elaborately fortified networks of Plevnas. It is so on all frontiers. The system of defence has been elaborated with infinite skill and absolute disregard of financial considerations. Whether it will be a German army endeavouring to make its way into Moscow and St. Petersburg, or a Russian army striking at Berlin or at Vienna, or a German army invading France – in every case the invading army would find itself confronted by lines upon lines of fortresses and fortified camps, behind which would stand arrayed forces equal or superior in number to those which it could bring into the field against them. These fortresses would have to be taken or masked. "Now it is calculated that to take a modern fortress adequately defended, even by superior forces, is an operation which cannot be put through in less than one hundred and twenty days – that is, supposing that everything goes well with the assailants. Any reverse or any interruption of the siege operations would, of course, prolong this period. But it is not merely that each fortress would have to be reduced, but every field would more or less become an improvised fortified camp. Even when an army was defeated it would retreat slowly, throwing up earthworks, behind which it would maintain a harassing fire upon its pursuers; and the long line of invisible sharp-shooters, whose presence would not be revealed even by the tell-tale puff of smoke, would inevitably retard any rapid advance on the part of the victors. It is indeed maintained by many competent authorities that there is no prospect of the victorious army being able to drive the defeated forces from the field of battle so completely as to establish itself in possession of the spoils of war. The advantage is always with the defending force, and every mile that the assailants advance from their base would increase their difficulties and strengthen their opponents. Long and harassing siege operations in a war of blockade would wear out the patience and exhaust the resources of armies." "But armies have stood long sieges before now," I objected. "Yes," said M. Bloch, "in the past; but we are talking of the future. Do not forget that the wear and tear would be terrible, and the modern man is much less capable of bearing it than were his ancestors, The majority of the population tends more and more to gravitate to cities, and the city dweller is by no means so capable of lying out at nights in damp and exposed positions as the peasant. Even in comparatively rapid campaigns sickness and exhaustion slay many more than either cold steel or rifle-bullets. It is inevitable that this should be the case. In two weeks' time after the French army is mobilised, it is the expectation of the best authorities that they would have 100,000 men in hospital, even if never a shot had been fired." "That I can well understand. I remember when reading Zola's 'La Debàcle' feeling that if the Germans had kept out of the way altogether and had simply made the French march after them hither and thither, the whole Napoleonic army would have gone to pieces before they ever came within firing distance of their foes." "Yes," said M. Bloch. "The strain of marching is very heavy. Remember that it is not mere marching, but marching under heavy loads. No infantry soldier should carry more than one-third of his own weight; but instead of the average burden of the fully accoutred private being 52 lb. it is nearer 80 1b., with the result that the mere carrying of weight probably kills more than fall in battle. The proportion of those who die from disease and those who lose their lives as the consequence of wounds received in fighting is usually two or three to one. In the Franco-German war there were four times as many died from sickness and exhaustion as those who lost their lives in battle. In the Russo-Turkish war the proportion was as 16 to 44. In the recent Spanish war in Cuba the proportion was still greater. There were ten who died from disease for one who fell in action. The average mortality from sickness tends to increase with the prolongation of the campaign. Men can stand a short campaign, but when it is long it demoralises them, destroys the spirit of self-sacrifice which sustained them at the first in the opening weeks, and produces a thoroughly bad spirit which reacts upon their physical health. At present there is some regard paid to humanity, if only by the provision of ambulances, and the presence of hospital attendants, nurses, and doctors. But in the war of the future these humanities will go the wall." "What!" I said, "do you think there will be no care for the wounded?" "There will be practically no care for the wounded," said M. Bloch, "for it will be impossible to find adequate shelter for the Red Cross hospital tent or for the hospital orderlies. It will be impossible to take wounded men out of the zone of fire without exposing the Red Cross men to certain death. The consequence is they will be left to lie where they fall, and they may lie for days. Happy they will be if they are killed outright. Why, even in the last great war the provision for attendance on the wounded was shamefully inadequate. After Gravelotte there were for some time only four doctors to attend to 10,000 wounded men, and the state of things after Sadowa was horrible in the extreme. It is all very well to inveigh against this as inhumanity, but what are you to do when in the opinion of such a distinguished army physician as Dr. Billroth it would be necessary to have as many hospital attendants as there are soldiers in the fighting line? What is much more likely to be done is that the dying and the dead will be utilised as ramparts to strengthen the shelter trenches. This was actually done at the battle of Worth, where Dr. Porth, chief military physician of the Bavarian army, reported that he found in some places in the battlefield veritable ramparts built up of soldiers who had fallen by the side of their comrades, and in order to get them out of the way they had piled them one upon the top of the other, and had taken shelter behind their bodies. Some of these unfortunates built into this terrible rampart were only wounded, but the pressure of the superincumbent mass soon relieved them from their sufferings." "What a horrible story!" "Yes," said M. Bloch; "but I believe that war will be decided not by these things – not even by fighting-men at all – but by the factors of which they at present take far too little account." "And what may those factors be?" I asked. "Primarily, the quality of toughness or capacity of endurance, of patience under privation, of stubbornness under reverse and disappointment. That element in the civil population will be, more than anything else, the deciding factor in modern war. The men at the front will very speedily be brought to a deadlock. Then will come the question as to how long the people at home will be able to keep on providing the men at the front with the necessaries of life. That is the first factor. The second factor, which perhaps might take precedence of the moral qualities, is whether or not it is physically possible for the population left behind to supply the armies in front with what they need to carry on the campaign." "But have they not always done it in the past?" M. Bloch shook his head impatiently. "What is the use of talking about the past when you are dealing with an altogether new set of considerations? Consider for one moment what nations were a hundred years ago and what they are to-day. In those days before railways, telegraphs, steamships, etc., were invented, each nation was more or less a homogeneous, self-contained, self-sufficing unit. Europe was built in a series of water-tight compartments. Each country sufficed for its own needs, grew its own wheat, fattened its own cattle, supplied itself for its own needs within its own frontiers. All that is changed; with the exception of Russia and Austria there is not one country in Europe which is not absolutely dependent for its beef and its bread supplies from beyond the frontiers. You, of course, in England are absolutely dependent upon supplies from over sea. But you are only one degree worse off than Germany in that respect. In 1895, if the Germans had been unable to obtain any wheat except that which was grown in the

Fatherland, they would have lacked bread for one hundred and two days out of the three hundred and sixty-five. Every year the interdependence of nations upon each other for the necessaries of life is greater than it ever was before. Germany at present is dependent upon Russia for two and a half months' supply of wheat in every year. That supply would, of course, be immediately cut off if Russia and Germany went to war; and a similar state of things prevails between other nations in relation to other commodities. Hence the first thing that war would do would be to deprive the Powers that made it of all opportunity of benefiting by the products of the nations against whom they were fighting." "Yes," I objected, "but the world is wide, and would it not be possible to obtain food and to spare from neutral nations?" "That assumes," said M. Bloch, "first that the machinery of supply and distribution remains unaffected by war. Secondly, that the capacity for paying for supplies remains unimpaired. Neither of those things is true. For you, of course, it is an absolute necessity that you should be able to bring in food from beyond the seas; and possibly with the aid of your fleet you may be able to do it, although I fear the rate of war premium will materially enhance the cost of the cargoes. The other nations are not so fortunate. It was proposed some time ago, I know, in Germany, that in case of war they should endeavour to replace the loss of Russian wheat by importing Indian wheat through the Suez Canal – an operation which in the face of the French and Russian cruisers might not be very easy of execution. But even supposing that it was possible to import food, who is to pay for it? And that is the final crux of the whole question." "But," again I objected, "has the lack of money ever prevented nations going to war? I remember well when Lord Derby, in 1876, was quite confident that Russia would never go to war on behalf of Bulgaria because of the state of the Russian finances; but the Russo-Turkish war took place all the same, and there have been many great wars waged by nations which were bankrupt, and victories won by conquerors who had not a coin in their treasury." "You are always appealing to precedents which do not apply. Modern society, which is organised on a credit basis, and modern war, which cannot be waged excepting at a ruinous expenditure, offer no points of analogy compared with those times of which you speak. Have you calculated for one moment what it costs to maintain a soldier as an efficient fighting man in the field of battle? The estimate of the best authorities is that you cannot feed him and keep him going under ten francs a day – say, eight shillings a day. Supposing that the Triple and Dual Alliance mobilise their armies, we should have at once confronting us an expenditure for the mere maintenance of troops under arms of £4,000,000 a day falling upon the five nations. That is to say, that in one year of war under modern conditions the

Powers would spend £1,460,000,000 sterling merely in feeding their soldiers, without reckoning all the other expenses that must be incurred in the course of the campaign. This figure is interesting as enabling us to compare the cost of modern wars with the cost of previous wars. Take all the wars that have been waged in Europe from the battle of Waterloo down to the end of the Russo-Turkish war, and the total expenditure does not amount to more than £1,250,000,000 sterling, a colossal burden no doubt, but one which is nearly £200,000,000 less than that which would be entailed by the mere victualling of the armies that would be set on foot in the war which we are supposed to be discussing. Could any of the five nations, even the richest, stand that strain?" "But could they not borrow and issue paper money?" "Very well," said M. Bloch, "they would try to do so, no doubt, but the immediate consequence of war would be to send securities all round down from 25 to 50 per cent., and in such a tumbling market it would be difficult to float loans. Recourse would therefore have to be had to forced loans and unconvertible paper money. We should be back to the days of the assignats, a temporary expedient which would aggravate the difficulties with which we have to deal. Prices, for instance, would go up enormously, and so the cost, 8s. a day, would be nearer 20s. if all food had to be paid for in depreciated currency. But, apart from the question of paying for the necessary supplies, it is a grave question whether such supplies could be produced, and if they could be produced, whether they could be distributed." "What do you mean by 'distributed'?" I asked. "Distributed?" said M. Bloch. "Why, how are you to get the food into the mouths of the people who want it if you had (as you would have at the beginning of the war) taken over all the railways for military purposes? Even within the limits of Germany or of Russia there would be considerable difficulty in securing the transit of food-stuffs in war time, not merely to the camps, but to the great industrial centres. You do not seem to realise the extent to which the world has been changed by the modern industrial system. Down to the end of the last century the enormous majority of the population lived in their own fields, grew their own food, and each farm was a little granary. It was with individuals as it was with nations, and each homestead was a self-contained, self-providing unit. But nowadays all is changed. You have great industrial centres which produce absolutely nothing which human beings can eat. How much, for instance, do you grow in the metropolitan area for the feeding of London? Everything has to be brought by rail or by water to your markets. So it is more or less all over the Continent, especially in Germany and France. Now it so happens (and in this I am touching upon the political side of the question) that those districts which produce least food yield more Socialists to the acre than any other part of the country. It is those districts, rife with all elements of political discontent, which would be the first to feel the pinch of high prices and of lack of food. But this is a matter on which we will speak later on." "But do you think," I said, "that the railways would be so monopolised by the military authorities that they could not distribute provisions throughout the country?" "No," said M. Bloch. "It is not merely that they would be monopolised by their military authorities, but that they would be disorganised by the mobilisation of troops. You forget that the whole machinery of distribution and of production would be thrown out of gear by mobilisation; and this brings me to the second point upon which I insist – viz., the impossibility of producing the food. At the present moment Germany, for instance, just manages to produce sufficient food to feed her own population, with the aid of imports from abroad, for which she is able to pay by the proceeds of her own industry. But in the case of war with Russia she would not be able to buy two and a half months' supply of wheat from Russia, and therefore would have to pay much more for a similar supply of food in the neutral markets, providing she could obtain it. But she would have to buy much more than two and a half months' from Russia, because the nine months' corn which she produces at present is the product of the whole labour of all her able-bodied agricultural population; and how they work you in England do not quite realise. Do you know, for instance, that after the 'Büsstag,' or day of penitence and prayer, at the beginning of what we call the farmers' year or summer season, the whole German agricultural population in some districts work unremittingly fifteen hours a day seven days a week, without any cessation, without Sundays or holidays, until the harvest is gathered in; and even with all that unremitting toil they are only able to produce nine months' supply of grain. When you have mobilised the whole German army, you will diminish at least by half the strong hands available for labour in the field. In Russia we should not, of course, be in any such difficulty, and in the scrupulous observance of Sunday we have a reserve which would enable us to recoup ourselves for the loss of agricultural labour. We should lose, for instance, 17 per cent. of our peasants; but if those who were left worked on Sunday, in addition to weekdays, we should just be able to make up for the loss of the men who were taken to war. Germany has no such reserves, nor France; and hence it is that, speaking as a political economist, I feel extremely doubtful as to whether it would be possible for either Germany or France to feed their own population, to say nothing of their own soldiers, when once the whole machine of agricultural production had been broken up by the mobilisation *en masse* of the whole population." "But has this point never been considered by the sovereigns and statesmen of Europe?" I inquired. "You know," replied M. Bloch, "how it is with human beings. We shall all die, but how few care to think of death? It is one of the things inevitable which no one can alter by taking thought. So it is with this question. War once being regarded as unavoidable, the rulers shut their eyes to its consequences. Only once in recent history do I remember any attempt on the part of a European Government gravely to calculate the economic consequences of war under modern conditions. It was when M. Burdeau was in the French Ministry. He appointed a committee of economists for the purpose of ascertaining how the social organism would continue to function in a time of war, how from day to day their bread would be given to the French population. But no sooner had he begun his investigation than a strong objection was raised by the military authorities, and out of deference to their protests the inquiry was indefinitely suspended. Hence we are going forward blindfold, preparing all the while for a war without recognising the fact that the very fundamental first condition of being able to wage it does not exist. You might as well prepare for a naval war without being sure that you have a sea in which your ships can float as to continue to make preparations for a land war unless you have secured in advance the means by which your population shall live. Every great State would in time of war be in the position of a besieged city, and the factor which always decides sieges is the factor which will decide the modern war. Your soldiers may fight as they please; the ultimate decision is in the hands of *famine*." "Well, it is an old saying that 'armies always march upon their bellies,'" said I. "'Hunger is more terrible than iron, and the want of food destroys more armies than battles,' was a saying of the first Napoleon, which holds good to-day." "But," interrupted M. Bloch, "I am not speaking so much of the armies, I am speaking of the population that is behind the armies, which far outnumbers the armies and which is apt to control the policy of which the armies are but the executive instrument. How long do you think the populations of Paris or of Berlin or of the great manufacturing districts in Germany would stand the doubling of the price of their food, accompanied, as it would be, by a great stagnation of industry and all the feverish uncertainty and excitement of war? "What is the one characteristic of modern Europe? Is it not the growth of nervousness and a lack of phlegmatic endurance, of stoical apathy? The modern European feels more keenly and is much more excitable and impressionable than his forefathers. Upon this highly excitable, sensitive population you are going to inflict the miseries of hunger and all the horrors of war. At the same time you will enormously increase their taxes, and at the same time also you will expose your governing and directing classes to more than decimation at the hands of the enemy's sharpshooters. How long do you think your social fabric will remain stable under such circumstances? Believe me, the more the ultimate political and social consequences of the modern war are calmly contemplated, the more clearly will it be evident that if war is possible it is only possible, as I said before, at the price of suicide." "From which, therefore, it follows, in your opinion, M. Bloch, that the Peace Conference has not so much to discuss the question of peace as to inquire into whether or not war is possible?" "A committee of experts, chosen from the ablest representatives of the Powers sent to the Hague," replied M. Bloch, "would have very little difficulty in coming to a conclusion upon the facts which I have just set forth in my book. Those experts might be soldiers and political economists, or the inquiry might be divided into two heads, and the two questions relegated to different committees of specialists. I am quite sure that, as the result of such a dispassionate international investigation into the altered conditions of the problem, they could only arrive at one conclusion – viz., that the day when nations could hope to settle their disputes by appealing to the arbitrament of war has gone by: first, because from that tribunal no definite decision can speedily be secured; and secondly, the costs of the process are ruinous to both the suitors." "It is rather a happy idea, that of yours, M. Bloch," said I, "that of the last Court of Appeal of nations having broken down by the elaboration of its own procedure, the excessive costliness of the trial, and, what is much more serious than anything else, the impossibility of securing a definite verdict. Hitherto the great argument in favour of war is that it has been a tribunal capable of giving unmistakably a decision from which there was no appeal." "Whereas, according to my contention," said M. Bloch, "war has become a tribunal which by the very perfection of its own processes and the costliness of its methods can no longer render a decision of any kind. It may ruin the suitors, but the verdict is liable to be indefinitely postponed." "Therefore the ultimate Court of Appeal having broken down," I said, "it is necessary to constitute another, whose proceedings would not be absolutely inconsistent with economic necessity or with the urgent need for prompt and definite decision. But if this be admitted, what immense world-wide consequences would flow from such a decision." "Yes," said M. Bloch, "the nations would no longer go on wasting £250,000,000 sterling every year in preparing to wage a war which can only be waged at the price of suicide, that is to say, which cannot be waged at all, for no nation willingly commits suicide. Then we may hope for some active effort to be made in the direction of ameliorating the condition of the people. The fund liberated from the war-chest of the world could work marvels if it were utilised in the education of the people. At present, as you will see from the tables which I have compiled in my book, the proportion of money spent on education compared with that spent on war is very small.

In Russia, for instance, we have an immense deal to do in that direction. In some provinces no fewer than 90 per cent. of the recruits are illiterate. In fact, as you will see from what I have written, I have been as much attracted to this subject from the desire to improve the condition of the people as from any other source. Hence my book took in part the shape of an investigation of the moral, social, and material conditions in which the masses of the Russian peasants pass their lives. It is a painful picture, and one that cannot fail profoundly to touch the hearts of all those who have followed the results of my investigation. The condition of the mass of the people in every country leaves much to be desired, but especially is this the case in my own country, where the resources of civilisation have hardly been drawn upon for the improvement of the condition of the peasants." "Yet, M. Bloch, I think I gather from you that Russia was better able to support a war than more highly organised nations." "You are quite right," said M. Bloch. "It is true that Russia can, perhaps better than all other countries, contemplate the dangers or impossibilities of modern war; but that is precisely because she is not so highly organised and so advanced or developed in civilisation as her neighbours. Russia is the only country in Europe which produces sufficient food for her own people. She is not only able to produce enough grain to feed her own people, but she exports at present four millions of tons every year. A war which stopped the export trade would simply place this immense mass of food at the disposal of our own people, who would be more in danger of suffering from a plethora of food than from a scarcity. But nevertheless, although this is the case, the very backwardness of Russia renders it more important that she should avoid exposing her nascent civilisation to the tremendous strain of a great war. Practically we may be invulnerable, but if, when having beaten back our invaders, we were to endeavour in turn to carry the war across our frontiers, we should find ourselves confronted by the same difficulties which make offensive war increasingly difficult, not to say impossible. Neither is there any conceivable territorial or political result attainable by force of arms here or in Asia which would be any adequate compensation for the sacrifices which even a victorious war would entail." "All this may be true, but nations do not always count the cost before going to war." "No," said M. Bloch; "if they did, they would very seldom go to war. Take, for instance, the civil war in the United States of America. According to some calculations it would have cost the United States four milliards of francs, that is to say £160,000,000 sterling, to have bought up all their slaves at £200 a head, and emancipated them. Instead of taking that method of solving a dangerous and delicate problem, they appealed to the sword, with the result that it is estimated that the war occasioned the country losses of one kind and another amounting to twenty-five milliards of francs, or £1,000,000,000 sterling, to say nothing of all the bloodshed and misery entailed by that war. The cost of emancipation thus ciphered out at £1200 a head per slave instead of £200 per head, at which the bargain could easily have been arranged. The economic condition of our peasants in many of our provinces," continued M. Bloch, "is heartrending. Their ignorance, their innocence, their simplicity, render them an easy prey to money-lenders, who have in many cases succeeded in establishing a veritable system of slave labour." "How could that be?" 1 asked. "The serfs were emancipated in 1861." "Yes," said M. Bloch, "they were emancipated, but their emancipation without education left them an easy prey to the Kulaks, who advance money upon their labour. A peasant, for instance, has to pay his taxes, say, in winter time, and the Kulak will advance the twenty or thirty roubles which he may have to pay in return for what is called his 'summer labour.' The price of labour in Russia in summer is twice or thrice as much as it is in winter. The Kulak buys the summer labour at the winter rates, and then having purchased in advance the summer labour of the unfortunate peasant, he collects his chattels in droves and farms them out wherever he can dispose of them. It is veritable slavery. But even this is less terrible than that which can be witnessed in some provinces, where parents sell their children to speculators, who buy them up and send them to St. Petersburg and Moscow as calves are sent to market, where they are sold out for a term of years as apprentices to those who have no scruples against securing cheap labour on those terms. "No one who has seen anything of the squalor and wretchedness, the struggle with fever and famine, in the rural districts of Russia, especially when there has been a failure of harvest, can be other than passionate to divert for the benefit of the people some of the immense volume of wealth that is spent in preparing for this impossible war. The children of most Russian peasants come into the world almost like brute beasts, without any medical or skilled attendance at childbirth, and they are brought up hard in a way that fortunately you know little of in wealthy England. Can you imagine, for instance," said M. Bloch, speaking with great fervour and feeling, "the way in which infants are left inside the home of most Russian peasants, whose mothers have to leave them to labour in the fields? The child is left alone to roll about the earthen floor of the hut, and as it will cry for hunger, poultices of chewed black bread are tied round its hands and feet, so that the little creature may have something to suck at until its mother comes back from the fields. At every stage in life you find the same deplorable lack of what more prosperous nations regard as indispensable to human existence. In some provinces we have only thirty-seven doctors per million inhabitants, and as for nurses, schoolmasters, and other agents of civilisation, there are whole vast tracts in which they are absolutely unknown. All this makes our population hardy, no doubt – those who survive; but the infant mortality is frightful, and the life which the survivors lead is very hard and sometimes very terrible." "The contrasts between the vital statistics of Russia and of France are, I suppose, about as wide as could be imagined." "Yes," said M. Bloch. "But although the French system of limiting the family and keeping infant mortality down to a minimum has some great advantages, it has great disadvantages. In a limited family much greater pains are taken to preserve the life of the sickly children. Hence, instead of allowing them to be eliminated by natural process, whereby the race would be preserved from deterioration, they are sedulously kept alive, and the vitality of the nation is thereby diminished. In other respects our Russian people are very different from what you imagine. For instance, it may surprise you, but it is undoubtedly true, that the amount of spirit consumed by our people is very much less per head than that which is drunk in England, and also that the number of illegitimate births in Russia is lower per thousand than in an other country in Europe. This is due to the prevalence of early marriages, for our people marry so early that when our young men are taken for the army from 30 to 60 per cent. are married before they enter the ranks. You may smile," said M. Bloch, "at me for thinking that those questions must be considered in a discussion of the future war; but it is the moral stamina of a population which will ultimately decide its survival, and I therefore could not exclude the discussion of all the elements which contribute to the well-being of a population in endeavouring to forecast the future of war." "Now, M. Bloch, let us turn to another subject. We have talked hitherto about armies, and only about armies. What is your idea about navies?" "My idea about a navy," said M. Bloch, "is that unless you have a supreme navy, it is not worth while having one at all, and that a navy that is not supreme is only a hostage in the hands of the Power whose fleet is supreme. Hence, it seems to me that for Russia to spend millions in the endeavour to create a deep-sea fleet of sea-going battleships is a great mistake. The money had much better be used for other purposes." "What!" said I, "then, do you not think that Russia needs a navy?" "A navy, yes," said M. Bloch, "a navy for coast defence, perhaps, and also cruisers, but a fighting fleet of battleships, no. It is a folly to attempt to create such a navy, and the sooner that is recognised the better." "But," I persisted, "do you not agree with Captain Mahan in thinking that sea-power is the dominant factor in the destiny of nations?" "Do not let us theorise; let us look at facts," said M. Bloch. "What I see very plainly is that the navy may be almost ignored as a vital factor in a war to the death between Russia and any of her neighbours. Suppose, for instance, that we had a war with Germany. What would be the good of our fleet? Suppose that it is inferior to that of Germany, it will be either captured, or shut up in harbour, unable to go out. If it is superior to that of Germany, what better are we? Here we have history to guide us. We cannot hope to have such an unquestioned superiority at sea over the Germans as the French had in the war of 1870; but what use was the naval supremacy of France to the French in their death-grapple with the Germans? Why, so far from finding them useful, they absolutely laid their ironclads up in harbour and sent their crews to Paris to assist in the defence of the capital – and they did right. Germany was striking at the heart of France when she struck at Paris, and no amount of superiority over the German fleet on the part of the French could be counted for a moment as a set-off against the loss of their capital. So it will always be." "But," I objected, "could the German fleet not be utilised for the purpose of landing an expedition on the Russian coast?" "No doubt," said M. Bloch, "it might. But here again I may quote Count Moltke. When, in 1870, we were discussing the possibility of a French expedition to the shores of the Baltic, Moltke declared that, so far from regarding such an expedition with alarm, he would rather welcome it, because any diversion of French forces from the point where the decisive blow must be delivered would increase the German chances of success. Hence, if the Germans were to send an expeditionary force to Russian waters, it would only represent the subtraction of so many fighting men from the seat of war, where the real issue of the campaign would be decided. No; Russia would have no reason to fear any serious attack from the sea. That being so, what is the use of wasting all our resources upon ironclads which we could not use? It would have been much better to have gone on piling up expenditure on our army much more rapidly than we have upon our fleet. In 1876 we spent twenty-seven million roubles on the navy, and twenty years later we were spending sixty-seven millions, so that the naval expenditure had more than doubled, while the expenditure on the army had only increased fifty per cent." "Do you not think that a German, British, or Japanese fleet might seriously injure Russia by bombarding the coast towns?" "No," said M. Bloch. "Such coast towns as we have, and they are not many, are for the most part well defended, too well defended to be seriously attacked by an enemy's fleet. The experience of Crete does not increase our dread of the bombarding ironclad as a method likely to affect the issues of a campaign. Why, is it not true that the international fleet on one occasion fired 70 shells and only killed three men and wounded 15?" "And what about the protection of your commerce, M. Bloch?" "The protection of our commerce would have to be undertaken (if undertaken at all) by cruisers and not by battleships. Besides, there should be some regard paid to the value of the thing protected, and the insurance which you pay for it. At this moment our oversea mercantile marine is small, so small compared with that of England that, although you are spending twice as much on your navy as we do, your naval insurance rate (if we may so call it) only amounts to 16 francs per ton of merchant shipping, whereas with us the rate is as high as 130 francs; or if it is reckoned by a percentage upon the trade, our naval expenditure is twice as high as yours. And to what purpose?" "But, M. Bloch, supposing that our fleet is inferior in strength to the German fleet, and that it is wiped off the race of the sea. What then?" "What then?" said M. Bloch. "Why, we shall just be in the position that the Italians were in when they lost their fleet at Lissa to the Austrians. But what effect had that decisive naval victory upon the fortunes of the campaign? The fate of Austria was sealed by the battle of Sadowa, and all naval losses which we might incur would naturally be charged for in the indemnity which we should impose upon our defeated enemy if we came off victorious, and if we were beaten on land our defeat at sea would not be a material aggravation of our position." "But, M. Bloch, do not you think that you need a strong fleet in order to keep your channels of trade open?" "I do not believe," said M. Bloch, "that you can keep your channels of trade open, even with the strongest fleet. I grant that if you have a supreme fleet, you may at least have a chance of keeping the trade routes open, but if you have not a supreme fleet (and for Russia this is out of the question) you can do nothing, and Russia, fortunately being self-contained and self-supporting, could manage to subsist better, if her oversea trade were cut off; than any other country." "Then how would you apply your reasoning to England?" "England," said M. Bloch, "is in a different category from all the other nations. You only grow enough bread in your own country to feed your people for three months in the year. If you do not command the seas, if you cannot bring to your markets the food of the world, you are in the position of a huge beleaguered fortress with only three months' rations for the whole people. If you ask my opinion, I tell you frankly that I do not think your position is very enviable, not because of any danger from invasion, for I recognise the superiority of your fleet, but because it seems to me that any nation is in a very precarious position which has to depend for so much of its food upon countries across the sea. A single cruiser let loose upon one of your great trade routes would send up the price of provisions enormously, and although no one could hope to blockade the English ports, any interruption in the supply of raw material, any interference with the stream of food products which are indispensable for the sustenance of your people, would endanger you far more than the loss of a pitched battle. "It is true that you are prosperous; but there are many elements in your population the material condition of which leaves much to be desired, and with the stress and strain of industrial stagnation, caused by the closing of markets abroad and the rise in the price of food which would be inevitable under any circumstances, you might have as considerable internal difficulties as any of those which threaten your neighbours. But, there again, if (which God forbid) England should find herself at war, the factor which will decide the issue will not be the decisive battle; it will be pressure of want, the lack of food, in short, the economic results which must inevitably follow any great war in the present complex state of human civilisation. "In short," said M. Bloch, "I regard the economic factor as the dominant and decisive element in the matter. You cannot fight unless you can eat, and at the present moment you cannot feed your people and wage a great war. To a certain extent this is already recognised, so much so that there are a few general principles that it is worth while mentioning. First, you may take it for granted that the great war, if it ever breaks out, will not take place until after the harvest has been gathered. To mobilise in spring, or in early summer, would bring starvation too closely home to the population for any statesman to think of it. Secondly, whenever there is a bad harvest you may be sure there will be no war. Even with a full granary it will be very difficult for any nation to feed its troops, to say nothing of its home population. With a bad harvest it would be impossible. Hence, if ever you should see a rapid buying-up of bread-stuffs on the part of any nation, you may feel sure that there is danger ahead; but so long as there is no attempt made to secure reserve supplies of grain, you may regard with comparative equanimity the menaces of war." "Then, on the whole, you are hopeful concerning the future, M. Bloch?" "Yes," said he; "hopeful with the hope that is born not of fantasy or of Utopian dreaming, but from the painstaking examination of hard, disagreeable facts. The soldier is going down and the economist is going up. There is no doubt of it. Humanity has progressed beyond the stage in which war can any longer be regarded as a possible Court of Appeal. Even military service has lost much of its fascination. At one time war appealed to the imagination of man, and the poets and painters found no theme so tempting as depicting the heroism of the individual warrior, whose courage and might often turned the tide of battle and decided the destiny of nations. All that has long gone by the board. War has become more and more a matter of mechanical arrangement. Modern battles will be decided, so far as they can be decided at all, by men lying in improvised ditches which they have scooped out to protect themselves from the fire of a distant and invisible enemy. All the pomp and circumstance of glorious war disappeared when smokeless powder was invented. As a profession militarism is becoming less and less attractive. There is neither booty to be gained, nor promotion, with an ever increasing certainty of a disagreeable death, should war ever take place. "The old toast in the British Army used to be," I said, "Bloody war and quick promotion." "Yes," said M. Bloch, "as long as bloody war only killed out a certain percentage it meant more rapid promotion for the rest, but if it kills out too many the attraction fails, for there is no promotion to a dead man. Side by side with the drying up of the attractiveness of a military career there has gone on an increasing agitation against the whole system, an agitation which finds its most extreme exponents among the Socialists, whose chief stock-in-trade is to dwell upon the waste of industrial resources caused by the present organisation of society on a competitive basis, which they maintain naturally and necessarily results in the excessive burdens of our armed peace. What the Governments will all come to see soon more or less clearly is that if they persist in squandering the resources of their people in order to prepare for a war which has already become impossible without suicide, they will only be preparing the triumph of the socialist revolution."

BLOCH'S PREFACE TO HIS OWN BOOK (1898)

Natural philosophers declare that the atmosphere reveals at times the presence of a certain so-called cosmic dust. It influences the change of colours in the sky, it colours the sunlight with a bloody line, it penetrates our dwellings and our lungs, acts injuriously upon living organisms, and, falling even upon the summits of hills, leaves its traces upon their mantles of virgin snow.

In the public and private life of modern Europe something of the same kind reveals itself. A presentiment is felt that the present incessant growth of armaments must either call forth a war, ruinous both for conqueror and for conquered, and ending perhaps in general anarchy, or reduce the people to the most lamentable condition.

Is this unquiet state of mind the consequence of a mistaken or sickly condition of the nervous system of the modern man? Or is it justified by possible contingencies?

Such questions cannot be answered categorically. All would desire that the dangers caused by armaments were but a symptom which time will destroy. But even an unanimous desire cannot have the power to change the great concatenation of circumstances which are the cause of armaments, until the time shall come when, in the words of Von Thünen, the interests of nations and the interests of humanity shall cease to contend with one another, and culture shall have awakened a sense of the solidarity of the interests of all.

Such a state of affairs is unhappily still distant. It is true that the ruinousness of war under modern conditions is apparent to all. But this gives no sufficient guarantee that war will not break forth suddenly, even in opposition to the wishes of those who take part in it. Involuntarily we call to mind the words of the great Bacon, that "in the vanity of the world a greater field of action is open for folly than for reason, and frivolity always enjoys more influence than judgment." To-day these words are even more apposite than in the past. For Reason itself it is harder than before to find a path in the field of circumstances which change for ever. The speed with which relations change is a characteristic feature of our time. In modern times a few years see greater changes in the material and moral condition of masses than formerly took place in the course of centuries. This greater mobility of contemporary life is the consequence of better education, the activity of parliaments, of associations, and of the press, and the influence of improved communications. Under such influences the peoples of the world live lives not only their own, but the lives of others also; intellectual triumphs, economic progress, materialised among one people, react at once on the condition of others; the intellectual outlook widens as we ascend, as the seascape widens from a hill, and, like the sea, the whole world of culture drifts and fluctuates eternally.

Every change in conditions or disposition is affirmed only after a struggle of elements. An analysis of the history of mankind shows that from the year 1496 B.C. to the year 1861 of our era, that is, in a cycle of 3357 years, were but 227 years of peace and 3130 years of war: in other words, were thirteen years of war for every year of peace. Considered thus, the history of the lives of peoples presents a picture of uninterrupted struggle. War, it would appear, is a normal attribute to human life.

The position now has changed in much, but still the new continues to contend with the remnants of the old. The old order has changed and given place to the new. Siéyes compared the old order of things with a pyramid standing upon its apex, declaring that it must be given a more natural position and placed upon its base. This demand has been fulfilled in this sense, that the edifice of state has been placed upon foundations incomparably wider than before, affirmed on the rights and wills of millions of men, the so-named middle order of society.

It is natural that the greater the number of voices influencing the course of affairs the more complex is the sum of interests to be considered. The economic revolution caused by the application of steam has been the cause of entirely new and unexpected conditions between the different countries of the world and between the classes inhabiting them, enriching and strengthening some, impoverishing and weakening others, in measure as the new conditions permitted to each participation in the new distribution of revenues, capital, and influence.

With the innumerable voices which are now bound up in our public opinion, and the many different representatives of its interests, naturally appear very different views on militarism and its object, war. The propertied classes, in particular those whose importance and condition was established during the former distribution of power and former methods of acquisition, precisely those classes whom we call Conservatives, are inclined to confuse even the intellectual movement against militarism with aspirations for the subversion of social order. In this is sometimes given, they attribute, too great an importance to single and transitory phenomena, while no sufficient attention is turned on the dangerous fermentation of minds awakened by the present and constantly growing burdens of militarism.

On the other hand, agitators, seeking influence on the minds of the masses, having deduced from the new conditions with recklessness and even intentional misrepresentation the most extreme conclusions, deny all existing rights, and promise to the masses more than the most perfect institutions could give them. In striving to arouse the masses against militarism such agitators unceremoniously ascribe to every thinker who does not share their views selfish impulses, although in reality he may be following sincere convictions.

And although the masses are slow to surrender themselves to abstract reasoning, and act usually only under the influence of passion or disaster, there can be no doubt that this agitation, ceaselessly carried on in parliaments, on platforms, and in the press, penetrates more and more deeply the people, and awakens in it those feelings which in the midst of the disasters called forth by war might easily lead them to action. The evil of militarism serves to-day as the chief instrument of the activity of agitators, and a tangible object for attack, while in reality these agitators strive not only for the suppression of militarism, but for the destruction of the whole social order.

With such a position of affairs – that is, on the one hand, the ruinous competition in constantly increasing armaments, and, on the other, the social danger for all which grows under a general burden – it is necessary that influential and educated men should seriously attempt to give themselves a clear account of the effect of war under modern conditions; whether it will be possible to realise the aims of war, and whether the extermination of millions of men will not be wholly without result.

If, after consideration of all circumstances, we answer ourselves, "War with such conditions is impossible; armies could not sustain those cataclysms which a future war would call forth; the civil population could not bear the famine and interruption of industry," then we might ask the general question: "Why do the peoples more and more exhaust their strength in accumulating means of destruction which are valueless even to accomplish the ends for which they are prepared?"

It is very natural, that even a long time ago, in many Western European countries, in all ranks of society, many attempts have been made, partly theoretical and partly practical, to eliminate war from the future history of humanity. Philosophers and philanthropists, statesmen and revolutionaries, poets and artists, parliaments and congresses, more strongly and strongly every day insist upon the necessity of avoiding the bloodshed and disasters of war.

A time was when it seemed protests against war were assuming practical importance. But the desire for revenge awakened by the events of 1870 turned the disposition of peoples in another direction. Nevertheless the idea remains and continues to operate on minds. The voices of scholars and the efforts of philanthropists directed against war naturally found an echo among the lower orders of populations. In the twilight of imperfect knowledge fantastic visions appeared, of which agitators took advantage. This agitation increased every year.

In recent times war has become even more terrible than before in consequence of perfected weapons of destruction and systems of equipment and training utterly unknown in the past. What is graver still, the immensity of armies and the training of soldiers in entrenchment must call forth difficulties in provisioning and defence from climatic conditions.

It is true that certain military authors think that the bloodshed of the battlefield will be decreased in consequence of the greater distance between the combatants, that attacks by cavalry and with the bayonet are improbable in the present conditions of firearms, while retreat will be facilitated for a defeated army. But, even admitting this, which is by no means proved, there can be no doubt that with modern firearms the impression which battle makes on armies will be incomparably greater than before, while smokeless powder will change even the nature of these impressions. Infantry and artillery fire will have unprecedented force, while aid to the wounded will be made more difficult by the great range both of small-arms and of artillery. Smoke will no longer conceal from the survivors the terrible consequences of the battle, and every advance will be made with full appreciation of the probabilities of extermination. From this, and from the fact that the mass of soldiers will have but recently been called from the field, the factory, and the workshop, it will appear that even the psychical conditions of war have changed. Thus in the armies of Western states the agitation against war may extend even so far as the materialisation of socialistic theories subverting the bases of monarchies.

The thought of those convulsions which will be called forth by a war, and of the terrible means prepared for it, will hinder military enterprise, notwithstanding the passionate relations of the people to some of the questions in dispute among them. But on the other hand, the present conditions cannot continue to exist for ever. The peoples groan under the burdens of militarism. Europe is ever confronted with the necessity of drawing from the productive forces of the peoples new and new millions for military purposes. Hardly was the small-calibre rifle adopted when invention made a new advance, and there can be no doubt that soon the Great Powers will be compelled to adopt a weapon of still smaller calibre with double the present energy, allowing soldiers to carry a greater number of cartridges. At the same time we see in France and Germany preparation of new artillery to turn to the best advantage the new smokeless powder. Millions are expended on the construction of new battleships and cruisers. But every year brings such radical improvements in guns, in speed, and in coal-carrying capacity that vessels hardly launched are obsolete, and others must be built to replace them. In view of what we see in Germany, Italy, and Austria, we are compelled to ask, Can the present incessant demands for money from Parliament for armaments continue for ever without social outbreaks? And will not the present difficulty of carrying on war at last be replaced by an absolute impossibility, at least in those countries where high culture has increased the value of the life of every citizen? Thus, in the war of the future will appear not only quantitative differences in the number of armies but also qualitative differences which may have immense importance.

But what is still graver are the economic and social convulsions which war will call forth in consequence of the summons under the flag of almost the whole male population, the interruption of maritime communications, the stagnation in industry and trade, the increase in the price of the necessaries of life, and the destruction of credit. Will these convulsions not be so great that governments will find it impossible in the course of time indicated by military specialists as the probable duration of war to acquire means for maintaining their armies, satisfy the requirements of budgets, and at the same time feed the destitute remainder of the civil population?

Within the last twenty-five years such changes have taken place in the very nature of military operations that the future war will in no way be like its predecessors. In consequence of the adoption of improved artillery, explosive shells, and small-arms which allow the soldier to carry an immense number of cartridges, in consequence of the absence of concealing smoke, in consequence of the immense proportions which military operations must take as a result of the vastness of armies, such unquestioned authorities on military affairs as Moltke and Leer and many other eminent military writers declare that a future war will last many years.

But with modern political, social, and economic conditions it would be strange if there did not arise in England, Italy, Austria, Russia, Germany, and France – in one country from one reason, in another from another – factors which will disarrange the apparatus of war and prevent its continuance before the ends desired shall have been attained. This is a question of the first gravity, yet military writers entirely ignore it, attending only to the technical side of war.

In consequence of alliances concluded, all plans of activity are founded on the combined operations of allied armies. What will happen to combinations founded on united action when one or another of the allies is compelled to cease operations through insufficient means for resisting the social influences of war?

Thus we find that military questions are bound up with questions of economy. But military writers look on the future war only from the point of view of attaining certain objects by destroying the armies of the enemy; the economic and social consequences of war, if they are considered at all, are considered only as secondary objects. Even economists, in consequence of the difficulty of such a question, have made no single investigation resulting in a complete picture of the consequences of war. But this is in no way surprising.

Without acquaintance with the technicalities of warfare it is impossible to understand what will be its precise conditions, or to define the limits where the operation of defined laws will cease and accidental phenomena appear. A result could only be obtained by careful study of the very nature of war in all its phenomena. Twenty years ago such a task would have been comparatively easy. But the last two decades have witnessed immense changes equal to revolutions. First of all a fundamental change has taken place in the very elements which take part in war and from which its course depends. In a future war on the field of battle, instead of professional soldiers, will appear whole peoples with all their peculiar virtues and failings.

A full appreciation of the conditions of a future war is all the more difficult since on the one hand new methods of attack and defence, as yet insufficiently tested, will be employed. and, on the other hand, because former wars were carried on by means of long-service professional soldiers. But not only will a future war take the character of a struggle of whole nations living a wide and complex life, with military problems corresponding in complexity, but the arms and apparatus of destruction are the very finest result of the inventiveness and creative activity of mankind.

The elements contending in a future war will be all the moral and intellectual resources of nations, all the forces of modern civilisation, all technical improvements, feelings, characters, minds and wills – the combined fruit of the culture of the civilized world. It is thus that this question demands the attention of all society. In Western states, especially from the adoption of conscription, interest in military affairs has spread through all ranks of society.

Reasoning on the basis of future wars, military writers declare that the chief elements of warfare, although only in their general character, must be made known to the population, which in the event of war constitutes the army, and from whose activity depends the issue of campaigns. It is not enough that officers and soldiers actually on service know what they are to meet in a future war. In the ranks of armies in time of war will appear an immense proportion of officers and men from the reserves, who for many years have taken no part in military exercises. As a consequence of this, in every state appear popular compositions with the object of informing the public of the technique of modern war, all, almost without exception, neglecting the economic side of the question. Some prejudge a future war from the example of history. Such neglect, as a rule, the improvement of weapons and the increased complexity of strategy and tactics. Others, well informed as to the improvement of weapons, but neglecting inevitable conclusions, assume that war will last but a short time, and therefore pay no attention to the financial and economic perturbation which it will cause or its effects on the moral condition of the people.

The late General Fadeleff very justly pointed out the danger arising from such a state of affairs. "The opinion of the people of their strength has immense influence on the course of politics; this opinion is often frivolous and unfounded, though from it may depend the destiny of nations. Yet it is generally agreed that even the elements of military affairs constitute a speciality which must remain unknown by the public. But when the moment comes to express its opinion on war and peace, to balance the chances of success, it may be assumed that of ten military specialists whose authority is accepted nine will adopt the opinions of the social medium in which they live. Thus a public, entirely ignorant of military questions, often becomes the deciding factor in decision. To free oneself from the influence of public opinion in such matters is impossible." It was with the object of making accessible in some degree information accumulated on all matters directly or indirectly connected with war that the present work was undertaken, of which this volume is but an abridgment.

It is but a slight service to diagnose an illness and pronounce it incurable. The position of the European world, the organic strength of which is wasted, on the one hand, in the sacrifice of millions on preparations for war, and, on the other, in a destructive agitation which finds in militarism its apology and a fit instrument for acting on the minds of the people, must be admitted to be abnormal and even sickly. Is it possible that there can be no recovery from this?

We are deeply persuaded that a means of recovery exists if the European states would but set themselves the question – in what will result these armaments and this exhaustion, what will be the nature of a future war, can resource [*sic*] be had to war even now for the decision of questions in dispute, and is it possible to conceive the settlement of such questions by means of the cataclysm which, with modern means of destruction, a war between five Great Powers with ten millions of soldiers would cause?

Delay in the practical settlement of this question is impossible. And when a settlement is arrived at it will be shown that for twenty, forty years millions have been wasted yearly on fruitless armaments which cannot be employed, and by means of which the decision of international disputes is inconceivable. But then it will be too late; then such immense losses will have been sustained that Europe generally will be in a worse position than Italy to-day. Then, instead of the dangers of international war, other threatening symptoms will have appeared.

That war will become impossible in time – this is indicated by all. Its apparatus grows more rapidly than the productiveness of European states, and preparations will continue to swallow more and more of the income of peoples. Meantime the relations of the nations become closer and closer, their interdependence more plain, and their solidarity in any great convulsion will constantly grow.

That war will finally become impracticable is apparent. The question is more apposite – when will the recognition of this inevitable truth be spread among European governments and peoples? When the impossibility of resorting to war for the decision of international quarrels is apparent to all, other means will be devised.

This interview with Bloch preceded the publication in English of the sixth and concluding volume of his study on the Future of War, which appeared under the title 'Is War now Impossible?' in 1899. The interview was made by William T. Stead and was reprinted in 1991 in the Gregg Revivals Edition of Bloch's work, entitled 'Is War Now Impossible? Being an Abridgement of the War of the Future, in its Technical, Economic and Political Relations' (Aldershot 1991).

Stead, who is described (by Brian Bond) as a radical, crusading journalist, died later on the Titanic.

Bloch's unique influence arose from the combination within him of the skills of technical and social analysis and a strong political compaigning spirit. The full flavour of this mixture is found in the vivid imagery and acute observations of his own Preface. As distillation of his views on how technological change conditions, politics and social values resonate strongly with the "globalisation" debates of today.

3

THE IMPERIAL RESCRIPT

The maintenance of general peace, and a possible reduction of the excessive armaments which weigh upon all nations, present themselves in the existing condition of the whole world, as the ideal towards which the endeavors of all Governments should be directed.

The humanitarian and magnanimous ideas of His Majesty the Emperor, my August Master, have been won over to this view. In the conviction that this lofty aim is in conformity with the most essential interests and the legitimate views of all Powers, the Imperial Governments thinks that the present moment would be very favorable for seeking, by means of international discussion, the most effectual means of insuring to all peoples the benefits of a real and durable peace, and above all, of putting an end to the progressive development of the present armaments.

In the course of the last twenty years the longings for a general appeasement have become especially pronounced in the consciences of civilized nations. The preservation of peace has been put forward as the object of international policy; in its name great States have concluded between themselves powerful alliances; it is the better to guarantee peace that they have developed, in proportions hitherto unprecedented, their military forces, and still continue to increase them without shrinking from any sacrifice.

All these efforts nevertheless have not yet been able to bring about the beneficent results of the desired pacification. The financial charges following an upward march strike at the public prosperity at its very source.

The intellectual and physical strength of the nations, labor and capital, are the major part diverted from their natural application, and unproductively consumed. Hundreds of millions are devoted to acquiring terrible engines of destruction, which, though today regarded as the last word of science, are destined to-morrow to lose all value in consequence of some fresh discovery in the same field.

National culture, economic progress, and the production of wealth are either paralyzed or checked in their development. Moreover, in proportion as the armaments of each Power increase, so do they less and less fulfill the object which the Governments have set before themselves.

The economic crises, due in great part to the system of armaments *à l'outrance*, and the continual danger which lies in this massing of war material, are transforming the armed peace of our days into a crushing burden, which the peoples have more and more difficulty in bearing. It appears evident, then, that if this state of things were prolonged, it would inevitably lead to the very cataclysm which it is desired to avert, and to the horrors of which make every thinking man shudder in advance.

To put an end to these incessant armaments and to seek the means of warding off the calamities which are threatening the whole world, – such is the supreme duty which is to-day imposed on all States.

Filled with this idea, His Majesty has been pleased to order me to propose to all the Governments whose representatives are accredited to the Imperial Court, the meeting of a conference which would have to occupy itself with this grave problem.

This conference should be, by the help of God, a happy presage for the century which is about to open. It would converge in one powerful focus the efforts of all States which are sincerely seeking to make the great idea of universal peace triumph over the elements of trouble and discord.

It would, at the same time, confirm their agreement by the solemn establishment of the principles of justice and right, upon which repose the security of States and the welfare of peoples.

4

JAN BLOCH IN THE CENTURY'S CONTEXT

HRH the Prince of Orange

There are two reasons for this meeting. First, we are commemorating the legacy of Jan Bloch. In his study, *The Future of War in its Technical, Economic and Political Relations*, he gave Tsar Nicholas II the clear advice that war could no longer be waged successfully. That conviction led to the first Peace Conference, which was hosted by my great-grandmother, Queen Wilhelmina, in The Hague in May 1899.

Secondly, we are rethinking the phenomenon of war in today's context: after a century that has seen the most terrible wars, followed by the most hopeful attempts at overcoming them. Discussion will be on the future of military strategy and the nature of future conflicts, but mostly, I hope, on strengthening international governance in the next century. After all, reflecting on the future of war can serve no other purpose than furthering future peace.

Bloch was convinced that a military and technical revolution had taken place during the second half of the 19th century. The range, power and speed of firearms had increased. The invention of smokeless explosives had enhanced visibility on the battlefield, putting the defence in a better position. Conscription and railway transport would lead to mass movements of troops and weapons. Given these developments, successful warfare would no longer be possible, since even the so-called 'victors' would suffer severe losses. Bloch feared that warfare would destroy the very fabric of society.

His ideas ran counter to the cult of the offensive, which dominated military thinking in Europe at that time. With hindsight, we know that his analysis was correct. The First World War developed into an extremely bloody stalemate on the western front. The mood had been very optimistic at the start, yet the outcome was a long bloodletting that weakened the European state system that had dominated the world.

G. Prins and H. Tromp (eds.), The Future of War, 61-66.

These developments cast doubt on the possibility that war could be waged in any kind of rational way. They cast doubt also on Clausewitz's famous plea that war should be 'a continuation of politics with the admixture of other means'. Was controlled warfare, with limits on the hatred between peoples and the war aims of politicians, still possible?

What does this mean for us today? How has war been transformed by nuclear deterrence, the changing nature of conflict during the last decade and the influence of the media and information technology?

Warfare nowadays seems to take different forms in different parts of the world. We should perhaps draw a distinction between at least two different types of warfare.

First, *war between states*. Although it seems to have become less frequent, which is a hopeful sign, military aggression between states still exists. However, these days states are using their military apparatus in totally new ways.

The second form of war, *intra-state violence*, occurs much more frequently. It encompasses a continuum of violence ranging from terrorism and communal violence to anti-regime rebellion and civil war. These conflicts tend to become drawn out, and the dividing line between war and peace often becomes blurred. This kind of violence is the result of the inability of states to resolve internal conflicts in a peaceful manner. It is related to problems of political legitimacy, tensions between population groups and religions, and stagnation in socio-economic development. The most dramatic consequence of this kind of violence is complete state failure and even collapse. Although we may label these wars as internal, neighbouring countries can be drawn in. Indeed, the effects of these wars usually threaten peace and security in a wider region. Often, intra-state wars are accompanied by gross violations of human rights. Such humanitarian catastrophes may lead to involvement of the international community.

This century has also seen the most vicious forms of state terror, often under the guise of civil or external warfare. The human suffering this causes far exceeds our comprehension.

What opportunities are there in the contemporary international system to prevent and limit wars?

The conventions agreed at the two Hague Peace Conferences were intended to limit the damage after war had broken out (*ius in bellum*). They did not address the issue of the prevention of war (*ius ad bello*). The Geneva Conventions of 1949, and their follow-up in 1977, extended the rules governing warfare. However, bad governance in many states has led frequently to these regulations being ignored.

Immediately after the Second World War, the UN Charter attempted to eradicate the scourge of warfare between states. The intention was to equip the United Nations with armed forces provided by its member states. Due to the Cold War, however, this goal was never achieved. After the genocide in Rwanda in 1994, The Netherlands proposed that a rapid reaction force be established under UN command. This, too, has failed to materialise. However, progress has been made on the establishment of a rapidly deployable mission headquarters. Furthermore, a number of states are working presently on the establishment of a rapidly deployable peacekeeping brigade for the UN stand-by arrangement system.

So, even now that the Cold War has ended, we have to admit that the capacity of the international community to safeguard peace and security is rather restricted. I conclude my contribution by mentioning five sets of problems and dilemmas that we must address if we are to strengthen this capacity:

1   BEYOND CLASSIC DEFENCE

Classic defence tasks now have to be combined with new ones, such as conflict prevention and crisis response. How do you strike the right balance between the defence of your own territory (or treaty area) and these new tasks?

2   MILITARY PERSONNEL

How can these tasks be combined most effectively in operational terms? Sometimes a soldier is required to be a warrior. At other times, he (or she) has to act like a policeman or even a diplomat. It is not always easy to shift from one skill to the other. The armed forces, therefore, need a finely-balanced staffing policy.

Several western states abolished conscription after the end of the Cold War. The reasons were that not enough of those eligible for conscription were actually being called up, and that a professional army could be deployed much more easily for peace support operations. However, the end of conscription changed the relationship between the armed forces and other sectors of society. Professionalisation of the armed forces implies that military personnel must have high qualifications. This gives them advantages in the labour market after they have completed their term.

3   EQUIPMENT

We have to consider the requirements of equipment and technology. We seem to live in an era where 'manned arms' are being transformed into 'armed men'. This would imply a return to the era before the mechanisation and motorisation of armies. On the other hand, as I saw during my three visits to Bosnia-Herzegovina, heavy weapons and a willingness to use force are indispensable in 'peace enforcement' and 'state building' missions.

As for technology, opinions differ. Some military strategists argue that improvements in technology, leading to superiority in accuracy of weapons and to advantages in information and communications, should enable us to cope with the new kinds of threat. Others point to the limitations and weaknesses of technological solutions.

4   ROLE OF THE STATE

The fourth set of problems relates to the future of the state. States are having to cope with processes like globalisation, regional integration and decentralisation. The concept of sovereignty is, therefore, being broadened. For instance, in an integrating Europe, state power includes what has become known as 'sharing sovereignty'.

Intra-state violence has coincided with fragmentation of central authority in a number of societies. We, therefore, face the major challenge of increasing political leaders' capacities to deal with the political and economic demands of their citizens in non-violent ways.

5   INTERNATIONAL ORGANISATIONS

Finally, strong and reliable states remain necessary to increase the capacity of international organisations.

Fortunately, since the end of the Cold War, the United Nations has become a forum for cooperation between the great powers of the world. In view of its continuing shortage of capacity, we should also welcome the fact that the UN can now rely increasingly on regional organisations, such as the Organisation for Security and Cooperation in Europe (OSCE). Similarly, organisations capable of engaging in military operations, such as NATO in Bosnia-Herzegovina, have been willing to implement UN Security Council resolutions. We must be thankful also for the cooperation between NATO and its former adversaries. In the case of Russia, the Permanent Joint Council is a major accomplishment. In the new security context, the prevention of armed conflict requires much of our time and energy. We must find new formulas for arms limitation, to help to guarantee military stability.

I would like to return to European integration. Is this not a perfect example of our human potential to transcend the deep-seated reflexes of war, of how it is possible to establish democracy, stability and wealth among former adversaries? Is this not the only real answer to the silent questions of the millions of war dead this century has seen? This process can serve both as a sign of hope and as a practical example to those entangled in the many different conflicts raging around the world.

European cooperation involves, among other things, politics (the furthering of democracy), economics (aimed at prosperity) and security (military cooperation). Peace results not only from military and economic cooperation, but also from democracy. The spread of democracy to central and eastern Europe can, therefore, be considered a major contribution to stability, as is reflected, for example, in the framework of the Council of Europe and the OSCE.

I wish you every success in your deliberations at this conference. I am sure that you will raise the right questions and start giving the world some new answers.

Let me finish with Tolstoy. In *War and Peace*, he showed himself to be highly sceptical about the human capacity to regulate warfare. He wrote that:

'No solution could be found for the most obvious question that occurs to one at once on examining any historical event; that is, how did millions of men come to combine to commit crimes, murders, wars, and so on?' (p. 1132).

The difficulties we encounter in preventing, limiting and ending war should give us an additional impetus to search for peace.

PART I

JAN BLOCH IN HIS OWN TIME

FROM ST PETERSBURG TO THE HAGUE: BLOCH AND THE FIRST HAGUE PEACE CONFERENCE (1899)

Peter van den Dungen

It is singularly appropriate that the first conference ever to be devoted to the memory of Jan Bloch is being held in St Petersburg. It was in this city that his great work, *The Future of War,*[1] was first published a century ago, in 1898.

Moreover, the fact that the conference is part of the celebration and commemoration of another centenary – the Peace Conference which was held in The Hague in 1899 – also makes St Petersburg a felicitous choice of venue. The First Hague Peace Conference resulted from the Imperial Rescript which the Russian Foreign Minister, Count Mouraviev, handed to all the diplomatic representatives at the Court in St Petersburg during their weekly reception at the Foreign Office, on 24 August 1898 (12 August, old style).[2]

---

1   The German and French translations appeared under the title *War*. Bloch explained the reason for this change to W.T. Stead, as follows: 'When I went to look over the proofs at the printing establishment in Germany where the German edition is being printed, the foreman printer came to speak to me. It was just after the Tsar's Rescript had appeared. "Sir", he said, "do you not think that your book is now misnamed? You call it *Die Zukunft des Krieges*". Why so? I replied. "Because", he said, "after the Tsar's Rescript there should be no more wars. And if so, how can you speak of the Future of War?" I was so impressed by the man's remark that I call my book simply *War* – for war, I hope, has no more future'. W.T. Stead, *The United States of Europe on the eve of the parliament of peace* (London, 'Review of Reviews' Office, 1899), p. 137.
2   For the text of the Rescript, and its sequel (the Circular by Mouraviev), see J.B. Scott (ed.), *Texts of the peace conferences at The Hague, 1899 and 1907* (Boston, Ginn, 1908), pp. 1-4.

G. Prins and H. Tromp (eds.), The Future of War, 69-83.
© 2000 *Kluwer Law International. Printed in the Netherlands.*

The publication of *The Future of War* and the issuing of the Rescript in the same city at about the same time[3] caused contemporary commentators to assume the existence of a strong link between the two events. Later on, diplomatic historians have cast doubt upon this. It is the purpose of this chapter to substantiate the original proposition, *i.e.* that Bloch's work inspired the Rescript.

The present contribution will not document Bloch's involvement (as a private individual) in the conference in The Hague. However, his significance for that event can be properly assessed only by focusing on his role in St Petersburg in the period before the conference, as well as that in The Hague during the conference.

Against the general background of the First World War, disinterest and neglect have largely been the fate of Bloch himself, one of the *dramatis personae* of the whole conference. A major contributory factor in this process has been the imposition in Russia of a doctrinaire ideology, which had little regard for 'bourgeois pacifists' following the 1917 revolution. It is perhaps not surprising that its beneficiaries were not particularly keen to keep alive the memory of one who had appealed to the instinct of self-preservation of Europe's ruling classes in his warnings that future war meant, inevitably, revolution.[4] Despite Bloch's failure to make leaders heed his message, it may well have been recognition of the potential dangers inherent in the very notion of the existence of independent peace workers, which led the editors of the *Great Soviet Encyclopaedia* to delete from the entry on him any references to Bloch's involvement in war and peace issues. To describe him as an author of economic and statistical works, and a director of railway companies, whilst keeping entirely silent on *The Future of War*, The Hague Peace Conference, or the International Museum of War and Peace, which he founded in Lucerne (to mention only the most prominent of his peace efforts), is not only misleading but farcical.[5] For peace researchers in the Soviet Union, Leninist-Marxist orthodoxy dictated that the foundations for the scientific study of war and peace originated with Lenin; pre-revolutionary, non-Marxist theorists such as Bloch, Yakov Novikow,

---

3   According to one contemporary St Petersburg source, the book was in the bookshops a week before the Rescript was announced. *Cf. infra.*
4   There was a copy of Bloch's work in Lenin's library in the Kremlin.
5   *Great Soviet Encyclopedia* (New York, Macmillan, 1973, vol. 3), p. 365. This is a translation of the third edition.

or Pitirim Sorokin (or radical anti-militarists of Christian-anarchist persuasion such as Tolstoy) were therefore fully ignored.[6]

From the day the Rescript was made public, speculation was rife about its real origins and purposes. Tsar Nicholas II's call for a peace conference was met with almost universal disbelief and cynicism among his fellow sovereigns, political leaders, and the public at large. Not idealism but *Realpolitik* was widely regarded as underlying the Russian call for a general agreement 'to put an end to [the] incessant armaments and to seek the means of warding off the calamities which are threatening the whole world'.[7] In particular, the country's financial inability to match the recent modernisation, which had taken place in the army of the Austrian empire, and the need to invest scarce economic resources for the country's industrial development, have been identified as the immediate causes of the Russian move.

Those who have preferred to interpret it in a more straightforward and charitable manner have had no problem in pointing out that the idea of limitation of armaments was in the air, and had been voiced earlier in the decade by other statesmen in Europe. It is possible, and even likely, that there were other motives, including in Russia itself the fact that high-ranking officials in the Foreign Ministry, such as Basily and Michael Priklonsky, had expressed similar sentiments. But it seems that the single most important factor which persuaded the Tsar was Bloch's thesis. In the words of a contemporary commentator and Russian expert: 'His book may or may not have been the only means by which the Tsar was converted to peace, but what is certain is that it materially contributed to bring about this remarkable change in the Russian monarch'.[8]

As soon as his Rescript was issued, commentators both in Russia and abroad echoed this view. For instance, when the *Daily Telegraph* in London published

---

6   Unlike in the West, where Bloch's book was hailed, in the words of a leading peace researcher, as 'the first truly scientific treatment of international politics' (J. David Singer). See P. van den Dungen, 'Peace research and the search for peace: Some critical observations', 2 *International Journal on World Peace,* No. 3 (July-September), 1985, 44; Peter van den Dungen, 'Jean de Bloch: a 19th century peace researcher', 15 *Peace Research*, No. 3 (September), 1983, 22-24.

7   Scott, o.c., p. 2.

8   'The "impossibility" of war. John Bloch's book. By a friend of the author'. The *Daily Telegraph,* 11 January 1900. The author was almost certainly E.J. Dillon.

a detailed review of the original publication upon its first appearance in the autumn of 1898 (the only English newspaper which paid attention to this event), it did so under the heading: 'The Book that converted the Tsar'.[9] Bloch's precise role must remain an open question, but in the meantime what is known about the Tsar's familiarity with *The Future of War* and its author suggests that his role must have been a very considerable one.

Yet, this familiarity has been, if not altogether denied, rather understated by several historians of the First Hague Peace Conference. For instance, Thomas Ford and several decades later Dan L. Morrill confine themselves to the comment that 'the Tsar was supposed to have read his monumental work'.[10] There has never been any need to be so circumspect on this particular point, which has been well documented in published sources from the start.

Bloch himself always declined the honour, which many paid him in The Hague and elsewhere, of having been the inspiration for the Rescript. On such occasions he explained that its core ideas were the result of a general evolution which had made a growing number of people realise that the days of the foolish and costly war system were numbered. This modesty was merely that: it was Bloch who personally alerted Nicholas II to the findings of his study – at a time when his study was not yet concluded, and, no less remarkable, even before the Crown Prince had succeeded to the throne in 1894.

The first results of Bloch's research were published in Warsaw in 1893-94 in a series of articles in the journal *Biblioteka Warszawska*. In the same years, a Russian translation was published in ten consecutive issues of *Russkij Westnik* under the title 'The future of war, its economic causes and consequences'. With the help of a Russian admiral (who had secured the approval of Tsar Alexander III for this), the Crown Prince had become interested in these articles.[11] It is

---

9   *Ibid.*

10 T.K. Ford, 'The genesis of the First Hague Peace Conference', *Political Science Quarterly,* September 1936, 359; D.L. Morrill, 'Nicholas II and the call for the First Hague Peace Conference', *Journal of Modern History,* June 1974, 296. Also Sandi E.Cooper wrote that 'Nicholas apparently knew Bloch's work'. See the introduction in her (ed.) *Arbitration or war? Contemporary reactions to the Hague Peace Conference of 1899* (New York, Garland, 1972), p. 9.

11 A.H. Fried, 'Meine Unterredung mit Staatsrath v. Bloch', 8 *Die Waffen nieder!,* No. 6, 1899, 232.

not known whether Bloch actually discussed his work with the Crown Prince at this early stage; this seems unlikely. However, Bloch was able to expound his views before the Prince's father. Bloch reported in his conversation with Stead that Alexander III listened courteously, but made no remarks.[12] Very different was the reaction of his son who, when Tsar, invited Bloch and engaged him in lively discussion. This seems to have happened for the first time when Bloch presented the Tsar with a full set of the completed work, about Easter 1898.[13] Bloch mentioned to Stead that, whereas Alexander III had not had the quickness of mind necessary to grasp the full significance of his teachings, Nicholas II 'listened for two long hours ... questioned him minutely upon the various points which he brought forward, and showed a firm grasp of the subject which astonished and delighted' Bloch.[14] In The Hague, Bloch gave a lively description of his audience with the Tsar when Bertha von Suttner asked him about this:

> 'Yes, the Tsar has studied the work thoroughly. When he received me in audience, the maps and tables from the book lay spread out on the tables, and he had me carefully explain all the figures and diagrams. I explained until I was tired out, but Nicholas II did not grow weary. He kept asking new questions or throwing in observations which testified to his deep appreciation and interest. "So *this* is the way the next war would develop", he said; "*those* would be the results, would they?"'[15]

At the time, it was also reported that the censor had initially refused permission for the work to be published and that Bloch eventually obtained the help of the Tsar in having this decision overturned. It is not clear exactly when the audience to which Bloch referred in his conversation with von Suttner did take place, or what its purpose was. In particular, it may or may not have been in relation to the censorship problem. The former possibility is implied in a most interesting private letter, which the Austrian ambassador in St Petersburg sent to the Foreign Ministry in Vienna on 31 August 1898, one week after the publication of the Rescript. He writes that Bloch's 'first audience with the Tsar lasted two hours, and His Imperial Majesty has commanded the publication of the

---

12 Stead, *The United States of Europe*, o.c., p. 133.
13 Fried, o.c., p. 232.
14 W.T. Stead, 'Character sketch. The late M. Jean Bloch', *The Review of Reviews*, 15 February 1902, 142.
15 B. von Suttner, *Memoirs* (Boston, Ginn, 1910, vol. 2), p. 252.

text, and the work has been in the bookshops for two weeks. As a result, Herr von Bloch has been received by the Tsar on five further occasions in long audiences, and later in May on many occasions by the Tsarina'.[16] On the assumption that the Austrian ambassador was correctly informed, the number of audiences which the Tsar accorded Bloch is a telling indication of his personal interest (as Bloch confirmed). There can be little doubt that by the time of the conference in The Hague, knowledge of their meetings, which had become widespread in government and diplomatic circles in the Russian capital, strongly contributed to the impression that Bloch was 'the father of the conference'. This is what he was called in St Petersburg, wrote the Dutch ambassador to his Minister in a letter on 1 May 1899.[17]

One of the key themes of Bloch's work was the need to bring about a halt in the increasing armaments burden, in order to free resources for the improvement of the standard of living of the multitude of poor Russian peasants. In his conversation with Stead, Bloch remarked: 'Nothing could exceed the keen, sustained, sympathetic attention with which the Emperor listened to his lengthy exposition of the immensity of the work which needs to be done before the mass of his subjects could be brought up to the standard of the more prosperous people'.[18] That this subject was close to Bloch's own heart is clear from the following passage:

> 'In fact, as you will see from what I have written, I have been as much attracted to this subject [the study of war] from the desire to improve the condition of the people as from any other source. Hence my book took in part the shape of an investigation of the moral, social, and material conditions in which the masses of the Russian peasants pass their lives. It is a painful picture, and one that cannot fail profoundly to touch the hearts of all those who have followed the results of my investigation'.[19]

---

16 Quoted in B. Kempf, *Suffragette for peace. The life of Bertha von Suttner* (London, Oswald Wolff, 1972), p. 45.

17 Van Stoetwegen to de Beaufort (Letter in Archives of Dutch Ministry of Foreign Affairs).

18 Stead, *United States of Europe*, o.c., p. 164.

19 Bloch, *Modern weapons and modern war. Being an abridgement of 'The War of the Future in its Technical, Economic and Political Relations'*. With a prefatory conversation with the author by W.T. Stead (London, Grant Richards, 1900), LI-LII. This text originally appeared under the title 'Has war become impossible?' in a

This and other central concerns of Bloch are echoed in the Imperial Rescript. Indeed, if the more than 3,000 pages of Bloch's work had to be compressed a thousandfold (and written in a language befitting a Tsar), it would be difficult to improve on the Rescript. It is hard not to agree with Bertha von Suttner who compared specific passages of Bloch's work with the Rescript and concluded that 'at times, [the] words are almost the same, and the spirit is identical'.[20] Another contemporary analyst commented that 'it looks almost as if de Bloch were one of the co-authors of the great manifesto'.[21]

The references above to the wider goals of Bloch's enterprise, as well as the statement in the letter from the Austrian ambassador that Bloch 'on many occasions' was also received by the Tsarina, invite a brief consideration of her possible role in the Tsar's decision to propose a peace conference. Indeed, the evidence available seems to suggest that an enquiry about Bloch's influence on the Tsar would not be complete if it failed to take into account his contacts with the Tsarina (as well as the influence of the latter on her husband). Bloch's compassion for the poor is well attested to by the nature of several of his earlier studies, by social welfare schemes, which he instituted for his employees, and, generally, by his philanthropic and humanitarian disposition. It was this aspect of his character and activity that had brought him into close contact with Empress Alexandra. There is evidence to suggest that, following the publication of Bloch's study of future war, she acted as a conduit for his ideas and helped him to persuade her husband to propose a peace conference. Prominent figures at the heart of the Imperial foreign and defence establishment, including the Minister of War, Kuropatkin, Foreign Minister Mouraviev, and Priklonsky, have all testified (sometimes on the basis of the Tsar's own admission) that he discussed disarmament and the Rescript with his wife. From a conversation with the Tsarina, Priklonsky gained the firm impression that she had had a decisive influence on the Tsar's judgment in these matters.[22]

---

supplement to *The Review of Reviews* which he edited (Vol.19, 15 May 1899, 1-16).

20   B. von Suttner, *Die Haager Friedensconferenz. Tagebuchblätter* (Dresden & Leipzig, E. Pierson, 1901, 2nd ed.), p. 34.

21   Dr Alexis Markov, as quoted in A. von Wegener, 'Die Komödie der ersten Haager Abrüstungskonferenz. Aus dem Tagebuch des russischen Kriegsministers Kuropatkin', *Berliner Monatshefte* (April), 1934, 322.

22   M. Priklonsky, 'Die Vorgeschichte der ersten Haager Friedenskonferenz', *Die Friedens-Warte* (May), 1929, 131.

The argument can be summarised thus far as follows: Bloch's role must be rehabilitated. Then, his significance for The Hague Peace Conference will be seen to reside in the fact that, through his writings and teachings, he had convinced the Tsar that his prediction that war had become suicidal was correct as were its chief corollaries, namely, the need for halting the incessant and nefarious increase in armaments, and for finding alternative ways for settling conflicts between states. Since such a programme could only be successfully pursued, if at all, as part of an international agreement, the idea for a peace conference was a logical step.

The apogée of Bloch's political influence came on 24 August 1898 when Mouraviev announced the Imperial Rescript. History is littered with official peace appeals, many – perhaps most – of doubtful sincerity. What lends unique character to Tsar Nicholas II's proposal is the strength of the foundations upon which it was built. However, the conference which the monarch proposed failed to be the expected 'happy presage for the century which is about to open'.[23] Instead, it brought that suicidal war, which Bloch believed the world would be sufficiently rational to avoid, and the pains of which are still keenly felt today, more than 80 years after its conclusion. Much of what Bloch predicted in the event that his warnings were not heeded has come to pass, first and foremost in Russia itself with the 'triumph of the socialist revolution'.[24]

Bloch's role was not over. He was active behind the scenes in order to ensure that the conference would take place. According to some accounts, he played a significant role, at home and abroad, in rescuing the very proposal for a conference. The Rescript of 24 August had caused widespread consternation and embarrassment in the chancelleries of Europe (especially in France), which caused Mouraviev to propose to the Tsar the abandonment of the whole plan. Although Nicholas II initially agreed with his Foreign Minister, he was hesitating to sign an official note of cancellation. In the meantime, Bloch, who had been confidentially informed about these developments by Basily (the presumed drafter of the Rescript), severely reproached Mouraviev – who denied that the idea for a conference had been given up. Bloch subsequently travelled to Paris and

---

23   Scott, o.c., p. 2.
24   Bloch's concluding words in his conversation with Stead. Cf. *Modern weapons and modern war*, o.c., p. LXII.

'allegedly succeeded, singlehandedly, in persuading the French to support the conference'.[25]

So wrote the German ambassador in St Petersburg, von Radolin, on 13 July 1899 (when the conference in The Hague was in its final stages) in a most revealing letter to his Chancellor, von Hohenlohe. The letter is clear evidence that, with the conference almost concluded, the question of its origins and of the Tsar's motives in calling it, was still being keenly pursued. Von Radolin had gathered his information from a discussion he had had with Komarow, a high functionary of the Russian Foreign Ministry. Since Komarow told von Radolin that Mouraviev and Kuropatkin had travelled to Paris shortly after the Rescript was issued in order to calm a panic reaction among French officials, the reference to Bloch's 'singlehanded' conversion of the latter seems somewhat of an exaggeration. However, Komarow may well have spoken the truth once it is realised what Bloch had argued in Paris. Although there does not seem to be a record of this, it is not difficult to fathom the essence of his approach. In Bloch's view, the purpose of the conference was to come to an agreement to investigate the nature of future war in all its dimensions, in other words, to study war as he had done. This was far removed from any concrete proposal for arms limitation, and, therefore, the conference held no danger, certainly not for the immediate future, for the national interest of any country. In fact, Bloch might well have attempted to ingratiate himself with the French by recalling that such an idea, in embryonic form, had first been suggested in France itself. As he informed W.T. Stead in the autumn of 1898, shortly after the Rescript was announced:

'In France some years ago, when M. de Freycinet was Prime Minister ... a proposal was made to appoint a Committee of Economists to report upon the economic results that would follow an outbreak of war. But the soldiers vetoed it. They do not wish to have the consequences of war brought home to the knowledge of the people. But that is what the Peace Conference ought to do'.[26]

With a main obstacle (French intransigence) apparently overcome, and the Russian Foreign Minister himself brought back into line, the plans for the con-

---

25   Johannes Lepsius *et al.* (eds), *Die Grosse Politik der Europäischen Kabinette, 1871-1914* (Berlin, Deutsche Verlagsgesellschaft für Politik und Geschichte, 1924, vol. XV), pp. 351-352.
26   Stead, *United States of Europe*, o.c., p. 136.

ference could go forward. On the assumption that Komarow's account is largely accurate, Bloch can be credited with a second, major, achievement – namely, to have rescued the (proposal for a) conference.[27] Indeed, it is his efforts in this regard which could equally well have earned him the *soubriquet* 'father of the conference'.

From the accounts available, it appears that Bloch was not involved, certainly not in any formal way, in the third and crucial stage of the conference preparations – the drafting of the agenda. Since he was not a member of the government or a civil servant, it is not surprising that he took no part in the deliberations, which resulted in Mouraviev's circular of 11 January 1899 (30 December 1898, old style). The Foreign Minister seemed to be fully in accord with Bloch's views on the conference (*cf. infra*). Since the Rescript had expressed so well Bloch's own ideas, he could be confident that they would inform the shaping of the specific programme. In this, Bloch was mistaken, and when he *did* intervene following the publication of the circular it was too late.

The so-called Second Manifesto specified eight points for the conference to address. It reflected, perhaps to a considerable extent, elements of an agreement, which Kuropatkin had concluded with his French counterpart, Chanoine, in the course of his visit to Paris. This agreement contained, for instance, a prohibition on the throwing of projectiles or explosives from balloons. In fact, six of the eight agenda points concerned matters of a similar kind about the regulation and limitation of warfare. Only the first point was about a possible 'freeze', for a limited period of time, of the level of armaments and the size of military budgets, and only the last point referred to the possible employment of means which could prevent armed conflict between states. Had French approval for the conference been at the price of a dilution of the original aims of the conference (which found a cautious expression in the first and last points only)? In that case, Bloch's Paris mission had not really achieved its goal.

---

27 William Langer called Komarow's story 'apparently trustworthy'. Cf. *The diplomacy of imperialism, 1890-1902* (New York, Alfred A. Knopf, 1951, 2nd ed.), p. 584. Similarly, Frieda Hoffmann wrote in her *Beiträge zur Vorgeschichte der ersten Haager Friedenskonferenz von 1899* (Hamburg, Hans Christian, 1935), p. 26 that she believed that the details given by Komarow 'can be assumed to be correct'. In the light of the important information about Bloch's role which Komarow provides, it is astonishing that his comments in this regard have been consistently ignored in the literature.

Bloch's reaction to the circular is described in two ambassadorial letters from St Petersburg, already referred to above. Von Radolin quoted Komarow as saying:

> 'Mr Bloch is totally exasperated at the dubiousness and superficiality of this document, and sees himself impelled to send the Emperor a memorandum which is said to be a masterpiece. He points out that the note of [11 January] is an absurdity and unlikely to lead to any practical result. Being himself of a mystical disposition, Mr Bloch plays on the mystical inclinations of the Emperor and convinces him through his memorandum that the entire programme is wrongly conceived.'[28]

Van Stoetwegen, the Dutch Ambassador, had been talking with Bloch who told him that the eight points 'have been wrongly chosen, even more badly drafted, show a slapdash approach, lack unity, do not comply with the Emperor's ideas, and will be the reason why the conference is destined to fail miserably'.[29] He called Bloch 'a very remarkable man', and singled him out as someone who would provide Russia with the trump card.[30]

Bloch was not the only one who expressed his unhappiness with the turn of events. Bertha von Suttner wrote that the agenda had reduced the forthcoming diplomatic gathering in The Hague to the level of a Red Cross conference:

> 'Here, also those who are not opponents of war and militarism, and who believe in the inevitability of war, want to cooperate. The six points in question have been drafted ... out of diplomatic consideration for the doubters and the half-hearted'.[31]

She had a personal reason to feel disappointed because Mouraviev had clearly given her a different impression of the aims of the planned conference during their meeting in Vienna in the autumn of 1898, after the Rescript had been issued. She quoted the minister as saying:

---

28   Lepsius, *Die Grosse Politik* , o.c., p. 352.
29   Cf. note 17 above.
30   Perhaps the Ambassador assumed that Bloch would be a member of the Russian delegation, which was not the case.
31   B. von Suttner, 'Zur Vorgeschichte der Haager Konferenz', *Deutsche Revue* (December), 1901, 352; *Memoirs*, o.c., p. 228.

'a war in the future is surely a thing of horror and ruin – really an impossible thing; to take care of the present huge armies in the field is impracticable. The first result of a war waged between the great powers will be starvation'.

She

'detected the echo of Bloch's doctrine in those last words, and that justifies the assumption that the work of the Russian councilor had helped to give the impulse to the drawing up of the rescript. Only Bloch had added to the word "starvation" two others, "revolution" and "anarchy"'.[32]

At about the same time, Bloch's own ideas for the conference were explained at length in his fascinating (and for many readers at the time, no doubt also startling) interview with Stead, reproduced in the introductory section of this book. Its chief goal had to be that participants ascertained and certified the proposition that war had become suicidal. He told Stead:

'What people have not realised, is that modern war is something altogether different from all the wars that have been fought since the world began. If I were to prescribe the right way in which to educate a soldier today, I should begin by burning all military history before 1875. Nothing that happened before then affords any instruction as to what will happen now. ... my idea of what might be done with the most advantage is, that the Congress after its first meeting should appoint a committee or committees of the ablest of its members to conduct what would be an international enquiry into the extent to which modern warfare ... has practically become impossible without sacrifices of life hitherto unheard of on the battlefield, without total dislocation of the fabric of society, and without inevitable bankruptcy and revolution.'[33]

That the Russian government had, in fact, originally intended to organise the conference in the manner prescribed above is evident from a letter which Sir C. Scott, the British Ambassador to St Petersburg, sent to the First Lord of the Treasury, Arthur Balfour, shortly after the Rescript was announced. He quoted the Russian Foreign Minister as saying that 'it might be found desirable to

---

32   *Memoirs*, o.c., pp. 218-219.
33   Stead, *United States of Europe*, o.c., pp. 134-136.

appoint a preliminary commission of experts, military, financial and commercial to formulate subjects for discussion'.[34]

Whatever the precise circumstances which may explain the great discrepancy between the conference idea as shared (at least at the time when the Rescript appeared) by Bloch, Mouraviev, and the Tsar, on the one hand, and the contents of the Circular, on the other hand, there was no alternative but to proceed on the basis of the latter. Uncertainty, confusion, and plain chaos seem to sum up the state of Russian diplomacy in preparation for the meeting in The Hague four months later, something which did not fail to leave its mark at the conference.[35]

Even at this late stage Bloch, typically, did not give up. Having come this far, he continued to pursue his great idea singlemindedly. Five weeks before the opening of the conference he informed von Suttner:

'In my opinion it would be best for an agitation to be made, to the end that the Conference *in pleno*, or that single states, should inaugurate an investigation as to the possibility of carrying through a great war. At this moment the governments are not humble enough, public opinion is not as yet ripe enough, to be able to obtain results from the Conference. It would be much more practical if the sessions could be postponed until autumn, so as to let the separate states have time for arranging investigations and preparing public opinion.'[36]

One week before the opening, he sent a telegram to von Suttner, which reveals that he had already decided on his next move in case the conference refused

---

34 G.P. Gooch and Harold Temperley (eds.), *British documents on the origins of the War, 1898-1914* (London, HMSO, 1927, vol. 1), p. 217.

35 Andrew D. White, who was head of the United States delegation, remarked: 'It was found that all was haphazard; that no adequate studies had been made, no project prepared'. *Autobiography of Andrew Dickson White* (New York, The Century Co., 1905, vol. 2), p. 28. It is highly unlikely that he would have commented in this way if the preparations for the conference had been entrusted to Bloch (to whom the matters White complained about were also an anathema), who showed throughout his life consummate skills in undertaking systematic and exhaustive investigations and translating their findings into highly practical projects.

36 *Memoirs*, o.c., pp. 235-236.

to institute the investigations for which he had been calling. He would then himself set up a committee to undertake the work. He informed her:

> 'I have letters from Prussian generals which show that the idea is already ripe. I am ready to guarantee the expenses. It would be very desirable, using Vienna as a rendezvous, to secure a number of names of political economists and statisticians, and, if possible, of military men. I think that, for execution of the plan, reporters on special divisions of my work, or independent workers, should be nominated, who subsequently should be coordinated through a central committee. Any other method, however, equally acceptable.'[37]

It seems that Bloch did not pursue this plan although, two months after the conference, in October 1899, he spoke at a meeting of the French Association for Political Economy where he invited members to answer a number of specific questions regarding the economic consequences of a future war.[38] Also on this occasion he expressed his frustration and disbelief that the opinions of outstanding military experts on the character of future war had not been heard at the conference in The Hague. It seems that in the estimation of diplomats this subject was beyond their competence, while their military advisers were lacking the authority, the courage, and the will to bring something as controversial as this out into the open. This was all the more irritating for Bloch in view of the fact that some of the most eminent military experts broadly agreed with him. In fact, his book had received high praise from a committee of Russian experts to whom it had been submitted by the Minister of War for examination.[39] The result was communicated to the Tsar in the form of a report in which the committee stated, according to Bloch that while in dealing with so very many questions it was impossible to avoid some mistakes, it was their opinion that the book was a very useful one, and that it was most desirable that it should be placed in the hands of all staff officers. They also added an expression of

----

37 *Memoirs*, o.c., pp. 239-240.
38 Charles Letort, 'Société d'Economie Politique. Réunion du 5 octobre 1899', *Journal des Economistes* (15 October), 1899, 122-124.
39 It was upon Bloch's request that the Tsar had submitted his work to the Minister of War for an expert opinion. *Cf.* Bloch, *Modern weapons and modern war*, o.c., p. XIII. It does appear that this request was made after the decision of the censor had been reversed, and that therefore the verdict of the Ministry played no role in lifting the ban on publication.

opinion that no book could contribute so much to the success of the Conference or to the information of those who were to take part in its deliberations.[40]

General Miliutin, who had been the Russian Minister of War for 18 years, in a letter which he sent to Bloch shortly before the conference, expressed the view that:

> 'The main object of your work has been to draw a picture, faithful but terrible, of that war which in a future more or less near will ruin Europe in order to allow recent inventions to be utilized. For that very reason your book would have an immense and beneficent effect if it could influence the directing spheres, the men who shape the policy of States, and above all other, the Delegates to the Conference at The Hague.'[41]

However, Miliutin knew better than most the pervasive influence of the military, and he feared that 'the appalling consequences which may be expected to follow the catastrophe are not capable of turning back the obstinate fanatics of militarism from the road which they have mapped out for themselves'.

We know how prophetic his words were. At The Hague, and in the few years which were left to Bloch, he moved heaven and earth to make his contemporaries see that the next great wars would be 'like a *rendez-vous* with death'.[42] The Great War was just that.

---

40 *Ibid.*
41 Quoted in Jean de Bloch, 'The wars of the future', *The Contemporary Review* (September), 1901, 312.
42 Johann von Bloch, *Der Krieg* (Berlin, Puttkammer & Mühlbrecht, 1899, vol. 1), p. xv.

6

BLOCH THE MAN:
A BIOGRAPHICAL APPRECIATION

Andrzej Werner

'Joy, hope, suspicion – above all, astonishment – were the world's prevailing emotions when it learned on 29 August 1898 that the young Tsar of Russia, Nicholas II, had issued a call to the nations to join in a conference on the limitations of armaments.' So wrote Barbara Tuchman in her dazzling depiction of the world before the Great War.[1] All capitals were taken by surprise by what *Le Temps* called this 'flash of lightning out of the North'. The pressure of Russian expansion had been felt from Alaska to India, from Turkey to Poland. 'The Tsar with an olive branch', it was said in Vienna, 'that is something new in history'. Similar reactions, signs of surprise, admiration and respect had also accompanied the numerous publications and statements made by the Tsar's principal mentor in matters of great war, Jan Bloch.[2] This chapter will briefly review Bloch's main arguments, set within a brief biographical account of Tsar Nicholas's remarkable Polish subject.

---

1   B.W. Tuchman, *The Proud Tower. A Portrait of the World before the War: 1890-1914* (Toronto/NewYork/London, Batman, 1972), p. 268.
2   Bloch used pen-names depending on the country of publication. So, in Germany he was Johann von Bloch; in France Jean de Bloch; in England John Bloch. In Russia, as a Polish subject of the Tsar, he was listed in official documents and in the Russian press as Ivan Stanislavovitch Bliokh, in Cyrillic, of course. But by birth his name was Jan Gottlib Bloch, Jan Bloch for short. He was so named in the Latin alphabet in Poland and in other Russian provinces where the Latin alphabet was in use. On Bloch, see his cousin, Michael Bloch's, biographical article in H. Josephson (ed.), *Bibliographical Dictionary of Modern Peace Leaders* (Westport, Greenwood Press, 1985), pp. 84-85.

G. Prins and H. Tromp (eds.), The Future of War, 85-100.
© 2000 *Kluwer Law International. Printed in the Netherlands.*

1   BLOCH'S CONCEPTION OF WAR

Liés dévoués pacifiques was the name which Eli Ducommun gave to the group
of activists who helped to stimulate The Hague Conference. Among them, Bloch
stood out. This 'Russian Cobden'[3] was also a Warsaw banker, an entrepreneur,
and, in particular, the 'king of Polish railroads'. He was distinguished in many
ways, which strongly influenced the manner in which he approached issues
of war and peace. In contrast to his better-known contemporaries among
industrialists-philanthropists, such as Alfred Nobel and Andrew Carnegie, Bloch
not only gave money to the cause of peace but, before he took the decision
to oppose war in its modern guise, he undertook his own thorough and extensive
researches and investigations of wars. This gave his efforts a unique authority;
for Bloch's extensive work deprived military or political authorities of their
monopoly in speaking unchallenged on issues of war. Bloch's consultations,
readings and experiments, done in laboratories and on testing grounds,
examining the physical characteristics of the new weaponry, drove him towards
his fundamental conclusion that war among the European powers in the
industrial age would be different and far more disastrous than any fought in
the past. Due to technical innovation, this war would be able to mobilise the
fighting parties comprehensively. The governments, he saw, did not realise this
and organisationally and conceptually they were not prepared to face such
calamity. Future war, Bloch predicted, would demand huge resources and sacrifices, which, combined with the colossal human casualties that would be
incurred might bring about the collapse of economies and international trade.
Socially, he foresaw that populations, exhausted by such war, might be prone
to public unrest, strikes and even disintegration. Presciently, he foresaw the
collapse of the fighting empires and the eruption of social and political revolutions.

Therefore, Bloch argued that it was urgent to stop the arms race and instead
to seek for ways in which conflict might be resolved peacefully. He advocated
wide use of arbitration and the setting up of an international tribunal.

These bold and coherent arguments together, supported by volumes of analysis
and fact, were published in Bloch's monumental six volume treatise entitled

---

3   Bloch was called Cobden by W.T. Stead, in W.T. Stead, 'Character sketch. The
     late M. Jean Bloch', 25 *Review of Reviews* (February), 1902, 136.

The Future of War in its Technical, Economic and Political Relations. The treatise appeared in its first Russian edition in 1898[4] and was then translated from Russian into French and German and its entirety, and the sixth volume, which contains the summary and conclusions, into English. In the form of extracts and pamphlets, it was also available in Dutch, Swedish and Danish.[5]

Bloch's originality lay in his insistence on treating war as a social phenomenon, which could not be understood piecemeal. War, he argued, had to be examined in the round. Today, we would say that Bloch advocated an interdisciplinary approach, in contrast to those specialist studies, which focus exclusively on technical matters. 'They look upon future war from one point-of-view only: how to reach the aim of destroying the enemy by arms. Economic and social consequences are only considered by the way, as secondary' (p. x of the introduction to *The Future War*).[6] Bloch conducted a thorough search of the literature and did not find the comprehensive analyses that he sought. This was no source of satisfaction. Bloch did not aspire to be, in particular, a pioneer in the study of war or ideas on war, and he regretted the absence of such analyses, because he thought that if all the main issues relating to great power war were only clearly explained, it would 'sober public opinion and support peace aspirations of all governments' (p. ix of the introduction). Bloch adhered to the maxim that you should study your enemy closely. In consequence, he was in no sense biased against military men. Indeed, wherever he could he quoted them, since they were those able to give best witness to the phenomenon of future war. But this did not constrain him from criticism. The more so, because he thought 'in today's conditions of war, it would be a crime to begin offensive actions or become involved in fighting without studying first the consequences of what could happen after beginning such a war' (p. ix of the introduction).

---

4   I. S. Bliokh, *Boudouschtchaia voina v tekhnitcheskom, ekonomitcheskom i politicheskom otnocheniaikch* (St Petersburg, Efron, 1898).

5   P. van den Dungen, *A Bibliography of the Pacifist Writings of Jean de Bloch* (London, Housmans, 1977).

6   All quotations here are taken from the Polish original, *Przyszla wojna pod wzgledem technicznym, politycznym i ekonomicznym* (Crakow, Gebethner i Wolff, 1899 vol.6; 1900 vol.1-5). It was published abroad to avoid Russian censorship that had denied Bloch the printing of a Russian edition in St Petersburg. Not to run further risks, Bloch published his Polish original in Cracow, which was then in Austria and under a much more liberal regime.

In Bloch's judgment, the key characteristic, which would distinguish future war from the past, was its comprehensive embrace of all aspects of society: he was the first to see that the 20th century could be a century of 'total war'. It would, in effect, make it impossible for any to escape its reach. Therefore, he directed his message not only to the Tsar, but to all European sovereigns and governments, and to non-European ones as well. His work presented the serious consequences that major war would have for trading powers. Indeed, the whole of volume 3 is devoted to war at sea and maritime questions.

Bloch warned also against the menace of arms races that were being generated by the rapid pace of technical and technological progress at the end of the 19th century. He warned of the economic burdens and the political tensions that arms races would cause for European states, and that they could, in fact, weaken economies and thus bring war closer rather than deter it. It was his remarkable comprehensive sweep, which therefore drove the importance of examining the causes of international conflicts and disputes, as well as the practical conduct of future war with the new weaponry; and this inclusiveness and reach is a distinctive characteristic of his work. In the highest sense, Bloch, like an engineer, applied the rigour and comprehensiveness of an engineer's approach to study to the subject of future war. This made *The Future War* different from all other studies.

2   THE FUTURE WAR

Bloch's great work sets out, in a clear and logical sequence, the implication of his working assumption that future war could only be understood in the round.

The first three volumes are devoted to war and strictly military-technical questions. Volume 1 contains descriptions and analyses of war making. It is concerned with the design and functioning of small arms, or artillery, cavalry and infantry. It describes the improvements and potentials of shelters and fortifications in future war, as well as the role of logistics required to sustain these mass armies. Volume 2 discusses land wars in detail, and 3 war at sea. Altogether, these three volumes cover almost 2,000 pages.

Volume 4 then turns to the causes of wars. It discusses projected economic difficulties of the main European countries, which might result from war, and estimates the economic and financial burdens for budgets and populations that would arise. It indicates also the possible sources of taxation and other finance to meet these colossal war costs. Volume 4 then reviews existing patterns of procurement, and shows them to be hugely inadequate for the requirements of new mass armies. It also argues that civil populations could not be successfully sustained, especially in the event of siege of large cities – an argument made in St Petersburg a generation before the moment when, temporarily named Leningrad, the city was to demonstrate the truth of the proposition.

Volume 5 dealt with efforts to oppose wars. Bloch reviewed the causes of wars and the likely causes of outbreak, and then focused on the nature of likely losses in war. This enabled him in the final volume, which has been in historical terms the single most influential in the series, to concentrate on how wars, thus described and predicted, might be avoided. In Volume 6, Bloch gave readers arguments in favour of and against an international tribunal of arbitration, as well as discussing other ways of resolving conflicts peacefully between states.

In total, the huge work ran to 3,271 pages in its Polish edition, and is, as such, the largest work in Polish military literature, as well as one of the longest and most comprehensive studies on the nature of war ever published.[7]

All six volumes have detailed and descriptive tables of contents, and in Volume 6, Chapter 7 Bloch gives a *résumé* of the whole work. Thus, if one possessed Volume 6, one did not necessarily need to study all the previous volumes in order to learn Bloch's main findings, and to understand the depth of the knowledge underpinning his anti-war message.

3 A SURPRISING SORT OF SCHOLAR

As I noted at the beginning of this chapter, Bloch's studies and anti-war activities were greeted both with surprise and interest. Interest attached to the substantive nature of his arguments; but surprise, reasonably enough, attached to Bloch's own career and motivation. Why did a railway tycoon devote so many years of his life and so much of his wealth to the cause of European

---

7   J. Bugajski, 'Geneza pismiennictwa wojskowego Jana Blocha (Genesis of Jan Bloch's military writings), *Zeszyty naukowe* WAT, No. 15, 1967, 129-130.

peace? Who was this extraordinary man from a borderland of Imperial Russia? How did Bloch, who was not the graduate of an elite school nor had any military service, acquire such prodigious knowledge and expertise? And how, in the 1890s, could he write such a penetrating multi-volume work on war in Russia, with its long imperial military traditions, and, indeed, with a new war in prospect? Furthermore, in a country with pervasive censorship and no place for political parties or parliaments, how did Bloch, an intellectual *parvenu* born to a poor Jewish family in Radom in Poland, cause Tsar Nicholas II and his wife, Alexandra Teodorovna, and the court to become interested in his books and his ideas? In sum, what was it in Bloch's life, which prepared him to wage war against war at the end of his life?

To start with, it is helpful to know who Bloch was *not*. Certainly he was not a man of war. He did not aspire to be close to war, although he was no novice in military questions before he undertook his war studies beginning in 1891 at the age of 55. These studies were not undertaken as a source of pleasure. They were caused by the threat of a new war approaching Warsaw, which was where he lived since 1850. Before that, in his many publications he did not study war as such, and those studies undertaken in 1891 had not looked as if they consummated Bloch's earlier research plans or dreams. Not that his war studies were *idées fixes* of an ageing gentleman, as many thought sarcastically. But the most important thing was that, once seized of his mission, Bloch was exceptionally well-qualified, both in talents and by his experience and life successes, to undertake these great researches.

Almost from the beginning of his business career, Bloch had had contacts with the military administration. It began in St Petersburg, where, at the age of 26, he earned his first million roubles. Although railway projects were not administered by the military, the line was a strategic asset and, as such, Bloch and other contractors had to prepare their offers and submissions not only to meet technical and commercial specifications, but also to meet military requirements and instructions. This was necessary in order to win contracts, and had been determined in Russia since the beginning of the railway age by the demands of the Empire's territorial expansion. It was an internal security priority for the protection of Tsardom against its oppressed population. So, his early railway projects constituted Bloch's 'university' of political and military thought.

The decision to build the first railway in Russia from St Petersburg to Moscow was taken late, despite very pressing transport and economic needs. It was rumoured that what lay behind this hesitance was the opinion of Michel Cheva-lier, the French economist who was frequently quoted in the Tsar's court. He warned that 'the most democratic institution is the railway', and the authorities, to be sure, were not interested in the free movement of their subjects. It was hardly the British example. In 1830, by means of the railway, they could trans-port an army corps in two hours instead of two days from Manchester to Liver-pool for boarding onto ships in order to suppress the Irish uprisings. It was this demonstration of the military utility of railways that he induced Tsar Nicholas I finally to give his consent to *Nicolayevskaia zheleznaia doroga*, the line named after him.

When Bloch came to St Petersburg in 1856, the new Tsar Alexander II gave permission for railway development within the framework of his limited liberal reforms. So, Bloch began his swift and unusual career on the back of this 'post-Sevastopol thaw'. The new Minister of Finance, Nicolas Reutern, who, after studies in America, was regarded as a political liberal, was quick to announce boldly that the future railway network in Russia would be aimed to make 'the Empire feel safe within its widespread borders and let it have an impact on South and West Europe in accordance with its historical mission'.[8] This policy was, in its technical form, facilitated by Bloch from the start.

First, was construction of the important line between St Petersburg and Warsaw, where the Bloch's lived. Next, came connections from the heartland of Russia to borders with Prussia, Austria and Turkey, whose lands encircled the Polish provinces which, at that time, constituted the most extended salient of Russia into the West. So, with such long and broad experience, Bloch was no novice in questions of the military interest.

This 'railway university' had other good consequences for Bloch. During his work, he acquired much insight into the skills and know-how of management and conduct of very large groups of workers. Working conditions on the railway in those days were military by nature. They could have become more demanding when, for example, in the 1860s, in the face of national uprisings of Poles and Lithuanians, the authorities ordered the speed-up of completion of the St Petersburg-Warsaw line, the project in which Bloch took part. Then work was

---

8   M. Ch. Reutern, *Biografitcheskii otcherk* (St Petersburg, 1910), p. 162.

conducted at such a tempo that the best engineers and sappers could be proud of it, as a contribution to war effort.

Another side of the coin was the scale of the projects in which he was engaged. It required putting down no less than 1,300 km of rail, and the management and employment of 40,000 people. Great skills of organisation and logistics were needed to meet such demanding schedules, and to do this job on time. Therefore, Bloch, after such a training, could forecast well the sorts of problems in victualling the supporting both armies and civil populations in the context of future war.

Bloch's qualification for his researches on the future of war were not only technical. He was also a prolific writer, and had published one book every two years in recent years. But his aim in the great project was essentially political: many of his activities and writings show that he was a reformer at heart and, indeed, his earlier publications did influence Russian decisions on railways and finance. Books had enabled him to adduce the support of other authors and thus to bolster his public stance. This was especially true in the case of his first book, in which he presented in detail a competent and bold description of the state of Russian railways. He seems to have been a good publicist. This book he translated and published in Paris, where it brought him a Grand Médaille at the Geographical Congress. This international distinction impressed St Petersburg, and Bloch was granted the title of Counsellor of State, in the rank of General-Major, and given membership of the Learned Committee of the Ministry of Finance at the age of 39.

To consolidate his position, Bloch continued with his work on railways and on railway reform. Now possessing easier access to official statistics through his own statistical office, Bloch amazed the railway community in 1878 (three years after his Paris medal) by commencing a five volume study on the impact of railways on the Russian economy, the last volume being published in 1880.

He progressed from railways to a broader analysis of Russian imperial finances. This too was a work with political purpose. Prodigious energy was required to produce and publish in 1882 his four volume study on Russia's finances in the 19th century. This work was his most important in the field of economics, it appeared also in France where it too was honoured, this time with a Médaille d'Or at the World Exhibition in Paris in 1882.

In consequence, in Russia Bloch's political stock rose further. St Petersburg, of course, was much more interested in his practical judgments and proposals for change than in his historical perspectives. His reformist posture and pragmatic proposals, well-grounded in the political and social realities of Russia, were popular. He was even spoken of as a potential candidate for the post of Minister of Finance. If Bloch did aspire to this public position later, we shall never know. But, in fact, the post was held by two of his former employees, from 1887-1892: his close partner Ivan A. Vyshnegradzki, Director of the Petersburg Institute of Technology; and, from 1892-1903, by the unfriendly Sergei J. Count Witte, who also became Prime Minister of Russia. Artur Eisenbach used to say 'If Russia were England, Bloch would be Disraeli'.

Was Bloch disappointed or embittered by this turn of events? We do not know. Instead, we can judge from the continuing outpourings of his writings that his vigour in public life was not diminished. What had changed? He was losing his passion to produce change in economic and financial reform in St Petersburg. His last three economics books on credit, land debt and banks in land reform were published in 1890, 1891 and 1895, respectively. But, by then his interest was turning to the study of war.

By the end of 1880 Bloch was confronted with another great public challenge, which became his most precarious engagement excepting in *The Future of War*. Although a Christian since his youth, he could not abide the discrimination that the Jewish population could suffer were the Russian law of 1882, on economic activities and domicile, extended to the Polish kingdom where Jews had enjoyed equal treatment since 1862. The task of preventing this was not easy at all, even for Bloch. First, the change was petitioned to the Tsar by Governor General, Josef Vladimirovich Hurko, of Warsaw. Further efforts to postpone the new law had to be undertaken in the poisonous climate of pogroms. Last but not least, Bloch's engagement on behalf of the Jews brought him vocal and bitter personal attack in the right-wing press, but it did not stop him.[9] He activated his contacts in St Petersburg. Warsaw Stock Exchange figures and data were collected and carefully elaborated to demonstrate how broad and important was the role of the Jews in Russia's commerce and economy, and what great harm would be done if the new law were extended to

---

9   R. Kolodziejczyk, *Jan Bloch 1836-1902, Szkic do portretu 'Króla polskich kolei'* (Warsaw, PWN, 1983), p. 166-186.

Polish provinces. In effect, a form of petition was submitted in St Petersburg, where Bloch finally obtained Tsar Alexander III's refusal of Governor General Hurko's request.

Although hurt by this unpleasant criticism, Bloch returned home the moral victor. He was also seen as an unyielding public campaigner and an experienced exponent of citizen diplomacy, traits which were later to serve him well in his last and greatest fight against future war.

4   TOWARDS THE FUTURE OF WAR

Bloch never served in the army, nor was he directly involved in warfare before he started his famous studies on war in 1891. He was close to the front for the first time when he was 41, during the Russo-Turkish in 1877, when, as President of the South-Western Railway Company, he accompanied Tsar Alexander II and his staff to inspect the army. For Bloch's future war interests, it was important that he could listen to officers of the highest rank and learn their opinions about war, its mechanisms and rules, and to note to his surprise that their self-assertion did not correspond with the competence in management, organisation or logistics that he knew from his 'railway university' education.

When the Tsar was offered optimistic forecasts about the quick ending of war, Bloch distanced himself. Events proved Bloch's observations to be correct. It took longer to beat the Turks and the cost was higher than anticipated, for even slight delays in the transportation of Russian troops to Plevna, the strongest Turkish fortress in Bulgaria, made a difference. It enabled Oman-Pasha, its defender, to strengthen his garrison so much that the costs of three unsuccessful Russian attacks with great losses meant that a painful siege had to be borne. Bloch remembered examples like this when he got involved in 1888 in defence plans for Warsaw, where he lived. In about 1882, the city was elevated to the status of a fortress. Only a citadel and a few forts remained from the Polish uprisings of 1830-31. However, when Germany made an alliance with Austria, and later in 1883 when they formed the triple alliance with Italy, Warsaw received an outer ring of fortifications and an inner one after 1886. This development was met with interest by all inhabitants, but also not without anxiety, since no plans on issues crucial to the fate of Warsaw had been disclosed by the authorities. For it happened that Warsaw was militarily not just another town-fortress. Like a large part of the Polish kingdom, it was situated geographically so far West as to be surrounded by Austria and Germany, and so, in effect, Warsaw was a central part of the forward theatre in future conflict and its strategic axis. This being so, the city had to be proof against the siege which might last not for weeks but months or longer. So the fate of 600,000 civilians required due and careful attention.

In 1888, the ever-practical Bloch obtained, in the name of Warsaw trades people, official consent for a corporate debate on some of these issues: how would food be collected and distributed? What other provisions would be available during a siege? How would the civil guard to set up and regulated? It took more than two years before a mixed Commission was set up in 1891, with Bloch as a member. The Commission learned that more than half a million people would have to be evacuated, with practically no provisions at all. To Bloch's surprise and anger the officials were not troubled by this. Similarly, by the possible fate of the 50,000 who would be left in Warsaw. He realised also that the authors of the Warsaw defence plan had not studied the experience of siege and the fall of Paris, which was much better prepared to fight than Warsaw was, nor that of Plevna during the Turkish war, in which General Hurko was one of the leading Russian commanders. Moreover, Bloch had reason to believe that these experiences were simply not known. In effect, the final report of the Commission, prepared by its military members, was impractical and many key questions were simply not elaborated. Therefore, Bloch was very personally exercised by these events and refused to put his signature to the report. Instead, with the consent of General Hurko, he committed himself to write his own study on the defence of Warsaw. This work was the first step in his studies on the road to *The Future of War*.[10]

Bloch's essay focused on practical and civilian sides of the plans for the defence of Warsaw, and, in particular, on those that were contested by Bloch during the work of the Commission. He did not reject that report entirely. As a local resident, he felt a duty to point out things, which he thought were overlooked or did not receive enough attention, although they were vital. So, Bloch's attention was devoted to the fate of those 50,000 people who would stay in Warsaw, as well as the half million who would become evacuees. These parts of his Warsaw *Memorial* included the experiences drawn from his own work

---

10   J. Bugajski, 'Warszawa w wojskowej tworczosci Jana Blocha (Warsaw in the military works of Jan Bloch)', *Rocznik Warszawski*, No. XI, 1972, 208.

on the railways and logistics, and made wide reference to his books on railways and finance. In sum, in the *Memorial* on the defence of Warsaw, Bloch produced a list of requirements and a detailed agenda for further work. The submission was presented to Governor Hurko by the end of 1891. Bloch lost his campaign, for he was told politely that many of his suggestions could not be carried out at all and those that could would not be, due to lack of funds. However, it was fresh in their memories that Bloch had in 1888 succeeded in having General Hurko's petition on the Jews overruled by the Tsar. The Warsaw generals did not wish to make of him a public enemy, and so they advised him to continue his studies on the economic side of the city's defences and, in particular, his observations on the new nature and character of war that might come.

We may judge that, in his mind, Bloch agreed with this and decided to proceed with further work, but he did not intend to engage himself in any full-scale war studies. He complained of being tired. His economic book on *Land and its Indebtedness* was due to be finished soon. It did not mean that he stopped caring about Warsaw's future. He still did and very much. After his *Memorial* was put into abeyance by the generals, he talked about writing a pamphlet or a medium-sized book about all the critical issues that, in his opinion, should have been faced by the civil and military administration of Warsaw, or by any other town-fortress at that time.[11] He intended to put his observations on the broader scene in the context of the French and Turkish experiences of Paris and Plevna. Bloch was thus turning himself from being a stern critic of Warsaw's lack of preparation into an author, who, if not instructing, was advising his compatriots and officers of other states under siege, pointing out what they should study and do. As he was always careful about his facts, he had, of course, ordered in Paris a set of the official reports.

Bloch's theme was 'War'. He planned to write for no more than a few weeks, but in fact it took him three years,[12] and the content and form of what finally emerged were very different from what he had earlier planned. After reading several official volumes that had arrived from France with detailed descriptions of the Paris siege, Bloch's interest was raised to such an extent that he now

---

11 L. Straszewicz, 'Jan Bloch. Wspomnienie (Recollection)', *Zycie I Sztuka*, No. 1, 1902, 3.
12 J. Bugajski, *op.cit.*, p. 209.

became a committed student, although not yet to the point where the issues of war and peace had overwhelmed his other concerns.

We know from his contemporaries that he worked feverishly. He turned out books by day and night. He studied war: he did it with great passion. He studied the construction of cannon; the role of cavalry in the face of modern weapons; the significance balloons to fortresses and so on, and it lasted for years.[13] In effect, this was the moment at which war displaced his economic and financial interests, and even his business duties.

More and more new books were bought and imported: even entire libraries. His assistants and his statistical office worked flat out. Experiments and tests were ordered and studied. A wide correspondence took place, both within and outside Russia, and, as Bloch's knowledge grew, he realised that he and other economists were not looking at war broadly enough to review its military and technical aspects with the same care as they explored others. In *The Future War* he indicated too, albeit indirectly, that he dealt with military matters of war in his earlier books on economy, railways and finance. He thought wrongly that his fragmentary knowledge of the technical side of war was enough to form a comprehensive and balanced judgment. It was not.

Despite his strong fascination with the *minutiae* of the technical side of war, and the progress in weapons and war technologies, Bloch had not yet decided to enter into fully-fledged war study. He kept on elaborating its economic and political causes and consequences.

But other forces were active on his agenda. A future European war was getting closer. Works on the Russo-French military alliance had advanced. In August 1892, the general staffs agreed on a common strategy in the event of a German attack on either party, and soon the text of a formal alliance was concluded and signed in January 1894. Thus, the political situation in Europe was set and polarised. Confronting the triple alliance of Austria, Germany and Italy, there stood two outer powers: Imperial Russia, through the Balkans to the Baltics and the Republic of France from the North Sea to the Mediterranean. Only the United Kingdom had not yet made up its mind which side to join. But Russia was, in any case, on a collision with Britain in Asia and the Far East. All these

---

13   L. Straszewicz, *op.cit.*, p. 3.

menacing developments coincided with Bloch's assiduous self-education. We may guess that, between 1892, when his *post-Memorial* work started, and 1893, when he became aware of an entirely different and new character of war, he changed his personal attitude about the war to come. He became sceptical at least, if not yet in open hostility.

He interrupted his work on the book, and by early 1893 had prepared a series of articles for publication under the title 'The Future War and its Economic Causes and Consequences', regarded as his first vocal warning to the public and the military of the new dimensions of war, which would be so much more disastrous for people, the economy, trade and finances.

Unexpectedly, his campaign against this future war could not begin. The barrier was hard to overcome, because there was no Russian censor in Warsaw who could read Bloch's articles on this mix of economics, politics and the military and give his approval to it, thus declaring that its message was not against the interests of the Russian Empire. After trying in other places than Warsaw with the same result, a frustrated Bloch turned to General A.K. Puzyrevski, the Chief-of-Staff of the Warsaw Military Region, previously his opponent, with a request to read his material. Finally the General consented.

Bloch's articles could then be published in *Biblioteka Warszawska*, the Warsaw social-literary monthly, between March 1893 and September 1894. They also appeared in *Russkij Viestnik* in St Petersburg. Bloch, however, went much further beyond and published his works in Germany, now Russia's enemy, in *Jahrbücher für Deutsche Armee und Marine* in 1894-95 as Johann von Bloch, and as Jean de Bloch in the friendly French *Revue du Cercle Militaire*.

Reaction to the campaign was disappointing. Just a few responses came in Russia and abroad and no debate started, despite the importance of the issues being raised. Bloch comforted himself that many younger officers and politicians, who shared his opinions and anxieties, could not voice them until those of high rank or position had done so. But these elders again did not wish to discuss Bloch's theses in public, in order not to weaken the national spirit to fight: so the endeavour was blocked. It seemed that for Bloch's opponents and adversaries ignoring his statements was the safest and most convenient course of action.

But this did not stop him from continuing his work. By 1895 he had decided to end his research and to frame his results as a direct assault on the highest authority in Russia: Bloch sought to place his views before the Tsar and his advisors in St Petersburg. It was a lesson that he drew from his previous experience in lobbying and, as we know, he was right. So the military threw a wet blanket over his works, whilst Bloch, for his part, continued with his anti-war research and studies, publishing them in full in 1898, despite Russia's strong militarism, the current arms race and preparations for war.

Given his access to the corridors of power, through his membership of the Learned Committee of the Ministry of Finance, Bloch was in a position to place his opinions and arguments in the ears of a wide range of senior Russian government officials. He focused on those who he believed to have doubts or anxieties about the current pro-war policy.

It was at this juncture, in 1894, that the author of this policy, Tsar Alexander III, died and was succeeded by young Nicholas II, who was known to be a different sort of person. He was both less militaristic and less decisive than his predecessor and under the influence of others, above all of his wife, Alexandra Teodorovna. Expecting more changes, Bloch concentrated with more energies on ending his studies, in order to have the work finished and at his disposal for further lobbying. To do this, he now needed to classify all his observations and opinions. In particular, he needed to set the technical and political framework of his work. As he did so, after several months, Bloch, to his surprise (in the opinion of his contemporaries), 'returned to his point of departure, meaning to issues of the economic consequences of war. A couple of years of steady and persistent work brought him to such heights that he could now see a new broad horizon, all in other shapes and colours than seen at the beginning'.[14] All this meant that he had to undertake a major reappraisal, rereading the hundreds of pages written so far. But he did not demur. On the contrary, he finally decided by 1896 that the economic aspects of war would not be the main theme of his book. Future war would be presented in its entirety, meaning in its technical, economic and political aspects. This reappraisal brought Bloch to his cardinal and most important and famous opinion that, for the great powers, future war would be simply impossible: it would be so destructive, so costly in human and material losses that economies would be

---

14 L. Straszewicz, *op.cit.*, p. 4.

in ruins and societies pushed to unrest, revolutions and collapsed states. So, faced with such calamaties, European monarchs and government could not expect that war might be for them 'the continuation of state policy by other means', as Clausewitz had defined it. This, even for Bloch, was a challenging conclusion.

In Russia, in particular, his conclusion that future war might lead reliably to social unrest was of considerable interest to the Court. The chapter in Volume 5, entitled 'Socialism, anarchism, propaganda against militarism', was intensely read, and it is reported that these issues attracted the close interest of the Tsar. At the same time, one should recollect that all six volumes of Bloch's work were later to be found in Lenin's personal reference library at the Kremlin.

The manner in which Bloch successfully introduced his arguments to Tsar Nicholas and the manner in which his case both propelled and underpinned the issue of the Imperial Rescript of 1898 is explained in more detail in the accompanying chapter by Professor van den Dungen. That The Hague Conferences failed to deflect the momentum towards war is a matter of history. So, too, that, when in September 1916, H.G. Wells wrote his reports of the Great War from the trenches near Soissons and Arras he chose to describe the bloody positional warfare that he witnessed as 'Bloch's war'.[15] What more precise but bitter recognition of the accuracy of Bloch's studies, conducted 20 years before, could one seek? But, alas, as Professor Sir Michael Howard observed on Bloch, 'like so many pessimistic prophets (including those of air power a generation later) Bloch underestimated the capacities of human societies to adjust themselves to adverse circumstances.'[16] *Plus ça change, plus c'est la même chose.* Be that as it may, for Bloch, like Nobel before him, it meant a 'fatal return to barbarism'.

---

15 H.G. Wells, 'Der Krieg Blochs', 18 *Die Friedens-Warte*, No. 5 (May), 1969.
16 M. Howard, 'Men against fire: expectations of war in 1914', 9 *International Security*, No. 1 (Summer), 1984, 44.

7

BLOCH'S INFLUENCE AMONG THE
GERMAN ANTI-WAR DISSIDENTS

Jutta Birmele

Jan Bloch is regarded as the only military thinker in the Russian Empire before
the First World War who succeeded in attracting attention outside Russia. No
sooner had the full-length German edition appeared one year after its publication
in Russian in 1888 than Bloch's book *Der Krieg* became the object of intense
discussion among the principal representatives of the pacifist movement, liberal
critics of Imperial Germany, government representatives, and military strategists
and writers. This chapter presents a survey of responses in Germany, and suggests why Bloch's book became 'the Bible' for one faction of the pacifists,
particularly for Alfred Fried, while others (for example Ludwig Quidde) felt
uneasy about Bloch's conclusions and above all about the absence of an
emphatic ethical base in favour of a utilitarian thesis. Bloch thus became a
catalyst whose reception in Germany brought to the surface fundamental differences in the peace (and war) philosophy before the First World War. He also
contributed to increased public discussion of the assessment of the military and
economic feasability of war.

Bloch's thesis (what we would now describe as the 'balance of terror' or
'mutually assured destruction', due to the technology and economic dimensions
that modern warfare had taken on) was embraced by Alfred Fried and others
in the German peace movement, who felt uneasy about the much-satirised
humanitarian and melodramatic *Die Waffen Nieder*-crusade undertaken primarily
by Bertha von Suttner, and sought a scientific basis for campaigning in favour
of disarmament and international arbitration as a decisive step towards a
peaceful international arrangement. In other words, the German pacifists
expected Bloch's work, based on 12 years of statistical and practical invest-

G. Prins and H. Tromp (eds.), The Future of War, 101-108.
© 2000 *Kluwer Law International. Printed in the Netherlands.*

igation into modern warfare[1] to move the issue of pacifism from the 'lunatic fringe' into the mainstream of German political life. Through the adoption of Bloch's rational thesis as 'scientific evidence', it was hoped to establish legitimacy for the 'peace movement' in the eyes of the political establishment, and gain the status of a serious political opposition. Only by engaging military planners and proponents of military culture in constructive dialogue could the peace advocates hope to influence the political climate in favour of a revision.

To appreciate the formidable obstacles faced by German pacifists, it may be instructive to recall the climate and dominant attitudes that shaped the political culture of Wilhelmine Germany at the end of the 19th century that later on culminated in the overwhelming show of popular support for the decision for war in 1914. Germany's political culture promoted a pattern of attitudes toward conflict resolution that denied, more than in other western countries, any fertile ground to pacifism.[2] Political culture refers to the collective beliefs, values and symbols, which define the meaning of political choices. They enter into the collective reasoning of a culture's citizenry and into the style and operating codes of its leadership.[3] In the 1890s, accentuated by the political vacuum left by Bismarck's departure, certain perceptions gained largely unquestioned validity:

·   with the acquisition of colonies, Germany had entered into an era of imperialist politics, and *Weltpolitik* implied the risk of international confrontation;[4]
·   increasingly, with the Franco-Russian Military Convention of 1892-93, the vision of Germany as a beleaguered fortress took shape;[5]

---

1   I.F. Clarke, *Voices Prophesying War. Future Wars 1763-3749* (Oxford/New York, Oxford University Press, 1992), p. 114.
2   R. Chickering, *Imperial Germany and a World without War. The Peace Movement and Germany Society 1892-1914* (Princeton, Princeton University Press, 1975), p. 37.
3   S. Verba, 'Comparative political culture' in: Pye & Verba (eds), *Political Culture and Political Development* (Princeton, Princeton University Press, 1965), p. 513.
4   See R. Chickering *Imperial Germany and a World without War*, p. 96.
5   Between 1891 and 1894, a number of Franco-Russian staff talks, agreements and treaties had alarmed the Germany political and military leadership. G. E. Rothenberg, 'Moltke, Schleiffen, and the Doctrine of Strategic Envelopment', in: Paret (ed.), *Makers of Modern Strategy* (Princeton, Princeton University press, 1986), p. 12.

- the worst-case scenario of a two-front war became an obsession for military strategists and was made public by numerous articles in the general press.
- Germany, as a dynamic, new economic power, was surrounded by aggressive enemies envious of Germany's accomplishments;
- Germany had a particularly virtuous, even superior culture and, therefore, a 'civilising world mission';
- to secure and support German interests, if necessary by 'force of arms', the nation must at all times be kept in military readiness;
- Germany's vulnerability, due to her geographic position and the numerical strength of her likely enemies, required domestic unity and justified suppression of divisiveness and alternate views.

When the German delegation entered The Hague Peace Conference in 1899 they did so on the back of;

- recent increases in Germany's military strength (1893-1897), compensating for her relative loss of power due to the changing international treaty system which disfavoured Germany;[6]
- Bülow's *Weltmacht* concept, announced in December 1897;
- Confident that the long depression had given way to an upsurge in the German economy;
- the Tirpitz Plan of 1898 for a German navy, as a lever for a 'great overseas policy'.

Massive mobilisation of public opinion, through manipulation from above, as well as through a groundswell of pan-German grassroots organisations, took place from the 1890s onwards. Against these huge numbers, the pacifists were an insignificant faction of German society. Around 1900, it is estimated that only 5,000 people in Germany actively advocated this position,[7] with only 2-300 engaged in any agenda, while veterans' organisations already had 1.5 million members,[8] and other patriotic and militarist associations, like the Navy League, were attracting huge numbers.

---

6   S. Förster, *Der Doppelte Militarismus. Die Deutsche Heeresrüstungspolitik zwischen Status-Quo, Sicherung und Aggression 1890-1913* (Stuttgart, Franz Steiner Verlag, 1985), pp. 28-74, 297.

7   R. Chickering, *ibid.*, p. 53

8   D. Düding, 'Die Kriegvereine im wilhelminischen Reich und ihr Beitrag zu Militarisierung der deutschen Gesellschaft', in: Dülffer & Holl (eds), *Bereit zum Krieg* (Göttingen, Vanderhoeck & Ruprecht, 1986), p. 101.

The venerable Helmut von Moltke held that 'war is part of God's order'. With-out war, the world would stagnate and lose itself in materialism,[9] a sentiment that became throughly entrenched in commonly held German opinion. Heinrich von Treitschke, the foremost state historian, claimed that it was 'the weary, spiritless, and exhausted ages which have played with the dream of perpetual peace'.[10] Theodor Mommsen, as quoted by Fried, summed up what probably characterised the overwhelmingly hostile attitude of the *Bildungsbürger* about the proposed peace conference: 'a misprint in world history'.[11]

Anyone countering the emotionally-charged self-perception of the German nation risked being accused of disloyalty or even treason. To be sure, pacifists shared many of the values of the dominant German belief system and were at pains to demonstrate their patriotism and loyalty.

By the time Fried's *Handbuch der Friedensbewegung* appeared in 1905, Fried had strictly abandoned moralism in favour of 'scientific' reasons (inter-nationalising of capitalism and free trade as the best guarantee for peace). Fried, a self-taught man who lacked the credentials of a university education, was particularly eager to position himself in the realm of academic credentials. Jacob Novikow, the Russian sociologist, had a considerable influence in shaping Fried's pacifist ideology. Novikow predicted that the growing economic inter-dependency would invariably lead to a new international world order, a world federation, and that war would become a phenomenon of the past. The spectre of a natural evolution into a global community without war was certainly devel-oped further in Bloch's study and supported by his extensive collection of data.

Fried's embrace of 'scientific pacifism' became an *exclusive* perspective in all of his Fried's publications, to the point where he would attack dissenting opinions, principally those with moral emphasis. Like scientific socialism (Marx-ism), scientific pacifism was expected to appeal to the contemporary public enchanted by *Wissenschaft* and craving certainty in the face of the uncertainty

---

9   H. von Moltke, *Gesammelte Schriften und Denkwürdigkeiten* (Berlin, 1892), Vol. 5, p. 194.

10 Quoted by F. v. Bernhardi in *Germany and the Next War* (London, Edward Arnold, 1914), p. 17.

11 A.H. Fried, *Handbuch der Friedensbewegung*, with a new introduction by D. Gas-man (New York, Garland Publishing, 1972), p. 205.

of massive technological, social, political and economic transformations. Presen-
ting himself as a 'realist' rather than an idealist, in Fried's eyes, served the cause
of working towards a world without war better than alienating the dominant
political culture of Wilhelmine Germany by attacking the emotional foundation
on which it rested. For example, in an effort to prove that pacifists shared a
common culture and equally felt loyal to their monarch, Fried and other
emphatically commended the Russian 'Friedensczar' for his manifesto and the
German 'Friedenskaiser' for his public support of The Hague Peace Conference.

Scientific pacifism clearly posed a problem for a faction of German pacifists,
whose ethical motivation it brushed aside. Ludwig Quidde, for example, hesit-
ated to concur with Bloch entirely. Without dismissing the validity of Bloch's
'scientific' reasoning, and acknowledging that historical developments would
facilitate the change of attitude towards war as a perversion[12], Quidde reaffirmed Kant's ethical motif as the compelling fundamental justification for
abandoning war as a legitimate instrument of politics. In Quidde's view, pacifism could not be separated from the issues of the enlightenment and the French
Revolution: freedom, equality, fraternity. In other words, pacifism was tied to
democracy, and, in this respect, Quidde's brand of pacifism, unlike Fried's,
posed a threat to the imperial political system. A peaceful order for Quidde's
faction in the German peace movement was not the natural outcome of an evolution but an act of will, the triumph of man's reason and moral consciousness
over his baser instincts, as Kant had postulated in his treatise, *Perpetual Peace*.
However, not until shortly before the First World War, and particularly by being
elected to the presidency of the Germany Peace Society, did Quidde's voice
emerge as a dominant force in shaping the ideology of the German 'peace movement'. By that time, a series of wars had put the thesis of scientific pacifism
on the defensive.

Liberal voices, such as that of Hans Delbrück, 'the foremost interpreter of
military affairs to the German people and civilian critic of the general staff',
as Gordon Craig has called him[13], tended to be devastatingly harsh in their
critique of Bloch's work as dilettantish and fancifully speculative. In an article

---

12   R. Chickering, *ibid.*, p. 106.
13   G.A. Craig, 'Delbrück: the military historian', in: Paret (ed.), *Makers of Modern
Strategy: from Machiavelli to the Nuclear Age* (Princeton, Princeton University
Press, 1986), p. 326.

for *Preussische Jahrbücher* 'War of the future and peace of the future', he took issue with Bloch's economic conclusions that economic interests of nations rendered war redundant: 'Economic damages will not prevent the war of the future, on the contrary, it will be an intensifier of warfare.'[14] Overall, 'from a scientific standpoint, the work does not have much to recommend it. It is a rather uncritical and poorly arranged collection of material; and although it is embellished with illustrations, the treatment is amateurish and overburdened with vast amounts of detail that have nothing to do with the actual problem. Moreover, the conclusions are extremely faulty and hastily drawn.'[15] Nothing could force sovereign states to submit to arbitration. 'What could arbitration do, where there is no right?' Power, as a determinant in international politics, would not be influenced by disarmament. On the contrary, disarmament, in Delbrück's opinion, would help to disguise the true assessment of relative power and contribute to international instability by creating an 'illusion of peace'.[16] Like other German liberals, *e.g.* Friedrich Naumann and Max Weber and much of the academic community, Delbrück fully supported German imperialism and *Weltpolitik*, preferably without war, but not shying away from risk of war: peace, as far as possible, but war if it should be necessary.[17]

Military circles in Germany rushed to refute Bloch's conclusions with intense scrutiny, and, based on a range of technical and strategic arguments, insisted that war continued to be entirely feasible.[18] On the topic of the length of a future war, the military community seems to have been divided, tilting, however, towards a short war.[19] Although the older Moltke, in his last address to the Reichstag in 1890, had predicted a long, drawn-out war that could last 'seven and perhaps thirty years',[20] military planning from the 1890s onwards reflected the experiences of 1870 that a future war would be determined by a decisive battle or two, contradicting Bloch's forecast of an entrenched, stalemated war.

---

14 H. Delbrück, 'Zukunftskrieg und Zukunftsfrieden', *Preussische Jahrbücher* (1899) 96, p. 221.
15 *Ibid.*, p. 208.
16 *Ibid.*, p. 221.
17 J. Dülfer, 'The debate on the First Hague Conference in Germany', in: Chatfield & van den Dungen (eds), *Peace Movements and Political Cultures* (University of Tennessee Press, 1988), p. 27.
18 R. Chickering, *ibid.*, p. 272f.
19 R. Chickering, *ibid.*, p. 391.
20 G.E. Rothenberg, *ibid.*, p. 310.

Disarmament and arbitration were rejected. Likewise, Bloch's (and subsequently the Russian Tsar's) suggestion that modern warfare was going to be economic suicide, was brushed aside. A particularly arrogant statement was made by the military expert of the German delegation, Groß von Schwarzhoff, at The Hague Peace Conference. In no way did Germany feel anxious about the military expenditure, she could well afford it: 'The German people are not crushed beneath the weight of expenditures and taxes. Quite the contrary; public and private wealth is growing, the general welfare and standard of living are rising from year-to-year.[21]

General Friedrich von Bernhardi, head of the military history section in the Great General Staff, was especially scathing in his critique of Bloch, a civilian, as amateurish. Bernhardi's influential book can be seen as a direct response to Bloch's thesis and to the German pacifists' embrace of Bloch's position. Pacifism was 'undermining the warlike spirit of the people' and materialism seduced the Germans into complacency, threatening to put an end to the glorious record of German history.[22] A world without war was simply unthinkable for the military careerist Bernhardi.[23] However, as Chickering has demonstrated, 'the antipathy towards the peace moment was less exuberant among the soldiers than it was elsewhere in Germany.'[24] In the press, efforts by pacifists, including the turn to 'scientific pacifism' on the basis of Bloch's work, were largely discredited in derisive terms such as *Friedensschwärmerei*, *Friedensfanatiker*, *Friedensapostel* or *Friedensduselei*,[25] and effectively destroyed any chance to move German pacifism into the range of mainstream culture at the time. As Fried lamented, the common attitude *'wenn Du den Frieden willst, rüste den Krieg'* prevailed.[26]

---

21 J. Brown Scott (ed.), *The Proceedings of the Hague Peace Conferences. The Conference of 1899*, translation of official texts (Oxford/New York, Oxford University Press, 1920), pp. 308ff, CF, GP, 15, 4259.

22 F. von Bernhardi, *Germany and the Next War*, transl. Allen H. Powles (London, Edward Arnold, 1914), p. 9.

23 'Wherever we open the pages of history we find proofs of the fact that wars, begun at the right moment with manly resolution, have effected the happiest results, both politically and socially.' *Ibid.*, p. 41.

24 R. Chickering, *ibid.*, p. 184.

25 R. Chickering, ibid., p. 185.

26 A. H. Fried, *Die Haager Conferenz. Ihre Bedeutung und ihre Ergebnisse* (Berlin, Hugo Bermühler, 1900), p. 60.

In spite of the negative reception within the German political and military establishment and the biased press, Bloch's work and The Hague Conference at least succeeded in focusing public attention on the feasibility and nature of war and on the existence of a rational opposition to war that could no longer be wholly dismissed as unpatriotic or lunatic. Eager to answer their critics, German pacifists took every opportunity to keep media attention on the issue of peace. With a revised theoretical underpinning (Fried's), the new systematic, scientific model, based on Bloch's work, hoped to overcome the image of hopelessly utopian sectarianism, which the public connected with symbols of olive branches, doves, angels, white flags, broken swords, ploughshares and poetry. That it did not succeed attests to the strength of engrained cultural hostility to peaceful conflict resolution in authoritarian German society, more than to the weakness of the German peace activists. Perhaps their trust in the power of Reason was naïve.[27] For the time being, the slogan *Die Waffen nieder* was replaced by *Organisiert die Welt*, based on Edwin D. Mead's book title, to emphasise a new organisational/technical/rational approach to world peace. As Bloch had remarked at the start of the Conference, the results would be more than satisfactory if the Conference just offered an opening for the peace idea, as the 'thin end of the peace wedge'.[28] Above all, Bloch's work, and The Hague Peace Conference with all the publicity it drew, gave German peace activists new confidence and direction in continuing their work. It took two world wars to strengthen sufficiently the 'peace wedge' and drive their agenda into the dominant German belief system.

---

27 '... daß man diese Idee nur solange bekämpfen kann, so lange man sie nicht versteht, und daß man sie vertheidigen wird von dem Augenblicke an, wo man sie erfasst hat. Dies allein berechtigt zu den schönsten Hoffnungen.' Fried, *ibid.*, p. 27.

28 P. van den Dungen, *The Making of Peace: Jean de Bloch and the First Hague Peace Conference* (Los Angeles, Center for the Study of Armament and Disarmament, 1983), p. 19.

PART II

TRANSFORMATION IN THE INTERNATIONAL ORDER

8

INTERNATIONAL ORGANISATIONS IN THE QUEST FOR PEACE

Carl Bildt

Reading Jan Bloch's work a century after it was published, it is indeed remarkable to note how accurate his predictions on the nature of a coming war turned out to be. Starting with very technical arguments, he ended with conclusions of profound political significance, which were very clearly at odds with the conventional wisdom of his day. Not only did he predict that a coming war would be a massive, long-lasting and brutal confrontation involving entire nations, but also that this would threaten the very fabric of our societies, paving the way for the social revolution which the empires of Europe had been doing their best to prevent ever since the Congress of Vienna system had been set up. Aware of the immense potential for destruction of entire societies in the new technologies of war, his call was for an international order, based on justice and arbitration, which would make war obsolete. His work paved the way for that call by Tsar Nicholas II, described by Dr van den Dungen, which led to the two Peace Conferences in The Hague in 1899 and 1907 that gave us not only the International Court of Justice but also the major elements of the laws of war which apply to this day.

In this respect, he was more successful in warning of dangers ahead than most other authors of his age, most of whom were just politely listened to, but with no action taken. But in a more profound way he failed, since the institutions set up and rules decided upon amounted to very little as the states of Europe steered towards that catastrophic civil war which started in 1914 and lasted for close to half a century. In his masterful *Diplomacy*, Henry Kissinger vividly describes the diplomatic and military 'doomsday machine' that the leaders of the empires managed to construct – by default far more than by design – and which led them not only to a war far worse than any one of them could ever have imagined, but also to the social revolution which Bloch had warned of in his book. The German, Russian, Austro-Hungarian and Ottoman empires all came crashing down as nations and societies were torn apart by the burdens

G. Prins and H. Tromp (eds.), The Future of War, 111-120.
© 2000 Kluwer Law International. Printed in the Netherlands.

of that horrible war, turning Bloch's warning into reality. The fateful communist *putsch* led first to civil war and then to the Stalinist dictatorship, which came to suppress Russia and haunt Europe until less than a decade ago.

The efforts to set up machinery to prevent war prior to the Great War were thus a failure. Bloch's warnings led to impressive efforts, but in the end they were unable to contain the pressures building up, and all the old order crumbled and disappeared as a result.

The doomsday machine ended the world as it had been known, and brought us into a new era.

As the horrors of the Great War become more apparent, the war aims with which the Anglo-Saxon world started came to be formulated in more radical terms. It was not only a war to restore a balance-of-power system, which had failed to prevent the war, but increasingly a war to end all wars, and to erect a new international system based on universal values rather than national interest. The Wilsonian model of international relations was undoubtedly a noble one (although elsewhere in this volume Edward Luttwak holds a different view). Although the diplomats of Versailles spent months redrawing maps, creating states and dealing with the details of structures in the different disputed corners of Europe, their main achievement was the League of Nations, which was supposed to end all wars, and usher the world into a new era of both peace and justice. But Wilson's idealism was defeated first by the isolationism of his own country. With the major power outside the system, it was bound to fail. And when the revanchism of France, as expressed in the harsh terms of the Treaty, fuelled the revanchism of Germany, it was hardly more than a question of time until the European conflict would restart, with even more powerful military technologies to spread the conflict further and faster over the entire continent and world. The glorious attempt of Versailles turned into little more than a lengthy cease-fire in that European civil war which came to dominate the first half of this century: on this Luttwak and I are in agreement.

Great wars produce great efforts to make peace. Out of the ruins of the League of Nations came the United Nations, now including all the powerful states of the world, and with ultimate power over the ultimate powers of the new organisation given to them. The UN system has been instrumental in resolving conflicts and creating the conditions for the development of nations and peoples during the past half-century. Blocked in its ability to develop into a universal system for conflict-resolution by the conflicts between the permanent members of its Security Council, it has nevertheless played a key role in key events during this long period of time. The scope of the efforts to secure peace has widened from Europe alone to the entire world. It has played a key role in the important process of decolonisation. It has given a voice and a role to nations and states which otherwise might have felt isolated in frustration at the margins of the international system. It has provided a forum for dialogue between all the nations of the world. But the UN has been much more than what we generally associate with these terms. It can be argued that the different organisations and arrangements that are part of the wider family of the UN have been even more successful in trying to shape a global order of cooperation and integration which, in the final analysis, also makes a vital contribution to the cause of peace.

The Bretton Woods institutions – the International Monetary Fund, the World Bank, what has evolved into the world trade organisations – have evolved into probably the most significant of international organisations. Together, they have shaped and reshaped an evolving international economic order, which so far has prevented the economic calamities that proved so disastrous during the interwar years, while at the same time improving the prospects for economic and social development for all those nations choosing to be a part of the system. For a long time, the Bretton Woods institutions and their framework for economic development were limited to those parts of the world following a western model of development. But as the old divisions have faded away, we are now beginning to see the entire world coming together in a common system of rules, obligations and frameworks for economic development and integration. Whatever the challenges we are face in the more restricted areas of security, this represents an achievement we should not forget and the importance of which we must not neglect.

When Bloch wrote about the threat to peace, his focus was distinctly a European one. Although our focus today must be global, it remains fair to say that questions of war and peace throughout history have to a large extent been debated against the background of the experience of European history. Bloch saw four big issues threatening the peace and stability of the continent of Europe. The first was the conflict between France and Germany over the disputed territory of Alsace and Lorraine – or Elsass and Lothringen. The second was what he referred to as the eastern question: the management of the decline of the Ottoman Empire and the political order of the areas formerly ruled by it.

The third was the question of the relationship between Russia and the rest of Europe. And the fourth was the emerging colonial question, then framed very much as the scramble for territory in Africa and Asia by European powers.

The big emerging issue of European security in those days, which Bloch failed to see, was how a system of stability and peace could accommodate the rise of Germany to the position of dominant nation in the western part of the continent. Previously a divided region in the heart of the continent, the combination of political unification and economic modernisation had suddenly started to lift Germany to the position of the strongest nations in Europe. The Peace of Versailles sought to solve the problem of Germany by suppressing it, and depriving it of economic and military resources. Germany soon broke out of the limitations of Versailles, launching a quest for the domination of the continent that was swifter and more powerful than any other such attempt in the past. After the defeat of Germany in 1945, the problem of Germany was solved through a combination of division and integration. Soon after the war had ended, Germany was *de facto* divided into two states. These were gradually integrated into two competing blocs, the one an extension of the Soviet system into virtually all the areas brought under the control of the Red Army, and the other a defensive alliance trying to deter war and protect democracy. Of far greater long-term importance than the division of Germany was her integration into a framework of close cooperation with her former enemies. It is this process of European integration during the past half-century that has solved not only the problem of Alsace and Lorraine, but also the wider problem of the place of Germany in Europe. The efforts at European integration represent not only a novel approach when it comes to the setting up of international organisations, but also when it comes to trying to secure peace in Europe. Within a group of nations sharing the same political core values, its system of economic and social integration also *de facto* rules out the possibility of the use of violence in inter-state relationships, thus securing peace between all nations part of the process of European integration.

However, we would be unwise to forget all the wars and conflicts of these areas during the past centuries. The great peace efforts of Westphalia, Utrecht and Vienna dealt with the perennial security issues of the areas now part of Europe to a very large extent. The European Union has proved itself the most important instrument for peace in our part of the world in our time. But the start was a difficult one. The Council of Europe never got the powers needed to be the true focus of the integration efforts. The European Defence Community failed.

It was only when the example of the Coal and Steel Community was applied much more widely – economic integration in order to achieve political ends – that it proved possible to move forward. Now, as we stand on the threshold of the 21st century, we can with a high degree of confidence say that the efforts that have led to the European Union, encompassing 15 European nations, have effectively removed the risks of war for a very large part of our continent. However, as some old problems in Europe have been solved others have resurfaced, and presented us with new challenges as we try to secure the absence of war in the future. It was the city Strasbourg that was the symbol and the centre of the conflict over Alsace (or Elsass) between France and Germany. Today, Strasbourg is the seat not only of the European Parliament, but also of the France-German joint brigade, trying to tie together the armies of nations that in the past fought each other so often. It is a fact filled with symbolism that key parts of this brigade have now been deployed from Strasbourg to Sarajevo, trying to secure the peace in that torn part of our Europe. In this simple fact of military deployment one observes not only that the first of the main threats to the peace of Europe seen by Bloch has been solved, but also that the second, restoring order to the regions of the former Ottoman Empire, has not.

Indeed, when we look at contemporary newspaper headlines, it looks as if we are about to be overwhelmed by the problems left as a legacy of the orders and disorders of the Ottoman Empire. From the problems of the peoples of Kosovo to the problems of the Kurds, we are dealing with the remaining issues of the political order of the vast area from the Danube to the Persian Gulf once under the rule of the Sublime Porte. If the first threat has been solved by a radically new approach in the form of economic and political integration within the European Union, the issues arising out of the second threat are now being dealt with by some sort of modern version of the Concert of Europe.

A century ago, it was the representatives of three empires that used to come together to discuss the implications of the different conflicts in the area, to issue edicts on how they should be solved, and to threaten different sorts of military action if their words were not taken seriously enough. Today, we see the United States, the key countries of the European Union and Russia coming together to discuss the implications of the different conflicts of the area, to issue edicts on how they should be solved, and to threaten different sorts of military action if their words are not taken seriously enough. The Concert of Europe of a century ago has turned into the Contact Group of today. The issues of this part of Europe are to some extent different from the issues in most other parts of Europe. The legacy not only of the Ottoman Empire over 500 years, but also the millennium of the Byzantine Empire which preceded it, has been a mosaic of cultures, religions and traditions in this area where East meets West, which has no equivalent elsewhere. To some extent, this mosaic could be held together within the framework of a multinational and multicultural empire. But when the multinational empires gave way to the nation states as the key principle of organisation, the tension between this principle and the multi-ethnic realities of the region started to produce the series of wars of which we have not yet seen the end. The choice for the region is simple, although stark. Either one tries to build new frameworks of integration and cooperation, or one continues down the road of setting up one new nation state after the other, with battles for borders being in effect battles for majority or minority status in the different states resulting from these conflicts.

Today, it is a question of the future of Kosovo. Tomorrow, it might well be the question of the future of some other part of this region. The jury is still out on the question of the possibilities of establishing a self-sustaining peace process in Bosnia. If one widens the perspective only so slightly, the immense challenge of the eastern Mediterranean, with Greece and Turkey entering into a new phase of bitterness over the Kurdish issue when they really need to come together over the Cyprus issue, underlies the magnitude of the challenge we are faced with in that wider area of Bloch's 'eastern question'. Indeed, over the years, we will increasingly be faced with the problems of order and disorder in the wider arch of instability stretching from Agadir on the Atlantic Ocean to Astrakhan on the Caspian Sea, where Europe meets Africa to where it meets Asia.

The third of Bloch's issues was the question of the relationship of Russia with the western parts of Europe. He concluded rightly – taking issue with others at the time – that war would never bring a solution. Russia needs all its resources for its long-term domestic reform and development, and will never be able to dominate the rest of the continent, while efforts by even the strongest adversary to conquer a Russia always able to mobilise reserves from its interior were always bound to fail. The lesson of Charles XII and Napoleon were to be relearned by Hitler.

Today, after the grim decades of Communism, Russia is again going through a transformation that is as important as it is difficult. It is shedding not only a system but also an empire, trying to come to terms with itself, and trying to find a new role in the emerging new international system. Leningrad was the symbol of the Communist coup that, for all its internationalist rhetoric, brought about not only the decline but also the isolation of Russia from the rest of the world. Apart from the occasional fellow traveller of the early years, there were few friends of the Soviet Union beyond the pay cheques of the NKVD or KGB. Now, the city is again St Petersburg. Founded by Peter the Great on a piece of land just taken from the Swedes, built in splendour by architects from Italy, deliberately turning its back on the inward-looking tradition of Muscovy, it was once the symbol of a new and modern Russia, wanting to be fully a part of the rest of Europe. The integration of Russia into structures of cooperative security and into Europe is a key task for the future. There are overwhelming reasons for the development of strong economic links between the European Union and Russia. And there are even stronger reasons for the development of political and security relationships between Russia and the emerging common foreign and security policy of the European Union, thus extending the system of security anchored in the relationship across the Atlantic.

A decade ago, the roundtable negotiations, which were to bring about the peaceful fall of the Soviet Empire in Europe, started in Warsaw, the last Soviet soldier left Afghanistan, and the blue-black-and white flag of Estonia was once again raised over the castle of Tallinn, thus signalling the end of the Soviet Union itself. Then, the talk was of the end of history and of a new Europe suddenly emerging. But today, ten years later, we are still in the midst of this the third attempt this century to bring about a lasting order of peace in Europe. Previous attempts to build lasting orders of peace have often been based on efforts to secure the dominance of one principle or another in the new international system created. The Congress of Vienna based its efforts on a concept of managed balance of power, which proved amazingly successful for a long period of time, but which ultimately failed. And the Congress of Versailles tried to dictate the noble principles of a Wilsonian state of affairs to the entire world, only to fail much faster and fall much further. Now, we are in the midst of a number of processes, the combination of which should bring the possibility of a prolonged period of the absence of major wars, although not necessarily of universal peace, and certainly not of stability in the more conservative sense of this word. It is not a question of one principle or one organisation or one structure. It is a question of a number of interdependent efforts to set up what will amount to a common system of cooperative security on our continent, with important consequences for the wider world.

The economic and financial dimension of the change should not be underestimated. When the finance ministers of the G7 group of nations decided to set up a global stability forum, or when the budget of the Russian Federation approved by the Duma takes for granted direct support by the International Monetary Fund, we see the gradual emergence of an increasingly tight global economic order, bringing together nations of the world otherwise in confrontation with each other. As the global trading system becomes more open, and the financial interdependence between states more pronounced, the scope for major conflict tends to be reduced even further, although it would be naïve to believe that economic integration alone can prevent conflicts and wars.

One of the key tasks ahead for security in Europe will be the fifth enlargement of the European Union, taking it out of the western Europe of the old Cold War over the heart of central and eastern Europe. It is a development with profound implications. It is a remarkable fact that there is today hardly any nation in the widely defined western part of Europe, which is not seeking or does not seek membership in the European Union. From Cyprus to Estonia, nations are negotiating and preparing for a step seen by them as crucial to their future peace and prosperity. Even in Norway, opinion polls register strength in support for membership in the European Union, which is remarkable. In Switzerland, which once saw isolation as something of a national virtue, the signs of change are also increasingly evident. There will be numerous problems along this road. The management of the new Euro currency, the development of a true common foreign and security policy, including a military capability, and substantial enlargement will have to be undertaken during the next few years. But it brings the promise of the process of integration over time being able to manage all the tensions and conflicts of that wider Europe to the West of Russia and the Ukraine and to the North of that area of the old eastern question.

Integration has many faces. Economic integration has been the key to the political efforts of the European Union during the past four decades, and the advent of the Euro will certainly not weaken this trend. With a common economy comes a common political responsibility, which will further develop the institutions necessary to make the management of this responsibility a natural part of our democratic systems of government. However, increasingly, we have to see military integration as a key part of the process of building a structure of peace in Europe. In the Europe of today, there are far more independent armies than there were in the Europe of yesterday. Bosnia is certainly an extreme example, but from having no army at all of its own a decade ago, it now *de facto* has three separate armies trying to control separate parts of its territory. A proliferation of independent armies brings with it increased risks of instability. But with the new as well as old challenges we face, and with the importance attached to cooperation between the United States, the European Union and Russia within the new Concert of the Contact Group, there are numerous reasons why we should try to build new structures of military co-operation. This will give us not only the instruments to deal with the crisis of today, but – perhaps even more importantly – also ensure that the young men and women in uniform tomorrow will see other young men and women in other uniforms not as enemies in conflict but as colleagues in cooperation.

The Franco-German brigade deployed from Strasbourg to Sarajevo is certainly one of the symbols of the conflicts solved as well as of the challenges remaining. But the soldiers of Russia, the United States, Poland, Sweden and Estonia, working together under joint command in another part of that region, point the way towards even more far-reaching arrangements for the future. Here, the key role will be played by the reformed NATO now gradually emerging. Whilst retaining important functions when it comes to deterring those seeking to address political problems through the use of force, its role will increasingly be to advance that crucial process of integration of the armed forces of Europe, moulding not only the members of NATO, but also its partners, into a military structure ready to address tasks jointly. The relationship with Russia will be of particular importance here. The solutions thrown up by history to the three European problems identified by Bloch come together in a new Concert for integration and cooperative security in Europe. The developing and deepening integration of the increasing number of members of the European Union must go hand in hand with continued strong links across the Atlantic and efforts to build new structures of cooperative security with Russia as well. The process of EU enlargement will clearly not be enough. A true common foreign and security policy will be a necessity, and we must soon be ready in earnest to proceed from the present policy of a patchwork of protectorates in the western Balkans to a truly regional policy of integration and reform. It is futile to search for an exit strategy from our commitments to that region – we must start to devise an entry strategy for it into the wider structures of Europe.

Needless to say, our concerns for security and stability are not limited to our common home or our common near abroad. We would be at least as affected by an implosion in Korea or an explosion in Kashmir as we are by the continued strife in Kosovo or the disputes over the issues of the Kurds. But it is only a Europe able to feel secure in its own part of the world that will have the energy and the resources to play a more active role in the search for peace and stability in the wider world. Furthermore, we should not forget the lesson of history, that Europe is not only one of the most promising places on this earth of ours, but also one of the most dangerous. It is by managing the challenges of this wider Europe that we can also learn to handle the challenges of the wider world – and the long-term challenges of our own societies. In the eastern questions are coming together all those issues of the meetings of civilisations and cultures which can bring, depending on how they are dealt with, either an explosion of conflict or an explosion of creativity, with recent history also providing an abundance of examples of both. There are parallels that we should not ignore between the problems of Bosnia, Brussels and Burundi. The juxtaposition of different cultures in the valleys of Bosnia, the suburbs of Brussels and the hills of Burundi all present us with problems with which we have not yet come to grips.

Bloch sought the establishment of systems of international law and arbitration. He succeeded – and they failed. The Great War brought the Old Order to its end. Since then, two further attempts at a new order of peace have failed. Now, we are in the midst of a third attempt. I am in no way arguing that we should give up Bloch's quest, and those of so many others, for universal justice and for a universal system of law. Indeed, the further development of the system of international law, not least in the area of human rights, is of the greatest long-term importance. But I am humbled by the experience of history, and convinced that the search for the ultimate good must not deflect us from the more immediate tasks with which we are confronted. If we can manage them, we will see a new pattern of cooperative security evolving, which might well give us better chances of peace and peaceful change in Europe than perhaps at any time during the millennium now coming to its end.

9

FROM INDEPENDENCE TO INTERDEPENDENCE: THE END OF SOVEREIGNTY?

Christoph Bertram

This is a strange combination: a collection of essays which is devoted both to the memory of Jan Bloch and to the future of war: to the prophet of the end of wars and now to their continuation! I will try to escape the tensions implied by asking what we have learnt about war and peace in the bloody century which began shortly after Bloch's writing suggested that war as a rational act of policy had come to an end. In so doing, I shall focus on the changes in the relationship between states primarily, but not exclusively in Europe, in order to identify what it was that turned the first half of the century into five decades of war and which, at the end of the Cold War, promises to provide a more resilient structure of peace.

My basic thesis will be very different from that of Jan Bloch. He argued that one major development, namely the technology of destruction, was changing in such a way that it would deprive the war-makers of any gain. It will also be different from that of Norman Angell who, a few years later, claimed that economic interdependence had rendered military conflict obsolete. If these eminent thinkers turned out to be so wrong in such a short time, it was because they focused on secondary causes of conflict, not on the primary one: the nature of the state system. Just as in domestic society, so in the international society the absence of rules, whose observance represents the priority common interest, is bound to produce competition, conflict, confrontation and potentially disaster. War can only be truly overcome if, as in the domestic sphere, the international sphere is ruled through joint institutions whose authority is in the primary interest of all members.

Here lies the reason why the prophecies of eternal peace at the turn of a previous century did not have a chance then and why they have it now as the 20th century turns into the 21st. It is because we now have in Europe strong common institutions to which member states are committed.

G. Prins and H. Tromp (eds.), The Future of War, 121-131.
© 2000 Kluwer Law International. Printed in the Netherlands.

That is not interdependence, it is the beginning of the end of sovereignty. It has brought about a remarkable change: Europe, once the most contested, war-infested part of the globe, has become its most peaceful. And it raises the wider question, namely whether – not identical but similar – structures of order, as those developed in the Euro-Atlantic region, can also help other parts of the world to acquire new and lasting stability and order.

1   STATES WITHOUT RULES

To demonstrate that it is the nature of the state system rather than a particular aspect of state power or impotence that stands between war and peace, it is worth remembering what the nature of the state system has been and in most parts of the world still is.

It is not, as the title of this chapter suggests, the difference between independence and interdependence which is decisive. Was it the independence of Europe's nation states from one another which propelled them into war at the dawn of our century? Certainly not. The Europe of the late 19th century displayed a very high degree of cross-dependence, economically, culturally and politically. The dynasties on Europe's thrones were linked by close family ties. Culture was cosmopolitan. Business expanded unrestricted across borders. There even was something akin to a common currency – the gold standard. Here, in the thickness of the European network, lay the root of the prophecies of lasting peace of which Bloch and Angell were the most prominent and Alfred Nobel, the man who served his fortune by producing dynamite and his conscience by establishing the Peace Prize, the most contradictory.

No, the old states of the old Europe were not at all independent, they were very interdependent indeed. Nations and societies had become interlocked. And yet this high degree of interaction did not serve as a sufficient barrier against interstate conflict. The mere fact that nations traded with each other, communicated with each other, that people mingled and mixed and the crowned houses intermarried with each other failed to create ties and interests strong enough to halt the slide into violence and war.

Quite the contrary. Obviously, the breeding ground for conflict is not, as anthropologists confirm, distance but closeness, not difference but similarity. Interdependence does not, it seems, create obstacles to strife but actually promotes it. Civil wars, when groups within what was once one society enter into conflict with each other, often produce the bloodiest atrocities – witness the events in the Balkans over the past few years, in Central Africa or in Chechenya, all between formerly closely intertwined ethnic groups. It is not the clash of civilizations which causes conflicts but the clash within common cultures. After all, the Europe that during the centuries engaged in so many wars also displayed a very high degree of social, ethnic, and religious homogeneity! Once the line between co-existence and confrontation is crossed, interdependence and inter-relationship actually seem to increase the ferocity of the conflict.

Why this is so? Perhaps because interdependence without additional institutional underpinning breeds resentment. National élites can no longer act autonomously unless they are willing to pay the price of major disadvantage. Interdependence, without the backing for structures for negotiation, encourages the fear that others are getting a better deal, that one is treated unfairly, that one's power and influence is slipping while that of others is growing. After all, it was precisely this fear of losing out in the competition of power that led the nations of Europe into the First World War. On the face of it, interdependence creates a community of interests. But it is a fragile community, unlikely to hold together during political and economic turbulence. Interdependence is no insurance against conflict.

2   THE IMPACT OF GLOBALISATION

Today we are entering a phase of even greater interdependence than that which applied 100 years ago. Then security was a matter of distance; far-away wars were not really of great concern. Today, modern missile technology, increasingly available to a growing number of states, brings distance within reach. Then, the economic fate of far-away countries was without relevance. Today, financial and economic turbulence in Asia and Latin America undermine the economic prospects of Europe and America as well. Then, most societies were ethnically homogenous. Now, most of our countries include citizens from well beyond our frontiers who are affected by conflicts back home. However far away things happen, they resonate close to us now.

Is the trend of globalisation unstoppable? The globalisation of communication certainly is, the globalisation of markets probably, too. When prosperity has become the highest value, globalisation is the price that has to be paid for it. Countries which try to stay aloof inevitably suffer economically. The price of backwardness is much higher than that of being exposed to the pressures and vagaries of the global market. So, the new, intense level of interchange which the world has reached today is likely to remain a fact of our life.

But if it is true that a high degree of interdependence is no barrier against conflict but possibly even a catalyst, then there is no cause for complacency. The need to succeed in the global market place opens national structures of power and society to interference from abroad. It exposes their inner weaknesses, accelerates their social unravelling, challenges their power structure. Perhaps, in the end, these pressures can only be met adequately by countries where power is based firmly on democratic legitimacy and accountability. It is in this sense that globalisation's logical companion is democracy.

But politics and logic do not always and certainly not always rapidly go hand in hand. Societies, as individuals, resent outside pressures. Precisely because globalisation penetrates the protective membrane that used to shield regimes and societies from the outside world, it can breed xenophobia, anxiety, revanchism. Thus, the economic pressures of globalisation may produce a political backlash, even in democratic societies, particularly once the promise of rapid new riches has collapsed – as today in many so-called 'emerging markets' in Asia, Latin America and Russia. This back-lash can take a variety of forms: renewed protectionism, political populism, anti-Westernism, religious fanaticism. The argument that those who indulge in these reactions will, in the end, be the losers in international competition holds little comfort. After all, those who fear to lose out have, in the past, often been those who chose violent responses to try to stop trends working against them.

Does that mean that globalisation increases the likelihood of future conflicts between states? Not automatically. First, globalisation reduces the power of traditional states. While military force is an instrument to deter and hinder invasions from abroad or to occupy foreign territory, it is quite meaningless against the dragons of global economic competition. Secondly, the impact of globalisation manifests itself not so much *between* states as *within* societies; it exacerbates social differences and promotes social tensions, thus further weakening the state and its ability to wage conflict beyond its borders.

Moreover, the globalisation of market forces coincides with, even favours, the development of global rules. Just look at the impressive range of new international regulations which have emerged over the past few years: the World Trade Organisation (WTO), the establishment of a international penal courts; the Chemical Weapons Convention; the agreement to prolong the Non-Proliferation Treaty indefinitely; the Comprehensive Test Ban Treaty; the Anti-Personnel-Mine Agreement; the evolution of humanitarian international law to permit interference in the internal affairs of other states; the current efforts to supervise global capital flows; the international steps to halt climate change.

Thus, the end of the Cold War has seen the beginning of new international, universal legal regimes. Perhaps it is that governments are increasingly realising that their interdependence has its corollary in common rules. Indeed, precisely because globalisation reaches deep into national societies, agreements of what is permissible interference and what unacceptable infringement are needed. It so happens that with the old East-West rivalry gone there is now a real chance to recognise common interests more clearly. As a result the – still loose – net of international law is pulling tighter. It is progressively restricting the latitude of states and companies, and it is offering procedures for the resolution of conflicts.

3   RULES AND INSTITUTIONS

The question, of course, is whether this tightening net of international regulation is sufficient to alter the nature of an international system which continues to remain based on the notion of sovereignty. Is the combination of global competition *plus* global competition rules enough to control tensions inherent in globalisation?

The answer is, I believe, negative. Globalisation may not by itself increase the likelihood of war, but nor does it decrease it. The rules it promotes are welcome but they are not, in themselves, sufficient to manage peace in the global village. Despite the weakening of the state, it is still the nature of the state system which creates the chief condition for war.

Is that system open to change? In 1996, the British diplomat Robert Cooper in a short but influential essay, 'The Post-Modern State and the World Order', differentiated between 'modern' and 'post-modern' states, and his distinction is helpful to our enquiry.

The modern state, according to Cooper, holds that the classical state system is still intact and should remain intact. For this group – and the large majority of developed countries belong to it – international law and loose multilateralism are both a sufficient as well as the maximum infringement on their freedom of manoeuvre. It is easy to spot the major members of this group: they think that the OSCE can serve as the main structure of European security (Russia); that multilateral commitments do not rule out unilateral action (United States); that good bilateral relations are all that is required for regional stability (China); that military deterrence is the only sensible guarantor against war (Israel).

The other group, that of the 'post-modern states', is much smaller. Its chief representatives are in Europe and have come together to form the European Union. Here, sovereignty is no longer the chief value of statehood. It is common prosperity and common stability. Here, the nation state's freedom of manoeuvre is being progressively reduced. The members, proud countries each with a long history of nationhood, have agreed on common borders towards the rest of the world, on a common currency, on a wide range of international initiatives, perhaps at some stage even on a common army. Between these 'post-modern states', the old state system has ceased to exist. Wars between them are no longer conceivable.

For the merely 'modern' states, however, war remains an option. Here, the 'profit' of war can still consist of status, prestige, of cutting a traditional rival down to size, of gaining territory. That the absence of objective gain should make major war obsolete has been the hope of many – past and present – prophets of peace. This hope has been repeatedly disappointed. It is obviously not enough to identify the absence of a rational incentive for peace. Instead, it is necessary to identify structures so strong that they are a positive disincentive to war. Interdependence, even one underpinned by global regulations, does not provide such a structure.

Now there is a growing and highly respectable school of thought in political science which argues that the old state system will be rendered peaceful once the new global regulations are combined with domestic democracy.

It is true that an increasing number of states today profess to a democratic structure or at least to a level of public accountability. That is, no doubt, good news. Democratic structures provide legitimacy to government, establish and maintain domestic stability, even encourage investment and prosperity. But does it mean that democracies do not go to war, at least not with one another? The record here is at least mixed. Were not all the major states fighting in the First World War more or less democratic – in the sense that all governments depended on parliamentary approval for the war effort? Were the various republics of the Former Yugoslavia not democratic in the sense that all their representatives were legitimated by public vote? Of course, none of these was up to the standards of modern democratic constitutions. But they all had political systems more or less empowering the part of the society that, in the 20th century, has paid the highest price for conflict – the public.

That democracy stands for domestic stability cannot be in doubt. But does it really serve as reliable barrier to inter-state conflict? True, democracy mandates the open conduct of public business. It establishes a division of power and thus imposes restraint on competing also bodies. It gives a voice to public opinion. Yet democratic public opinion can be mobilised for war! It is useful to remember that liberalism and nationalism can go hand in hand. Indeed, they have often done so in history, not least in the run up to the First World War. The outbreak of the bloody hostilities in the Balkans, the ferocity of ethnic cleansing is unthinkable without the long and intense barrage of opinion makers in what was a relatively free press, arguing for regional and ethnic incompatibility in a country in which regions and people used to exist quite peacefully together. The Balkans are no case for the clash of civilisations; they are a case for how an intense campaign of ethnic hatred can finally, once the first shot is fired, lead to bloody secession.

There is much to be said for the thesis, argued by an increasing number of academic studies, that true democracies – those in which the rule of law is deeply rooted, in which minorities are respected and equal members of society, and in which the culture of compromise and tolerance is firmly established – do not easily go to war against other, similarly true democracies. But, as Fareed Zakaria has convincingly shown, while the number of formal democracies is raising rapidly, they are not necessarily democracies as defined above. The formal criteria of domestic political regimes alone do not, therefore, offer much confidence when it comes to the avoidance of war. And, even where the material democratic credentials are convincing, they offer some plausibility but no guarantee of peaceful international behaviour.

The question is not, therefore, whether democracy contributes to the obsolescence of major war; it probably does. It is under what external conditions it is most capable of doing so. Democracy on its own, despite all its merits, seems insufficiently reliable to prevent conflict with other countries; it may even facilitate the outbreak of eternal strife once introduced newly in societies which emerge from decades of oppression.

4   DEMOCRACY AND SUPRA-NATIONALITY

The best system of assuring the absence of internal strife – democracy – is clearly one central ingredient. But what is the best system of assuring the absence of external conflict? Mere intergovernmental agreements, we have seen, are not enough to block wars, however useful they are in facilitating cooperation among states in times of peace.

In the natural sciences, a theory must be proven in the real world in order to be valid. On how best to achieve a state of durable peace we fortunately have an old theory that is been proven in recent practice. The theory is that of Immanuel Kant, the great philosopher, who defined the conditions for perpetual peace 200 years ago not very far from St Petersburg. The practice is that of the European Union and the Atlantic Alliance.

In his famous essay on perpetual peace, Kant identified two conditions in particular, one concerning the internal constitution, the other the external relationship of states. The natural state of relations among men and states, he argued, it not that of peace but of war. Peace, therefore, has to be deliberately founded.

One foundation is what Kant called the 'republican constitution' – what we would today call democracy. Its principles are these: 'First, the freedom of all members of society (as the people); secondly, the application of common legislation to all (as subjects); thirdly equal rights (as citizens).'

For good reason, those who emphasise the centrality of democracy for the avoidance of conflict refer to Kant. He already offered the chief reason why democratic rule tends to discourage belligerence: 'If the consent of the citizens is required to decide on whether or not to go to war, nothing is more natural than that they would think twice before beginning such a dangerous game, since they would have to decide that the misery of war fall upon themselves.'

The other foundation is what Kant calls 'the federalism of free states'. Here, he has in mind something much more than traditional inter-state law. Indeed, he dismisses the great international jurists revered in his time – Grotius, Pufen-dorf and Vattel are mentioned by name – as 'a bunch of dismal consolers.' A new quality of relations between states, he argues, is needed. His ideal would be a world republic, one which transposes the domestic rule of law to the global scale. But this, Kant recognises, is unrealistic to expect, 'since the states, based on their notion of international law, do not want it.' Kant's solution: an 'ever-enlarging federation of states ... to halt the stream of hostile attitudes.' Central to this theory of peace are the institutions which channel human behaviour towards peacefulness: Domestically, the institutions of democracy and the division of powers, externally the institution of federation and the pooling of power. Only institutions which safeguard agreed rules can pacify either men or states, not passing phenomena like technology of economic interest, Kant confirms.

It took almost two centuries before Kant's theories could be tested in the real world. For most of this period, Europe's nation states were busily proving one part of the theory correct – namely that the natural condition among states is war not peace. Only after they had been exhausted, impoverished and humiliated by war, did the countries of western Europe set out to prove the other part of the theory: that internal democracy plus external federalism can combine to provide reliable peace.

The European Economic Community of the late 1950s has evolved into the European Union of today, a group of states knit together by common values and strong institutions. This Union has achieved what few thought possible only a few years ago: a common market, common outside borders, a common currency. And it sets out – slowly, too slowly, but surely – to bring other countries in Europe into the community which share the same values and are ready to submit to the common institutions. The other hitherto exclusively western organisation, the North Atlantic Alliance, while still structured as a purely intergovernmental body, is gradually evolving in a similar direction. It, too, is opening its doors, albeit too slowly, to the new European democracies.

The centrality of common, resilient institutions for the maintenance of peace becomes clear when you consider their particular impact on the behaviour of states. First, where they exist, they are the natural conduit for governments conducting business with each other; in case of crisis they offer a ready procedure for getting together in sorting things out peacefully. Secondly, over time they create a habit of cooperation as well as vested interests among the members to make cooperation work. Moreover, they gain time for hard-pressed governments and thus help to avoid both *faits accomplis* and panic in a crisis. Finally, such groups are inherently incapable of launching an aggression against other states.

5   EUROPE: EXCEPTION OR EXAMPLE?

In contrast to a century ago, the future of war today does not lie in Europe. The region, defined by membership in the two major European structures of order, the European Union and NATO, is the safest part of the modern world.

One imperative following from this has already been noted by Kant: the need to expand the federation, to halt the stream of hostile attitude. It is in the interest of all European states, even those like Russia who profess otherwise, that the zone of stability created by the EU and NATO be enlarged to Central and East Europe, South-East Europe and to the Balkans. Indeed, if there is to be long-term stability in what once was Yugoslavia, that stability cannot provided by the presence of foreign troops, but will have to created by progressively bringing the various new republics into the European Union.

Yet there are obvious limits to this process of enlargement. The community of countries forming a federation must share the same values, be committed to the same degree of citizen rights, display a similar resilience of domestic institutions and a similar acceptance of strong common institutions. The Euro-Atlantic structure cannot become a global framework. It will have to remain regional.

Should, can other regions emulate the European model? As to whether they should, there can be only one answer: if it is true that in Europe the conditions for lasting peace are being established, why should other regions be deprived of similar blessings? Indeed, as if to prove once again Kant's theory, it is precisely in those parts of the world were similarly resilient multilateral structures are absent that the risk of new conflicts is particularly apparent: in the Middle East, in Central Asia, in Africa, in South and North-East Asia.

Ask yourselves where you expect the next conflicts to break out – and you will discover that this is where there are no strong regional underpinnings for regular, intense, durable state-to-state cooperation. And those tempted to reject the European model as just another example of European or western arrogance can rest assured: the West Europeans had luck not merit. They were only ready and willing to pool their precious sovereignties after having given to the rest of the world an example of enormous barbarity.

But can the European model of strong joint institutions be copied elsewhere? Traditions, culture, religion, historical experience are very different in different regions, and even in Europe the Anglo-Saxons find it much more difficult to accept the model that Kant and Monnet devised.

And yet, there has been no obstacle in the cultures, traditions, religions or historical experiences of other regions to import another, earlier, European model – that of the nation state. Why then should they be incapable of importing the device that can assure the peaceful co-existence of nation states within a region, that of supranational integration? Today, no state is independent, all are, and increasingly so, interdependent. The willingness of states to engage their neighbours in a common institutional structure, to transfer powers to common organs, to become committed to solving problems between them peacefully is essential to prevent elsewhere a repeat of what Europe went through in the first part of the 20th century. The end of complete sovereignty is the beginning of incomplete peace.

There is, of course, one uneasy aspect of the European experience, a nagging question as one wonders how soon states elsewhere will accept limits to their sovereignty. Can they, in contrast to the Europeans, reach that stage without having gone through the wars that shook and sobered Europe? Does there have to be a future of war for them before there can be a future of peace?

10

OUT OF AFRICA:
THE FATE OF THE STATE AND THE
INTERNATIONAL SYSTEM

Francis Deng

1   INTRODUCTION

The fate of the state and the international system in the post-Cold War era is
essentially dualistic in nature. Both domestically and externally, the state in
many parts of the world is confronted with the challenges of national identity
crisis and contested sovereignty. These challenges are rooted primarily in the
problems of racial, ethnic, cultural and religious diversities, rendered conflictual
by gross disparities in the shaping and sharing of power, national resources,
and the opportunities for social, cultural and economic development. During
the Cold War, there was a tendency to relate all the problems around the world
to the ideological confrontation of the super powers. In the post-Cold War era,
problems are now being better understood in their proper national and regional
context, where internal conflicts, violations of human rights, denial of democracy
and mismanagement of the economy are the pressing problem areas. In confronting these problems, the state is being pulled in opposite directions by the
demands of various local groups and the pressures of globalisation of the market
economy and universalising cultural trends. In this tug of war, the sub-regional
organisations are assuming an intermediary role between the state and the global
community. In Africa, the internal pressures against the state are compounded
by the demand for various forms of revivalism – cultural and religious. Since
the creation of the state fundamentally undermined Africa's indigenous values,
institutional structures, and patterns of behaviour, there is an increasing call
for appreciating and mobilizing them for political and economic development
as a broad-based process of self-enhancement from within. The assignment of
responsibility for addressing these challenges must also recognize the fundamental shift that has taken place in the post-Cold War era. Dependency is being
replaced by mutually beneficial partnership. This implies recasting sovereignty
as a concept of responsibility for the security and general welfare of the citizens,
with accountability at the regional and international levels.

G. Prins and H. Tromp (eds.), The Future of War, 133-145.
© 2000 *Kluwer Law International. Printed in the Netherlands.*

This conclusion derives from several interrelated research projects over nearly a decade. The first, conducted at the Brookings Institution, has focused on conflict resolution in Africa within a framework of interconnected policy areas; the second has been the work on the UN mandate on internal displacement which has been the responsibility of the Representative of the Secretary-General on Internally Displaced Persons, and the third is the initiative of the Africa Leadership Forum to develop a normative framework toward a Conference on Security, Stability, Development and Cooperation in Africa (CSSDCA), the so-called Helsinki-for-Africa process. While these have been the primary sources of my analytical themes, the observations made in this paper may have a wider relevance to the fate of the state in many parts of the developing and even some developed pluralistic states.

2   PROBLEM AREAS AND POLICY CHALLENGES

A policy analysis of the fate of the state in Africa must place the challenge in its proper context by addressing a series of pertinent questions: what are the critical problem areas confronting the state which call for analysis on the basis of which policies can be formulated for action? What are the root causes of these problems? What can be done about them? And where does the responsibility for addressing them lie? These questions can also be related to a series of subsidiary questions: are the sources of Africa's problems essentially internal or external? Commensurately, should solutions be sought internally or externally? If the solutions required are internal, to what extent should they be indigenously grounded or based on externally-oriented norms or prescriptions?

Africa's list of problems calling for urgent attention must place internal conflicts highest in the order of priorities, followed by human rights violations, dictatorial or authoritarian systems of governance, and flawed economic policies, all of which are closely interconnected in a chain of cause and effect. A correlative list of solutions would include conflict resolution, human rights protection, democracy and sustainable development.

The case is often made that Africa's problems are primarily the result of underdevelopment and abject poverty, which would place development highest on the list of priorities. Indeed, at independence the highest policy priority for Africa was economic development. 'African leaders adopted the ideology of development to replace that of independence,' Claude Ake wrote in a study he prepared for the Brookings Institution's Africa programme. 'But as it turned out, what was adopted was not so much an ideology of development as a strategy of power that merely capitalized on the objective need for development.'[1] African leaders saw human rights and democracy as luxuries to be sacrificed or postponed until Africans were sufficiently advanced. Development was presented in terms of the war against 'our real enemies' – poverty, ignorance and disease, which, in the words of one commentator, were regarded as 'the unholy trinity' against which the nationalist swords were drawn.'[2]

But despite the priority given to development, Africa's economic performance has been dismal, and, while the failure to live up to expectations can be attributed to many causes, bad governance in general and internal conflicts in particular are the most significant. Economic growth is impossible where war, insurgency and terrorism destroy lives and property at random, prevent agricultural production, create multitudes of refugees and displaced persons, and divert precious resources into massive arms purchases and military build ups. Whatever their priority, these problems, put together, portray a continent in crisis and desperately in need of rescue operations, a continent some would go as far as saying is not worth saving.[3]

Nevertheless, the recent developments on the continent in both politics and the economies indicate some positive turn of events. Africa is now perceived to be undergoing a renaissance that is transforming the continent. Conflict does

1   C. Ake, *Democracy and Development in Africa* (Washington, Brookings, 1996), pp. 8-9.
2   T. Mkandawire, 'Shifting commitments and national cohesion in African countries', unpublished paper, (Copenhagen, Center for Development Research, 1997), p. 10.
3   Following the article by Robert D. Kaplan, 'The Coming Anarchy,' *Atlantic Monthly*, (April 1994), UN Secretary-General Boutros Boutros-Ghali convened a meeting of a selected number of scholars and policy analysts, including Kaplan himself, with senior aides of the Secretary-General, to discuss Kaplan's thesis, the extent of its validity, and what, if any, the United Nations should do in response. The author was among the participants. Although Kaplan's thesis and conclusions were not shared by all the participants, the general tendency was sympathetic to his point of view and the principle of triage, bearing in mind that the international community had limited capacity to respond effectively to all the crises in the world. In this selection process, some countries, notably in Africa, were implicitly dispensable. Indeed, one participant went as far as saying that although he hated to say so, Rwanda did not really matter to world order.

indeed still divide countries, as we are witnessing today in the Great Lakes region, the Sudan and Sierra Leone, to mention only a few, but peace, reconciliation and development are increasingly becoming the trends. Increasing numbers of African countries have conducted multi-party elections that international observers have judged generally free and fair. Economic growth rates are rising, and the continent is striving to attract foreign investment. While Africa remains the poorest continent with the highest population growth rate, some countries are reaping the fruits of new market-oriented institutions and policies.[4] Omar Kabbaj, President of the African Development Bank, has stated, 'as a result of the economic reforms that a large number of countries have implemented over the last decade, Africa now seems to be on the verge of achieving sustained rates of economic growth that exceed population growth rates.'[5] Participants in the seminar at which he spoke concluded that these changes signal the dawn of a new era in Africa: 'The impressive stride that has been made towards political liberalization and democracy by over thirty countries in the region in the last decade is indeed a cause for optimism about the future.'[6]

Such views reflect a degree of calculated optimism that is being increasingly invoked as a policy tool. But, while optimism is a motivating and reinforcing factor, the shift in perspective on the conditions in Africa signals the potential danger of a reverse myth building. Wishful thinking, that does not permit an objective assessment of the situation and the development of practical and realistic solutions, can be very damaging. When such myths are exploded, as they are eventually bound to be, given their shaky foundation, the crisis becomes aggravated and alternative remedies rendered even more difficult.

The reality on the continent is much more varied than the contrasting perspectives of doom or 'impressive strides' warrant. What Africa needs is a proper diagnosis as a basis for effective treatment. While the glass is getting half full, it is still largely half empty, and calls for persistent and rigorous pursuit of political and economic reform.

---

4   The American Assembly, *Africa and U.S. National Interest*, Columbia University, The Ninetieth American Assembly, 13-16 March, 1997, p. 5.
5   O. Kabbaj, foreword to Kifle, Olukoshi and Wohlgemuth (eds), *A New Partnership for African Development* (Stockholm, Nordiska Afrikainstitutet, 1997), p. 5.
6   O. Kabbaj, *A New Partnership for African Development*, p. 11.

With respect to the causes of Africa's crises, it is widely recognised that the problems in Africa have their roots in state formation and the challenge of nation-building in the context of immense diversities and disparities. The system was first intended to serve the interests of the colonial powers. Independence granted political autonomy to the colonies while maintaining their linkage to the economies of former colonial powers through trade, investment, and largely tied aid.

As for the responsibility for solutions, there is a consensus that the problems are internal, and that however external their sources or continued linkages, the primary responsibility for solutions, especially in the post-Cold War era, falls first on the Africans themselves. The time has long since come to stop blaming colonialism for Africa's persistent problems.

The irony is that the principal modern agent of Africa's political and economic development and the interlocutor in the international arena is the state, itself a creature of foreign intervention. Although Africans have, for the most part, accepted the state with its colonially defined borders, African states lack the indigenous cultural roots for internal legitimacy. Even worse, citizen participation is for the most part minimal. Indeed, the state is often not representative or responsive to the demands and expectations of its domestic constituencies. It is important in this context to distinguish between recognising the unity and territorial integrity of the state and questioning its policy framework, which might be attributable to a regime or might be more structural. A structural problem would require a fundamental restructuring of the state to meet both the internal standards of good governance and the international requirements of responsible sovereignty.

Failure on the one level usually implies failure on the other. When a state fails to meet the standards prescribed for membership in the international community, and thereby exposes itself to external scrutiny and possible sanctions, it is likely to assert sovereignty and cultural relativism in an attempt to barricade itself against alleged foreign interference. Sovereignty has evolved enough not only to prescribe democratic representation, but also to justify outside intervention. The determining factor is, therefore, the political will of other states based on national interest or humanitarian concern. However, assertions of sovereignty can also be invoked by powers lacking the will to become involved. Since intervention is often costly in lives and material, it is convenient to avoid it unless imperative national interest dictates otherwise. Sovereignty then elicits benign conformity to the principle of noninterference or provides a convenient excuse for inaction. To circumvent the constraints of sovereignty against justifiable intervention, and, more importantly, to inspire or at least motivate governments and other controlling authorities such as insurgent movements to discharge their obligations, there is a need to prescribe 'normative sovereignty', or 'sovereignty as responsibility'.

If responsibility for Africa's problems is now being assigned to the Africans, as represented by their states, the logic should extend down to embrace citizen participation, what might be termed the challenge of localisation. This would broaden the basis of participation to include not only the wide array of organisations within the now popular notion of civil society, but also, and primarily, Africa's indigenous, territorially defined, local communities, with their organisational structures, value systems, institutional arrangements, and ways of using their human and material resources. Of course, the continuing goal for African development has been to widen the market through regional integration, but whatever the size of the market envisaged, development from the grass roots broadens the base of participation and mobilizes the population. Discussions about the development 'miracle' of Japan, South Korea, and other Asian countries nearly always emphasize the role of culture in mobilising human resources and 'releasing the energies of the people.' A culturally-oriented approach has the prospects of making effective use of the resources and energies of the traditional sector, presently untapped or under used, in the process of development.

3   THE CHALLENGE OF ETHNIC DIVERSITY

Africa is now facing international calls for democratisation, which poses a formidable challenge for pluralistic states that are acutely divided on ethnic or religious grounds. Because democracy has become closely associated with elections, in which Africans tend to vote on the basis of ethnic or religious identity, democracy risks becoming a dictatorship of numbers, with the majority imposing its will on the minority. For this reason, the suitability of democracy for African societies is being questioned, both within and outside the continent.[7] But Africans cannot accept dictatorship as the alternative. The assault on democracy is based on a narrow definition that places overwhelming emphasis on procedure, reflected in elections, then uses the negative consequences of this narrow definition to question democracy as a whole. A balanced perspective should draw a distinction between the principles of democracy and the institutional practices of implementation.

Among the principles of democracy that have gained universal validity are that governments rule in accordance with the will of the people, adhere to the rule of law, separation of powers, independence of the judiciary, and respect for fundamental human rights and civil liberties. These principles are safeguarded by transparency, freedom of expression (and the press), access to information, and accountability to the public. In the context of ethnic diversity, decentralisation down to the local level, combined with some method of ensuring the representation of those who would otherwise be excluded by the weight of electoral votes, would be necessary. In any case, democracy, however defined or practised, implies accommodation of differences and a special responsibility for the protection of minorities. In most African countries, the population is a conglomerate of many ethnic groups, which makes it difficult to speak of majority and minority. Given that these are countries still in the process of nation building, groups that find themselves threatened with a minority status would rather resist incorporation into such a stratifying state framework.

The main point, however, is that while democracy, broadly defined in terms of certain principles, is universally valued, it needs to be viewed in the context of African cultural realities to make it functional and sustainable. To place political reform, in particular democratisation, in the cultural context, one must examine indigenous African institutions and value systems and the way they have been used or undermined in order to determine whether they retain elements that could be integrated into the reform process. Perhaps the most outstanding characteristics of traditional African society, which the colonial rulers to some extent recognised and used to their advantage but which postcolonial states have disregarded and even discredited to their peril, are the

---

7   See for instance F. Zakaria, 'The rise of illiberal democracy', 76 *Foreign Affairs*, no. 6 (November-December, 1997) and Robert D. Kaplan, 'Was democracy just a moment?', *The Atlantic Monthly* (December, 1997).

autonomy of the component elements of the political and social order and the devolution of power and decision making to the local units through what might be described as a participatory mode of governance.

African political systems, whether empires, kingdoms, centralised states or stateless societies, were structured in a hierarchy in which the basic unit was the family, extended to the lineage and the clan, with the cluster of lineages and clans constituting territorial entities and ultimately nations. Despite the hierarchical nature of the system, these entities were generally governed by consensus and broad participation through group representation at the central level and village councils at the local level. In each village, extended families chose their heads, who would together form a council of elders, without whose authority the chief had no power. In the deliberations of the council, any adult was free to speak. The elders would keep on discussing an issue until they reached a consensus. 'The moral order was robustly collective', wrote Mamadou Dia. 'Majority rule, winner-take-all, or other forms of zero sum games were not acceptable alternatives to consensus decision making.'[8]

Under colonial rule, these characteristics of the indigenous systems were largely harnessed and contained by policies of indirect rule through which law and order and the administration of justice were maintained. But while indirect rule offered the people the opportunity to govern themselves, albeit to a limited extent, the intelligentsia that led the independence movement saw it as a divisive exploitation of tradition aimed at facilitating the divide-and-rule policies of the colonial masters. Consequently, at independence, African élites were eager to disavow tribalism as divisive. Unity was pursued in a way that assumed a myth-ical homogeneity or manipulated diversity. Kwame Nkrumah of Ghana outlawed parties organised on tribal or ethnic bases. Félix Houphouet-Boigny of Côte d'Ivoire coopted ethnic groups through shrewd distribution of ministerial posts, civil service jobs, social services, and development projects. Julius Nyerere, himself a scion of tribal chieftaincy, stamped out tribalism by fostering nationalistic pride in Tanganyika and later, Tanzania, born out of the union with Zanzibar. Jommo Kenyatta of Kenya forged a delicate alliance of ethnic groups behind the dominance of his Kenyan African National Union party. In South Africa, apartheid stratified races and ethnicities to an extent that was not

---

8   M. Dia, *Africa's Management in the 1990s and Beyond: Reconciling Indigenous and Transplanted Institutions* (Washington, DC, The World Bank, 1996), p. 41.

sustainable. Post-apartheid South Africa remains poised between a racially, ethnically, and tribally blind democratic system and a proud ethnic self-assertiveness, the prototype of which is represented and exploited by Zulu nationalism. Sudan offers an extreme example of an identity crisis resulting from mismanaged diversity. The rebellion of the SPLM/SPLA is essentially a resistance to the Arab-Islamic domination and the threat of assimilation.

In most African countries, the determination to preserve national unity following independence provided the motivation behind one-party rule, excessive centralisation of power, oppressive authoritarian regimes, and systematic violations of human rights and fundamental liberties. The participatory decision making in traditional African society was later alluded to by nationalist leaders to justify the one-party system, the rationale being that since Africans traditionally sat and debated until they all agreed, the multi-party system was antithetic to African culture. The delicate balance between the interest of the individual and that of the community was also tipped to give undue emphasis to the community's interest and used to justify the imported concept of socialism, euphemistically dubbed 'African Socialism'.

Managing ethnic diversity is one of the challenges post-colonial African governments were reluctant to face. Ethnicity acts as a pole around which group members mobilise and compete for state-controlled power, economic resources, positions, contracts, awards, and constitutional protections. It is founded on a subjective perception of common origins, historical memories, ties, and aspirations. An ethnic group suggests organised activities by people who share a common consciousness of a special identity, and jointly seek to maximise their corporate political, economic, and social interests. Ethnicity, or a sense of peoplehood, derives from combined remembrances of past experience and common aspirations, values, norms, and expectations. The validity of these beliefs is not as important to an overarching sense of affinity as the people's own ability to symbolise their closeness to each other.[9] Given its centrality and pervasiveness, ethnicity is a reality no country can completely afford to ignore. As a result, African governments have ambivalently tried to dismiss it, marginalise it, manipulate it, corrupt it, or combat it. But no strategic formula for its constructive use has been developed.

---

9   D. Rothchild, *Managing Ethnic Conflict in Africa* (Washington, Brookings, 1997), p. 4.

Ethnicity is a dynamic concept. In intergroup or cross-cultural situations, individuals tend to acquire multiple identities that change with contexts and according to the advantages and disadvantages encountered. In the process, some identities may disappear and new identities may emerge. Nevertheless, the fundamental characteristics of a given ethnic group, including its 'corporate' identity, continue. The individual may leave the group, live among other identity groups, acquire other symbols of identity, become integrated or assimilated, and perhaps even shed the labels of the original identity, but that does not affect the continuity of the group from which he or she originated. An educated Kikuyu may leave his tribe and go to the city or even live abroad. In the process, he might become a Christian, a Kenyan, an African or acquire other identities, but the Kikuyu remain as a group with a territory, a culture, and a social structure to which the individual who has left may even continue to owe a certain allegiance. Indeed, an overwhelming majority of Africans, however urbanised or modernised, belong to known 'tribal' origins and remain in one way or another connected to their groups. This flexibility or adaptability allows considerable room for moulding identity to suit changing conditions or to serve alternating objectives. This makes identity a resource capable of being used in a variety of ways, some constructive and some destructive, both by the individuals and the groups concerned and by policy makers.

Ethnic identities in themselves are not conflictual, just as individuals are not inherently in conflict merely because of their different characteristics. Rather, it is unmanaged or mismanaged competition for power, wealth, or status, broadly defined, that provides the basis for conflict. Analysts tend to hold one of two views of the role of ethnicity in these conflicts. Some see ethnicity as a source of conflict; others see it as a tool used by political entrepreneurs to promote their ambitions.[10] Ethnicity, especially when combined with territorial identity,

---

10   According to one source, ethnicity is important in African politics because it serves as an 'organizing principle of sound action', which makes it 'basically a political ... phenomenon.' (Chazan *et al.*, *Politics and Society in Contemporary Africa* [Boulder, CO, Lynne Rienner, 1988], p. 120, p. 110). UN Secretary-General, Kofi Annan, in a paper presented to an international conference on 'The Therapeutics of Conflict,' when he was still Under-Secretary-General for Peacekeeping Operations, observed: 'Many of [the civil wars] have also been perceived as showing strong symptoms of ethnic conflict. Ethnic conflict as a symptom is, at best, extremely difficult to assess... Ethnic differences are not in and of themselves either symptoms or causes of conflict; in societies where they are accepted and respected,

is a reality that exists independently of political manoeuvres, but it is also a resource for political manipulation and entrepreneurship. Ultimately, managing ethnicity remains a function of domestic governance. Unfortunately, managing diversity is a challenge of constitutionalism that African countries still need to address. At the moment, diversity is either ruthlessly suppressed, pushed under the rug and nervously ignored, or tactically and pragmatically accommodated. After Eritrea's breakaway, Ethiopia appears to be the only African country that is trying to confront the problem head-on by recognising territorially-based ethnic groups, granting them not only a large measure of autonomy, but also the constitutional right of self-determination, even to the extent of secession. Ethiopia's leaders assert emphatically that they are committed to the right of self-determination, wherever it leads. But it can also be argued that giving the people the right to determine their destiny leads them to believe that their interests will be safeguarded, which should give them a reason to choose unity.

4   TOWARDS A FRAMEWORK OF GRADUATED RESPONSIBILITY AND ACCOUNTABILITY

The emerging response of African leaders to the suffering of fellow Africans or the threat to regional security and stability suggests several actions. The first is the need to develop a policy framework that would oblige states to treat their citizens with dignity by ensuring their physical protection and enjoyment of democratic values, respecting fundamental rights and freedoms, and providing reasonable standards of social and economic welfare. These are what a citizen needs to feel a sense of belonging and loyalty to the nation. Although these norms should stipulate a special responsibility for the protection of minorities, conditions in Africa, where virtually every ethnic group is a minority in a multiplicity of ethnicities, demand inclusiveness on the basis of a national consensus.

This implies the second line of action: the creation of strong subregional arrangements for security and development cooperation. The foundation for these

---

people of vastly different backgrounds live peacefully and productively together. Ethnic differences become charged-conflictual-when they are used for political ends, when ethnic groups are intentionally placed in opposition to each other.' (K. Annan, 'The peacekeeping prescription', in Cahill (ed.), *Preventive Diplomacy* (New York, Basic Books, 1996), p. 176.

arrangements has already been laid by ECOWAS, IGAD and SADC, but they need to be strengthened. The support the international community has been giving to the peacemaking and peacekeeping activities of these organisations, although limited, suggests the much greater role that subregional organisations could play in promoting regional peace, security, stability, and development. Indeed, because they offer a more cohesive framework for setting standards and providing enforcement mechanisms, they could be the first tier in the development and implementation of the CSSDCA. Donor countries and the international community in general could assist financially and technically.

These principles, if adopted and acted on, should ensure a reasonable degree of national cohesion and stability, especially as other members of the regional community would act as watchdogs across national borders. Precisely because minimum conditions for peace and tranquility would be expected to result from such arrangements, states are likely to be more receptive to opening up their borders to those who, for whatever reasons, find themselves compelled or obliged to flee or leave their countries of origin.

Nation-building has internal and external dimensions. The internal dimension requires an inclusive framework that should involve all groups within the state, some of which have been sidestepped, excluded, or marginalised. The external dimension should begin with regional cooperation and rethinking the borders, not to question their legitimacy but rather to make them porous and responsive to regional dynamics. Ultimately, what Africa needs is a comprehensive policy framework, stipulating principles of state responsibility and accountability, with enforcement mechanisms as a basis for addressing realistically the continent's problems at the national and regional levels and in partnership with the international community.

A range of responses to the challenges of reform is emerging on the African scene. Some governments are responsive, others are resistant, and may others are straddling in between. The international community should support those African governments committed to economic reform, participatory democracy, respect for human rights, and responsible international partnership with positive incentives, discourage those bent on repression and resistance to reform with punitive sanctions, and offer a combination of carrots and sticks to those wavering in between. Already, the international community has made appreciable progress in responding to humanitarian tragedies, but much more needs to be done to make governments adhere to the responsibilities of sovereignty by ensuring the security, fundamental rights, civil liberties, and general welfare of their citizens and all those under their jurisdiction. Africa is recognisably a continent in crisis, beset with devastating ethnic and religious conflicts, repressive governments, gross violations of human rights, and dismal economic performance. But Africa is also going through a process of a Second Liberation struggle against its own dysfunctional systems of statehood and governance. Much is being done and the challenge of doing a great deal more has been embraced. Still, the structural constraints, the established patterns of behaviour on the part of the ruling élites, and a somewhat disengaging international community all combine to make the task of reform and transition formidable. A vital aspect of this task is a search for a normative framework that would provide guidance for good governance, better crisis-management, and more effective reform policies at the national and regional levels, with supportive action at the international level.

11

STATE MAKING, STATE FAILURE AND
REVOLUTION IN MILITARY AFFAIRS:
WAR AT THE END OF THE 20TH CENTURY

Mohammed Ayoob

War is a supremely political act, although war makers may harbour economic and other designs. Individual wars may have important economic consequences, and particular decisions to go to war or desist from it may be influenced by economic considerations as well. However, this should not detract from the fact that the decision to go to war is above all a political act, because it is primarily determined by the participants' judgments about the nature of an existing or preferred political order (which could be either domestic or international or both) and their assessments about the effectiveness and legitimacy of such an order.

This applies as much to internal as to interstate wars. Interstate wars are usually intimately related to existing balances of power (whether global or regional) and the desire on the part of participants either to change that balance or to reaffirm it.[1] It is the difference between changing or reaffirming an existing balance that distinguishes *status quo* powers from revisionist ones. Similarly, internal war, the most common type of war these days, is normally concerned with maintaining or changing the domestic political balance, in terms of the equilibrium between groups, regions, classes, etc., thus pitting the defenders of the *status quo* (whether in terms of regimes or boundaries) against those who challenge it.

Despite this fundamental characteristic that intrastate wars share with interstate ones, some scholars, such as Martin van Creveld, have argued that there has been a major 'transformation of war' in the past few decades, as interstate wars

---

1   See R. Gilpin, *War and Change in World Politics* (Cambridge, Cambridge University Press, 1981) and P. Kennedy, *The Rise and Fall of the Great Powers* (New York, Vintage Books, 1989).

G. Prins and H. Tromp (eds.), The Future of War, 147-166.
© 2000 *Kluwer Law International. Printed in the Netherlands.*

have become the exception and internal wars the rule in the system of states.[2] According to van Creveld, the prototypical Westphalian or Clausewitzian war was based upon the tripartite division among government, army, and people, which, in turn, was founded upon the functional differentiation typical of the Westphalian state. In such wars, professional armies fought each other as a result of decisions made by governments, and the people were usually bystanders who suffered the consequences of war and were affected by its outcome but were not participants in war.

Now, according to van Creveld, the era of interstate war in the Clausewitzian sense is over and the conventional armed forces of the great powers have been rendered redundant. I will return to this question later in the light of the performance of the admittedly high-tech, but still conventional forces of the major 'revolution in military affairs' (RMA) powers in the Gulf and in the Balkans. In the meantime, I am willing to admit that it is true that currently the most frequent and important form of war is 'low intensity conflict', much of it intrastate in character, in which the distinction between government, army and people is largely blurred.

According to van Creveld, pre-Westphalian wars were those waged in the early modern age 'precisely in order to determine who was, and who was not, entitled to use armed violence.'[3] He makes a clear-cut distinction between such wars and Westphalian wars in terms both of the participants in, and the conduct of, war. I believe that this division is overstated because it ignores the fact that war, especially in the Westphalian sense, was intimately connected with the making of modern states and the imposition of centralised political control, which was both essential for the extraction of resources as well as materially dependent upon such extraction. As such, state makers directed the use of force or organised violence as much against recalcitrant groups within their populations and against rival claimants for legitimacy in the same territory as against other states that contested their territorial claims.[4]

---

2   M. van Creveld, *The Transformation of War* (New York, Free Press, 1991).
3   M. van Creveld, *The Transformation of War*, p. 50.
4   For details, see C. Tilly (ed.), *The Formation of National States in Western Europe* (Princeton, Princeton University Press, 1975).

Intrastate and interstate wars have, therefore, been inextricably intertwined in the history of state making in modern Europe. In any case, in much of the modern period in Europe the distinction between internal and external wars was far more fuzzy than is the case today, because territorial domains were continuously contested (and changed hands often) without the notion of legitimacy privileging any one party over the other until quite late in that historical process.

Furthermore, as Charles Tilly has stated, 'Early in the state-making process, many parties shared the right to use violence, the practice of using it routinely to accomplish their ends, or both at once. The continuum ran from bandits and pirates to kings via tax collectors, regional power holders, and professional soldiers .... The distinctions between "legitimate" and "illegitimate" users of violence came clear only very slowly, in the process during which the state's armed forces became relatively unified and permanent.'[5]

Centralising states came to monopolise the right to use force quite late in the Westphalian era. As Janice Thomson has pointed out, even in the realm of external or extra-territorial violence, it was only 'In the course of the nineteenth century [that] nonstate violence was delegitimated and eliminated.'[6] This was done by outlawing piracy and dispensing with the services of mercenaries by raising 'national' and 'citizens' armies on the model of Napoleonic France. The state's monopoly over both internal and external violence was immeasurably strengthened by the crystallisation of international norms in the 19th century that made the state the sole legitimate repository of instruments of coercion within territorially demarcated political communities. States had tried to craft and augment these norms over a period of time in order to protect their position as the primary domestic and external actors, compelling obedience at home and monopolising the right to wage war abroad.[7]

---

5   C. Tilly, 'War making and state making as organized crime', in: Evans *et al.* (eds), *Bringing the State Back In*, (Cambridge, Cambridge University Press, 1985).

6   J. E. Thomson, *Mercenaries, Pirates, and Sovereigns* (Princeton, Princeton University Press, 1994), p. 143.

7   As Hedley Bull has pointed out, 'This came about in two stages: first the forging of the distinction between public war, or war waged on the authority of a public body, and private war, or war waged without any such authority, and the curtailment of the latter; and second, the emergence of the idea that the state was the only public body competent to confer such authority.' H. Bull, *The Anarchical Society* (New

Therefore, one needs to interpret Tilly's celebrated dictum that 'war made states and states made war' in full awareness of the historical context to which it refers.[8] This would lead one to conclude that what we now call internal war contributed to state making equally, if not more than interstate war. Construction and imposition of political order is, by necessity, more a domestic than an international activity.

Viewing the 'Westphalian state' as the culminating point of a process whose eventual triumph was uncertain until at least the beginning of the 19th century, rather than as an unproblematic given (as neo-realists tend to do), would also make one realise that there were various alternative models of political organisation over which the modern state triumphed largely because of the conjunction of a specific set of factors within a particular geographic location at a certain point in time (the concept of time in this context to be measured in centuries rather than months or years).[9] E.L. Jones has attempted to explain this combination of factors with reference to the interaction among economics, geopolitics and the natural environment in modern Europe.[10] Tilly has argued that the success of the modern state owed most to the fact that it was able to combine coercion and capital in a far more optimal fashion than competing forms of political organisation were able to do, thereby gaining crucial advantage over its competitors both in terms of resource mobilisation and the organisation and technology of warfare.[11]

Therefore, when analysed in its proper historical context, it becomes clear that the Westphalian state as it emerged in the early 20th century was vastly different, in terms of its capabilities and functions, from the state as it existed in the 17th century. Consequently, to quote Thomson, '[I]nternational relations specialists would do well to abandon the notion that the state is the state is the state. The national state that emerged in 1900 was a fundamentally different

---

York, Columbia University Press, 1977), p. 185.

8   For details of this argument, see C. Tilly, 'War making and state making as organized crime', *ibid.*, pp. 169-191.

9   For details, see H. Spruyt, *The Sovereign State and Its Competitors* (Princeton, Princeton University Press, 1994).

10 E.L. Jones, *The European Miracle* (Cambridge, Cambridge University Press, 1987), second edition.

11 C. Tilly, *Coercion, Capital and European States, AD 990-1990* (Oxford, Basil Blackwell, 1990).

entity from its predecessor.'[12] The intervening centuries since the Peace of Westphalia contributed tremendously to shaping the Westphalian state.

It was only with the consolidation of state power and the states' acquisition of unconditional legitimacy as the sole repository of political authority during the course of the 19th century in western Europe, which had by now become the heartland of the international political system, that wars appeared to take on an almost exclusive interstate character in which 'rational' actors took decisions on the basis of 'national interest' to 'declare' war on one or more of their peers. This ideal type, never fully realised in practice, seems to have run its course with the end of the Second World War. Nuclear weapons and the end of colonial rule in Asia and Africa created an international political context that contributed in two major ways to changing the character of war.

First, war among the major powers was all but ruled out because of a stable bipolarity, underwritten by the possession of Mutual Assured Destruction capability on the part of both superpowers.[13] Secondly, the process of decolonisation unleashed a new spate of conflicts intimately related to the process of state making that got underway among the late entrants into the system of states that now came to constitute the 'weak, intruder majority' within that system. This was almost a re-run of the state-making wars in early modern Europe, albeit within a vastly changed international context.[14] At the same time, many of the disputes and conflicts accompanying the process of concurrent state making among contiguous and proximate states in much of the Third World were exploited by the superpowers for their own strategic and political ends and, therefore, became enmeshed with the superpower rivalry known as the Cold War.

---

12 J.E. Thomson, *Mercenaries, Pirates, and Sovereigns*, p. 149.

13 J.L. Gaddis, 'The long peace: elements of stability in the postwar international system', in: Lynn-Jones and Miller (eds), *The Cold War and After* (Cambridge, MA, MIT Press, expanded edition, 1994). Despite the presence of nuclear weapons or because of them, the superpowers reached the brink of a nuclear war during the Cuban missile crisis. For details, see J.G. Blight, B.J. Allyn, and D.A. Welch, *Cuba on the Brink: Castro, the Missile Crisis and the Soviet Collapse* (New York, Pantheon Books, 1993).

14 For details, see M. Ayoob, *The Third World Security Predicament: State Making, Regional Conflict, and the International System* (Boulder, CO, Lynne Rienner, 1995).

The end of the Cold War in 1990, and the consequent removal of its overlay from regional affairs, made many analysts and scholars acutely aware of certain phenomena that they had tended to ignore because of their obsession with super-power competition. These included the high incidence of intrastate conflicts in the developing world and the fact that many Third World conflicts had lives of their own independent of great power rivalry, although not totally insulated from the latter. It is this realisation, and the apprehension that conflicts in the Third World may have unforeseen and highly negative consequences for the new global order being fashioned by the United States and its allies, that has led many scholars in the West to look afresh at the phenomena of conflict and war in the contemporary era.

Moreover, the disintegration of the Soviet Union and the dismemberment of Yugoslavia have led to the emergence of a substantial number of states that share the political characteristics of traditional Third World states, are at the same early stage of state making and, therefore, suffer from similar problems of lack of political legitimacy, domestic conflict and the intertwining of the latter with regional conflict.[15] The Third World conflict syndrome has, therefore, spread to the periphery of Europe making western analysts greatly apprehensive of its impact on the core areas of the global North.

A central argument of this paper is that one cannot grasp the nature of contemporary conflicts, and, therefore, the character of current wars, unless one is able to understand the process of concurrent state building among contiguous and proximate states in the Third World (including Central Asia, the Caucasus, and the Balkans) where most conflicts have been concentrated during the second half of the 20th century. As in western Europe between the 16th and the 18th centuries, most states in the Third World today are grappling above all with the issue of constructing and maintaining effective and legitimate political orders within territorially demarcated communities.

There are, however, major differences between the current Third World undertaking and that of the west European states at a corresponding stage in their state-making process. Third World states are obliged to undertake and complete their state-making venture within a radically shortened time-frame and in an

---

15 For details of this argument, see M. Ayoob, 'The new-old disorder in the third world', 1 *Global Governance*, no.1 (winter 1995), 59-77.

international context, both in terms of prevailing norms and a rigid hierarchical structure that is far more hostile to their state building enterprise than was the case when European states were at a comparable stage in their state-making odyssey. Currently, both international norms and structure make Third World states far more vulnerable to external penetration – normative, political, military, and economic – than was the case with early state makers thus subjecting their state making endeavors to a much greater degree of international intervention.[16]

However, in order to understand the process of state making and its relationship with conflict and war in the Third World, one has to go back to the colonial encounters that shaped the political geography of Asia, Africa and Latin America. The era of European expansion into what we now call the Third World made two things very clear. First, that non-European claims to what could amount to sovereignty were not recognised as a legal right by the European powers, even if in practice frequently they had to make concessions to the actual control of territorial domains by non-European rulers, at least until they managed to subjugate the latter. Secondly, that resistance to European colonisation was usually dismissed as either the acts of 'barbarians' or 'savages' who did not know what was good for them or as 'mutiny' against 'legally constituted authority', which by definition could only be European in character.[17]

With hindsight it is clear, however, that these violent encounters were not merely a part of the saga of European domination. More importantly, they formed the most crucial component of the state making process of the majority of states that inhabit the international system today. Both the geo-political contours of post-colonial states and the expectations of centralised control and administration (based on the ideal of the Westphalian state) within strictly

---

16 For details of this argument, see M. Ayoob, "The security predicament of the third world state: state making in a comparative perspective": in B. Job, *The Insecurity Dilemma: The National Security of Third World States* (Boulder, CO, Lynne Rienner, 1992), pp. 63-80.

17 The first explanation was typically provided by Spanish, Portuguese, and British settlers in the Americas, Australia and New Zealand, regarding the resistance put up by native inhabitants to European colonization and in justification of the cruelties inflicted upon them by the Europeans. The second was used to describe the more organized resistance to European domination and expansion mounted by indigenous forces, including erstwhile ruling classes, in more advanced Asian societies. This was epitomized in the British characterization of the major Indian uprising of 1857, that found its symbol in the last Moghul emperor, as the 'Sepoy mutiny'.

demarcated boundaries were established by the outcome of these colonial encounters.

As the overwhelming majority of post-colonial states have inherited the colonially established boundaries as well as the political orders established by the
colonial powers, they are the linear successors of the colonial proto-states and,
paradoxically, owe their existence in their present form to the colonially crafted
order, which many of their anti-colonial 'nationalist' leaders had vowed to overturn. They have also inherited and/or appropriated the legitimacy of the colonial
state, to the extent that it had succeeded in acquiring such legitimacy in the
eyes of the subjugated populations.

Consequently, the ruling elites in the post-colonial states are usually in a
position to dub their opponents, especially those who oppose the colonial boundaries of the post-colonial states, as rebels, insurgents, secessionists, etc., all
pejorative terms that detract from their opponents' standing in the eyes both
of their own populations and of the international community. More importantly,
such characterisation denies them any status under international law. In this
sense, colonial policies of territorial acquisition, resource extraction, and the
violence used to achieve these goals, have become both essential prerequisites
and integral components of the state making process in the Third World.

However, this process of state making has also created its obverse phenomenon,
namely, state breaking.[18] While not many attempts at the breaking of post-
colonial states, in other words secession, have succeeded, their persistence has
meant that intrastate war has become the primary form of conflict since the
Second World War not only in the Third World, but in the international system
as a whole. This is borne out by calculations made by a number of scholars
both regarding the concentration of conflicts in the Third World and the primacy
of internal conflicts among them.

To give but one example, Kalevi Holsti has calculated that out of 164 armed
conflicts world-wide between 1945 and 1995 all but five (three in western
Europe and two in eastern Europe) were located in either the traditional Third

---

18   For details of this argument, see M. Ayoob, 'State making, state breaking, and state
     failure', in: Crocker and Hampson (eds), *Managing Global Chaos* (Washington,
     DC, United States Institute of Peace Press, 1996), pp. 37-51.

World (Asia, Africa and Latin America) or in the new Third World (the Balkans and the non-European parts of the former Soviet Union), where state building is at an early stage as well. Holsti, however, excludes anti-colonial wars of national liberation from his data. If one includes those figures the concentration of conflicts in the Third World would appear to be even more dramatic. Furthermore, according to Holsti, 77 per cent of conflicts between 1945 and 1995 were internal in character, although 30 per cent of such intrastate conflicts involved external armed intervention. Once again, if one includes anti-colonial wars, which were quintessential internal wars of regime change but which Holsti excludes, the proportion of intrastate to interstate wars would be appreciably higher.[19]

These conflicts are related as much to state making as state breaking, and often it is all but impossible to distinguish the difference between the two. This is also the case because almost every effort at breaking an established post-colonial state has as its principal objective the setting up of a new state on a part of the existing state's territory that would usually have a different mix of, and, therefore, balance between, groups inhabiting the proposed state. This objective has spawned secessionist groups ranging from the Tamil Tigers in Sri Lanka to the Kosovo Liberation Army in the rump of Yugoslavia.

Most attempts at secession have been justified with reference to the right to self-determination of ethno-national groups, a doctrine first propagated by Woodrow Wilson at the end of the First World War, with respect to territories in eastern and south-eastern Europe that had been part of the defeated Austrian and Ottoman empires. The disintegration of the Soviet Union and Yugoslavia has led to the re-emergence of this doctrine with a vengeance in south-eastern Europe. Today's major powers are once again faced with the same problems that faced the great powers when they attempted to redraw the borders in Europe based on ethnic criteria after the First World War. The break up of multi-ethnic federations into mini-states, defined in terms of dominant ethnic majorities, has spawned the demand for micro-states based on ethnic purity to the exclusion of all other groups. This has led to ethnic cleansing, including massacres, wholesale expulsions of unwanted groups, and major refugee problems. It has vindi-

---

19   K.J. Holsti, *The State, War, and the State of War* (Cambridge, Cambridge University Press, 1996), pp. 22, 210-224.

cated William Pfaff's claim that 'The idea of the ethnic nation ... is a permanent provocation to war.'[20]

But such conflicts and wars are not new in the traditional Third World. In fact, many intrastate conflicts in post-colonial states have been initiated by self-defined ethnic groups demanding the right to self-determination, fed by the perception that they are being discriminated against by the dominant ethnic group. Most Third World societies are multi-ethnic in character. Therefore, failure to accommodate all major groups or to define national identities in inclusive, territorial terms, has usually led to a backlash from disempowered groups who begin by demanding autonomy but often end up calling for secession when their quest for autonomy is rebuffed.[21]

If the objective of secessionist groups is not the setting up of a new state, then it is redrawing the boundaries between contiguous states that would apportion a part of one state's territory to another, usually on the basis of the presumed 'ethnic' character of the majority of the population residing in that territory. These attempts have led to wars over Kashmir, the Ogaden and Bosnia, among a large number of others, that clearly demonstrate that secession and irredentism are two sides of the same coin.[22] It is this link between the two that makes it so difficult to distinguish between intrastate and interstate wars in much of the international system. Secession, as Horowitz has pointed out, 'lies squarely at the juncture of internal and international conflict.'[23]

Furthermore, if one looks behind many conflicts in the Third World that ostensibly appear to be interstate in character, one would find that the origins of many such conflicts are deeply rooted within the domestic polities of at least

---

20 W. Pfaff, 'Invitation to war', 73 *Foreign Affairs*, no. 3 (1993), 101.
21 For a well-reasoned and well-documented argument that institutional failures rather than cultural and historical animosities lie behind the collapse of interethnic understandings in multiethnic polities, see P. Bardhan, 'Method in the madness? A political-economy analysis of the ethnic conflicts in less developed countries', 25 *World Development* , no. 9, 1997, 1381-1398.
22 For the close relationship between secession and irredentism, see D.L. Horowitz, 'Irredentas and secessions: adjacent phenomena, neglected connections', in Chazan (ed.), *Irredentism and International Politics* (Boulder, CO, Lynne Rienner, 1991).
23 D.L. Horowitz, *Ethnic Groups in Conflict* (Berkeley, CA, University of California Press, 1985), p. 230.

one, if not both, of the participants. For example, the India-Pakistan war of 1971 had its origins in the civil war in East Pakistan. This led to a flood of millions of refugees into India and the subsequent Indian military intervention that resulted in the separation of Bangladesh from (West) Pakistan.

Similarly, the source of the Iran-Iraq War of 1980-88 can be traced to the Iraqi regime's fear of the demonstration effect of the Iranian Revolution on the Iraqi populace and the consequent threat to the Ba'athist regime. It was this apprehension, more than any other, that propelled Iraq into attacking Iran in 1980. Even the most high profile interstate dispute in the Third World, the Arab-Israeli conflict, in reality was, and continues to be, primarily a conflict between two state-building projects, the Zionist and the Palestinian, in the same territory that inevitably clashed with each other and in the process attracted the involvement of regional states as well as major powers.

These examples illustrate the fact that interstate conflicts in the Third World are quite often derivatives of the process of state making undertaken concurrently by contiguous and proximate states in various parts of the globe. The simultaneous nature of this process, which frequently includes the assertion of political and military control over demographic and territorial space contested by neighbouring states (Kashmir in the case of India and Pakistan, the Ogaden in the case of Somalia and Ethiopia, Nagarno-Karabakh in the case of Armenia and Azerbaijan), underlies many of the conflicts among countries in the Third World that appear to the outside observer to be instances of regional conflict tied to regional balance of power issues.

The arbitrary nature of colonially drawn boundaries has gravely exacerbated this problem by dividing groups with linguistic, religious, and other affinities between two or more usually contiguous states, thus making it very difficult for states not to be drawn into the internal conflicts of their neighbours, either because of domestic pressure or the flow of refugees from states in turmoil. The failure of many Third World states to assure the security of their populations, a function of their lack of 'empirical sovereignty', to use Robert Jackson's term, has also served to externalise internal conflicts because it has created mammoth human movements across borders, as for example in Central Africa during the 1990s.[24]

There is another critical link between concurrent state making and regional conflict *via* the notion of the regional balance of power: the more that balance is tilted in a particular state's favour, the easier it is for that state to enhance its state-building goals by successfully asserting its control at the expense of neighbouring states over contested territories and populations. Israel's example in the Middle East is eloquent testimony to the validity of this conclusion. The dynamics of regional balances have, therefore, become intertwined with the essentially domestic enterprise of state making and nation building, thus reinforcing the potential for conflict in both spheres.

The end of the Cold War has brought to the fore another variant of internal war that Donald Snow has termed 'uncivil wars' because, according to him, they 'often appear to be little more than rampages by groups within states against one another with little or no apparent ennobling purpose or outcome.'[25] According to Snow, 'these conflicts, and the participants therein, lack any clear political objectives as well as political ideology.' There is also 'an apparent absence of clear military objectives that can be translated into coherent strategies and tactics.'[26] Somalia, Liberia, Afghanistan, and Congo-Zaïre seem to fit this description almost perfectly.

These conflicts correlate closely with state failure, which is the direct consequence of the inability of political institutions to provide the minimum degree of order necessary to make life tolerable for the citizenry and peaceful, routine interactions among individuals possible. Furthermore, as Donald Snow has pointed out, 'The destabilization, even devolution to the status of failed states, is most likely to occur when states with previously strong coercive capability (strong states) but weak societal consensus (weak societies) loose their coercive hold.'[27]

---

24 For the difference between 'empirical' and 'juridical' sovereignty, see R. Jackson, *Quasi States: Sovereignty, International Relations and the Third World* (Cambridge, Cambridge University Press, 1990), chapters 1 and 2.
25 D.M. Snow, *Uncivil Wars: International Security and the New Internal Conflicts* (Boulder, CO, Lynne Rienner, 1996), pp. 1-2.
26 D.M. Snow, *Uncivil Wars*, p. 109.
27 D.M. Snow, *Uncivil Wars*, p. 102.

Many instances of state failure in the Third World, Somalia and Afghanistan among them, are good examples of states loosing their coercive capability precipitately, thus irretrievably eroding the residual legitimacy possessed by them. However, the coincidence of such state failure with the end of the Cold War provides a clue to a major factor that has contributed greatly to such failure and set off 'uncivil wars' in several locations in the Third World.

At the height of the Cold War, the superpowers attempted to shore up client governments in internally fragmented states ruled by narrowly based authoritarian regimes. One major instrument of such support was the transfer of large quantities of relatively sophisticated arms to friendly regimes. Such arms transfers sometimes led to countervailing transfers of weaponry by the rival superpower to forces opposed to the central authorities. Afghanistan during the 1980s came to epitomise this action-reaction phenomenon.

Past superpower policies of pouring arms into fragmented polities, however, became a major source of instability and disorder in the post-Cold War period when central authorities could no longer sustain themselves in power once their superpower patrons had lost interest in them. The presence in large quantities of relatively sophisticated weaponry, ranging from AK-47s to Stinger missiles, combined with the withdrawal of superpower support to weak and vulnerable regimes – support that was essential to prevent the central authorities from being overwhelmed by domestic rivals who, in turn, were divided among themselves – created near-total anarchy in countries like Afghanistan, Somalia, and Zaïre where central authority collapsed completely thereby turning these quasi-states into failed states.

However, the relationship between state failure and internal conflict is not a one way street with the former inevitably leading to the latter. The relationship is in many cases circular with the two phenomena feeding upon each other. State weakness provides the political space for the intensification of conflicts among political factions and/or ethnic groups, and the latter in turn further erodes the capacity of the state to maintain order and provide security to its citizens. Suffering from acute insecurity, individuals often turn to political factions, ethnic groups, and even criminal gangs (and sometimes it is difficult to distinguish among the three categories) to provide them with protection in exchange for their loyalty and contribution – financial, physical or both – to the 'war effort'.

Another dimension of state failure has a major impact upon the level of conflict within societies. Alex de Waal has pointed this out with great clarity in relation to Africa. He has argued that economic crisis in Africa has meant that 'governments find it more difficult to sustain and control armies, which then turn to local sources of provisioning. These include requisitioning, looting and taxing populations, involvement in commerce, and diverting humanitarian aid. Though the causes of war in Africa and the aims of the combatants are still almost exclusively phrased in terms of achieving state power and affecting constitutional change, the realities on the ground reflect more intense predatory behaviour by soldiers.'[28] This search for 'survival' on the part of unpaid or poorly paid soldiers, who command great coercive power in relation to the rest of the population, contributes to the reality and perception of state failure while serving a 'rational' purpose for those engaged in it.

Finally, state failure, like state making, must be viewed as a process not an event. In William Zartman's words, it is akin to 'a long-term degenerative disease'[29] rather than something that occurs at a particular point in time. Such an understanding of state failure will help one comprehend the fact that, as the Lebanese example demonstrates, the process is not irreversible. Furthermore, it will assist one to understand why this process is usually accompanied by long-drawn out 'uncivil wars', during which political factions fight over what they presume to be the state's carcass and the state attempts to revive itself drawing upon its residual capacity and legitimacy. If and when one faction succeeds in by and large subjugating the others, it usually dons the mantle of the state in order to legitimise the concentration of coercive power in its hands.

Similarly, if one views conflict and war as processes, and not merely in terms of final outcomes, one would conclude that there are usually groups, factions, and individuals that benefit economically, as well as politically, from the prolongation of wars, even of the 'uncivil' kind. They come to acquire a vested interest in perpetuating such conflicts. This is why 'Conflict entrepreneurs, as well as conflict victims, must be part of any analytical framework' devised to

---

28 A. de Waal, 'Contemporary warfare in Africa: changing context, changing strategies', 27 *IDS Bulletin*, no. 3, 1996, 6.

29 I.W. Zartman, 'Introduction: posing the problem of state collapse', in Zartman (ed.), *Collapsed States: The Disintegration and Restoration of Legitimate Authority* (Boulder, CO, Lynne Rienner, 1995).

study what has been termed 'complex political emergencies.'[30] Such a perspective can help unravel the 'rationality' behind what appear to the outside observer to be totally irrational conflicts.

One final dimension of the question of war at the end of the 20th century needs to be addressed. Since the end of the Cold War, it has become conventional wisdom to assume that the industrialised states operate on the basis of a neo-liberal understanding of international politics seeking absolute gains for all rather than relative gains at each other's expense. This means that not only war but major conflicts of interest among the industrialised states of the global North are ruled out for the foreseeable future. However, this framework does not apply to relations between the industrialised world and the Third World.

In its relationship with the Third World, the coalition of industrialised states, led by the United States, has no hesitation in adopting a very realist approach through which it attempts to preserve its relative advantage over the global South. James Richardson has captured this reality very lucidly. According to him,

> 'The realist dictum "the strong do what they can, the weak do what they must" draws attention to the dark shadows in North-South relations .... Realism survives not only in the North-South economic relations but also in the military preparedness of the major powers .... Self interest now appears to dictate that the leading powers remain associates rather than rivals, as balance of power logic would have required, but the anarchic system structure points to their retaining a military capability to protect their favored position against the less favored.'[31]

What does all this portend for the future of interstate war in the international system? It suggests that wars that pit major industrialised states against regionally ambitious or 'rogue' states in the Third World cannot be ruled out. The

---

30   J. Goodhand and D. Hulme, 'From wars to complex political emergencies: understanding conflict and peace-building in the new world disorder', 20 *Third World Quarterly*, no. 1 (February 1999), 19. The authors provide examples from Sudan, Liberia, and Afghanistan to demonstrate that conflict entrepreneurs benefit from internal war and thus possess a vested interest in their indefinite continuation.

31   J.L. Richardson, 'The end of geopolitics?', in: Leaver and Richardson (eds), *Charting the Post-Cold War Order*, (Boulder, CO, Westview, 1993).

American air attack on Libya in 1986 should have been seen as a precursor of things to come. The Gulf War of 1991 provided us with a model for this kind of war. Since that war, the United States and its allies have continued to deny the Iraqi state its right to exercise sovereign authority over large parts of the country. They have also prevented the revival of Iraq's military capabilities. Both these strategies demonstrate the type of punishment that is likely to be inflicted on 'rogue' states that fall foul of the dominant coalition in the post-Cold War era.

While all the factors that operated in the case of the Gulf War may not come together in the same fashion in most other regions of the Third World, there is more than a lurking suspicion among many important Third World states that if developments take place in other regions that are not to the liking of the global hegemon or the dominant coalition then similar military action cannot be ruled out in those cases as well. This feeling has been considerably strengthened as a result of US-led NATO military action against Serbia in 1999 and has led to the denunciation of NATO action not only by Russia and China, but by important regional powers like India as well.[32]

Such suspicion is linked to the perception that the major western powers are unwilling to countenance the emergence of strong powers in the Third World.[33] Humanitarian justifications for such military ventures are usually not given much credence in the Third World, especially since the doctrine of humanitarian intervention is seen to be applied selectively only to cases where the dominant coalition's strategic and/or economic interests seem to be at stake. The question is inevitably raised: Why Iraq (Kurds), Haïti, and the Balkans, and not Turkey

---

32 For the official Indian reaction condemning NATO action against Serbia, see K.K. Katyal, 'India criticises new doctrine', *Hindu*, 12 May 1999.

33 It is interesting to note in this context the argument made by Ian Lustick in relation to the Middle East. According to him, the intrusion of European colonialism and the policies followed by western great powers both during and after the colonial period effectively prevented the emergence of great powers (and one should add, strong states) in the Middle East. They did so by denying putative powers, that could challenge the concentration of military, political and economic power in Europe and North America, the option of successful war and expansion. I. S. Lustick, 'The absence of Middle Eastern great powers: political "backwardness" in historical perspective', 51 *International Organization*, no. 4 (autumn 1997), 653-683.

(Kurds), Rwanda, East Timor, and Tibet?[34] In much of the Third World, the Gulf War and the bombing of Serbia have become symbols of the western powers' desire to maintain their political and military supremacy in the international system and a warning to potential regional challengers to back-off or face the military and economic consequences of a devastating war.

It is obvious that the supremacy of the industrialised world, and specifically of its leader, the United States, is based on its huge technological superiority over the rest of the members of the international system. In the military sphere, this superiority is seen to be the cause as well as the consequence of the RMA, which is based on 'dramatic improvements in the accuracy and range of weaponry, the acuity of reconnaissance and surveillance, the ease of deception and suppression of the enemy's defenses, and the effectiveness of command and control.'[35]

This revolution assures RMA powers, the United States foremost among them, total control of the battlefield environment in times of war. As a result, offence dominates defence when an RMA power is engaged in combat with a non-RMA power. This was clearly demonstrated in the Gulf War during which high technology weapons deployed by the United States and its European allies, in conjunction with effective surveillance and command and control, rendered Iraqi defences totally impotent. The bombing of Serbia has driven home the same lesson.

RMA has demonstrated clearly that in the post-industrial era technological power is increasingly determined by proficiency in, and command over, information technology. As a result, power has become more fungible, and capabilities in various arenas have become more interlinked with each other than was the case even in the most advanced phase of the industrial era which coincided with the period of the Cold War.

---

34 For a reasoned critique of the application of the doctrine of humanitarian intervention in the 1990s, see F.J. Petersen, 'The façade of humanitarian intervention for human rights in a community of sovereign states', 15 *Arizona Journal of International and Comparative Law*, no. 3 (1998), 871-904.

35 J. Orme, 'The utility of force in a world of scarcity', 22 *International Security*, no. 3 (winter 1997-98), 145.

Paradoxically, therefore, in an era when one assumes that power is becoming more diffuse and disaggregated, it is in fact becoming more integrated and concentrated in the hands of those who control the 'system of systems' technology. This puts a great deal not merely of information but of knowledge at their command in an age when 'Knowledge, more than ever before, is power.'[36] No wonder the United States, with its preponderance in the field of information technology, appears to have become in the military sphere not only the lone superpower but the supreme power as we enter the 21st century.

The accentuation of inequality, as a result of RMA, between the industrialised North and the less developed South has led some Third World countries to search for the ultimate equaliser, in the form of nuclear weapons and ballistic missiles, that may, among other things, have some deterrent effect on what they consider to be the overbearing attitude, some would say the 'predatory' instincts, of the hegemonic coalition. It has also stimulated several of them to acquire the poor man's atom bomb, chemical and biological weapons, at least in part to deter the concert of industrialised powers from taking advantage of their military weakness.

As the RMA gap widens, the attraction of weapons of mass destruction (WMD), however rudimentary in character, can be expected to grow in a number of capitals in the Third World. The RMA powers may have inadvertently contributed to the spread of WMD and this is likely to have a major impact, as well as unintended consequences, as far as future conflicts in the international system are concerned. It is also likely to undermine both the nuclear non-proliferation and the missile technology control regimes as embodied in the NPT and the MTCR.

The foregoing analysis leads to several conclusions that are summarised below. First, one can predict with a reasonable amount of confidence that most (if not all) wars in the foreseeable future will continue to be concentrated in the Third World, defined to include not only the traditional areas of the Third World but the Balkans, the Caucasus, and Central Asia as well.

---

36 J.S. Nye, Jr., and W.A. Owens, 'America's information edge', 75 *Foreign Affairs*, no. 2 (March-April 1996), 20.

Secondly, it is clear that the majority of wars will be either intrastate in nature or will have a significant intrastate dimension to them. This is ordained by the fact that most Third World states are at an early stage of state making. Internal wars usually accompany attempts at state making because 'the lower the initial *level* of state power, the stronger the relationship between the *rate* of state expansion and collective violence.'[37] This is explained by the fact that attempts at expanding the control of the state are usually met by violent resistance by segments of the population that are reluctant to submit to a particular central authority. Such resistance in turn leads to violent retaliation on the part of the state and the spiral of violence usually escalates before one party or the other emerges triumphant.

Thirdly, the fact that contiguous and proximate states in the Third World are involved in the state making enterprise concurrently, when combined with the artificial nature of their boundaries and close trans-border affinities between many segments of their populations, makes it almost inevitable that many intra-state conflicts are likely to take on an interstate aspect as well. Furthermore, regional balances of power have come to be intimately connected with the state-making venture. States that are able to create favourable regional balances are in a position to achieve their state-making goals more quickly and easily than those that are not able to do so. This further augments the connection between regional and domestic politics tying regional conflicts with intrastate wars.

Fourthly, the rigid stratification in terms of the inequality of power between the industrialized North and the less developed South makes the latter's state building venture more difficult. It does so by permitting the major industrialised powers to intervene – politically, militarily, and economically – in the conflicts in the Third World for the former's strategic and/or economic reasons. Such intervention immensely complicates the process of state making in the Third World. Furthermore, as the Afghan and Somali cases demonstrate, the transfer by the major powers of relatively sophisticated weapons in large quantities to combatants within Third World states has contributed greatly to the emergence of the failed state phenomenon which is currently perceived as a major threat to international order.

---

37   Y. Cohen, B.R. Brown, and A.F.K. Organski, 'The paradoxical nature of state making: the violent creation of order', 75 *American Political Science Review*, no. 4 (1981), 905. Emphasis in the original.

Finally, the concentration of power in the industrialised world has provided the opportunity for the dominant coalition, led by the United States, to exploit the military advantage it has acquired through RMA *vis-à-vis* important Third World states and, thus, prevent the emergence of strong powers in the global South. Where this coalition feels that its strategic and/or economic interests may be threatened by emerging Third World powers, it has the capacity to take recourse to war, usually by employing missiles and high performing airplanes against which most Third World countries have no adequate defence. The Gulf War of 1991 may well be the model for such wars in the future. This imbalance has, however, made the nuclear option, as the ultimate equaliser, attractive to certain Third World states and may well become a major contributory factor to the spread of nuclear weapons (and other WMD) in the international system thus radically undermining the nuclear non-proliferation regime.

The future of war in the international system will, therefore, continue to be intimately connected to the process of state making in the Third World and the regional tensions that concurrent state making is likely to create in different parts of the Third World. It is also likely to be tied to the power inequalities between the global North and the global South based on the RMA phenomenon. This would permit the dominant coalition of industrial democracies to unilaterally take action against Third World states that they decide to define as 'rogue' states.

However, if more Third World countries succeed in attaining even modest nuclear weapons capability and combine it with unmanned delivery systems that can strike conventional forces in their vicinity, it could provide them with a rudimentary capacity to use nuclear weapons for tactical purposes. If this happens, it is likely to dilute the conventional military advantage possessed by the RMA powers. It may also establish a linkage between conventional and nuclear war-fighting capabilities, a connection that western strategists and statesmen have tried hard to prevent for the past 50 years.

PART III

TRANSFORMATION OF WAR

THREE CONTRASTING VIEWS AT THE LARGE SCALE

12

A BRIEF HISTORY OF WARFARE –
PAST, PRESENT, FUTURE

John Keegan

Where and when did war begin? Man is a potentially violent but not necessarily warlike creature. As he exists, *homo sapiens sapiens*, he has lived on earth for only about 40,000 years and he ceased to be anything but a hunter and gatherer much more recently, after the remission of the last Ice Age some 10,000 years ago. No-one agrees whether man the hunter was also man the warrior or not, although theorists take up the cudgels in earnest over the issue. Robert Audrey, the ethologist, believes that the hunter's adoption of the killing weapon, which mediated contact between man and prey, prepared the psychological basis for warfare. The behaviourists Tiger and Fox argue that the male hunting party was the archetype of all human organisations, which therefore has the idea of the use of violence for communal profit at their centre. These are theories only on, as it is becoming fashionable to say, inventions of the past. There are no true discoveries, nor can there be, for the evidence is irretrievable.

When evidence begins, it comes, as so often, from the Middle East. As the Ice Age was ending, Middle Eastern man was beginning to collect seeds systematically, then to transplant cereal grasses to more favourable habitats. Eight thousand years ago the process was so well advanced that something recognisable as farming was well established, as was the domestication of animals for meat and milk. Man was founding large collective settlements always near a source of water. He was also beginning to fortify, as we see in the excavated walls of Jericho which may be 9000 years old. Something had happened. What was it?

The best guess is that Jericho's neighbours had decided to prey on its wealth. They may have been robbers and destroyers; they may, more intelligently, have chosen to be violent parasites. What we may guess is that, while the inhabitants of Jericho were 'haves', hard-working 'haves', the outsiders were 'have-nots' who decided to help themselves. Helping yourself fits the pattern of a growing body of evidence about agriculture, city-building and warmaking that survives

G. Prins and H. Tromp (eds.), The Future of War, 171-180.
© 2000 *Kluwer Law International. Printed in the Netherlands.*

from the prehistory of the middle period between the founding of Jericho and the appearance of large-scale civilisation in the river lands of Mesopotamia 6,000 years later. Mesopotamia, the land between the rivers Tigris and Euphrates, offered farmers great advantages and great disadvantages. Its rich soil was watered by the annual flood, so assuring regular crops; the flood obeyed no rules, on an absolutely flat alluvial plain, so requiring the digging of irrigation channels if it were to be put to most profitable use. Irrigation ordained collective effect under central leadership. Since the floods were seen as divine handiwork, that leadership became priestly, so were born the theocratic so-called 'hydraulic' states of ancient Iraq.

Similar states were arising in Egypt, in the Punjab, in the Chinese river valleys. We know much about Egypt, but because its extraordinary location protected it from outside depredation, and its overpowering theocracy from domestic turmoil, its early history tells us little about early warfare. Iraq's, by contrast does. Its early cities seem not to have been walled. There was water and land enough for all, and predators lived far away, on the arid hills or in the deserts that surround the plain. Yet inter-city rivalries, perhaps provoked by population increase, did eventually lead to coalescences, and to the emergence of what pre-historians call 'empire', the empires of Sumer and then of Assur, Assyria.

The Sumerians flourished some 5,000 years ago. They had begun to practise writing, they had learnt the use of metal, they had begun to organise armies. All those things work together: writing was necessary for accounting, accounting was needed to record the collection of private and public wealth, public wealth needed protection by men with metal weapons, armed men needed to be organised for state purposes. Predators were gathering and pressing inward. As the Mesopotamian kingdoms expanded towards their high and arid natural boundaries, raiding into their rich lands by 'have-not' outsiders turned from a nuisance to a threat. The outsiders, moreover, were acquiring the means of long-range aggression. Some time before 2000 BC, the horse, hitherto a puny animal valued only for eating, had been domesticated and selectively bred into a beast of burden – and draught. A little later a draught-vehicle of military value appeared, the chariot. Outsiders who straddled the mountain margin of the irrigated empires on the one hand, of the horse-rearing steppe on the other, Hittites, Elamites, began to make long-distance depredations on the river empires. The empire struck back. River peoples had already identified reasons of their own for needing to venture off the plain: the need to trade, particularly for metal ores their stoneless soil did not yield, the need to acquire horses, perhaps the need to learn chariot technology. By the middle of the first millennium BC, 2500 years ago, Assyria had all those things. It also had in consequence an army of formidable power and long-range campaigning capability, armed with metal weapons, choked in metal armour, equipped with fast chariots and organised as a battle-winning striking force. Its external enemies learnt to fear it. They learnt to fear it most of all because the Assyrians had also mastered the most important of recent military technologies, the making of iron weapons, and the most revolutionary of recently developed mutualities between man and its animal kingdom, riding the horse. The Assyrian army was an iron army, a chariot army, an archery army – the ferocious composite bow was part of its arsenal – and it was also a *cavalry* army.

In that lay its undoing. Its external enemies were also by now cavalrymen, and had come to possess the composite bow, which may have been an Assyrian invention. At the end of the 7th century BC, Assyria was assailed from all sides by enemies and went down to defeat. Power in the Middle East passed rapidly to Persia, a kingdom which belonged more to the rough world of Asia's interior than to the civilisation of the irrigation societies. A great deal of power passed also to the horse peoples of the Central Asian Steppe proper who, through their victories over the Assyrians, had learnt that skill with the bow on horseback brought wealth unaccompanied by responsibility. A succession of such peoples, Cimmerians, Scythians – they were Assyria's destroyers – Huns, Avars, Alans and Magyars and eventually Mongols and Turks were, from their homeland on the Steppe, over the next 2,000 years, through their skills as horsemen and archers, to enjoy a free ride against the settled, busy hard-working, literate and civilised societies which had the bad luck to share a border with the steppe lands. Persia suffered as a result, so did the Indus valley civilisations, so did China, so eventually did Europe.

Until the fall of Assyria, warfare had chiefly been an activity in which the 'haves' had an upper hand over the 'have-nots'. The 'have-nots' of the poor and uncivilised regions wanted what the rich and civilised cultivated and accumulated, but they lacked the means to lay hands on it. The 'cavalry revolution', as William McNeil has characterised the phenomenon, changed that. It put pillagers on equal, often superior forms with states which depended for security on organised armies which, of their nature, lacked the relentless aggressiveness and acquisitiveness of the wild people outside. By the 3rd century BC, the Chin dynasty of China had already begun the effort to wall itself off from the steppe, an effort that was to persist, despite the fall of successive dynasties to steppe intruders, until the second millennium AD. The Roman empire would, from the 1st century AD onwards, also seek security within defended frontiers, though its enemies were not initially the horse peoples themselves but intermediate populations propelled westwards through the forest country by steppe pressure at their rear. These Teutonic 'barbarians', as the Romans called them, eventually found the force of desperation and, at Adrianople in 378, killed an emperor and destroyed the last of the western Roman field armies. It was this disaster which exposed Rome to attack by the first of the horse peoples to reach the West, the Huns under Attila, in the middle of the 5th century.

Attila, as we know, was defeated. His appearance on the borders of western civilisation, however, presaged 1,000 years of recurrent horse offensives against civilisation, by the Arabs – not strictly a horse people, but benefiting from their successes – against Byzantium and Persia, by Avars, Alans and Magyars against the Carolingian empire, by the Mongols, who successfully cast down the civilisations of the Islamic caliphate, Sassanian Persia, and the Sung dynasty of China, and by the Turks, who in the 15th century became the inheritors of Byzantium. The horse peoples inspired terror and disgust wherever they rode. Like the Vikings, who in the longship found a means of long-range aggression equivalent to the horse, they were pillagers and destroyers, true enemies of civilisation in all its aspects, economic, aesthetic, intellectual and spiritual. It was through their hands that warmaking became a scourge of the world, a denial of human creativity, a purely selfish assault on the world of the 'haves' by 'have-nots', who by the 15th century AD had in many cases become proud and rich 'haves' themselves.

To recapitulate: warfare had begun as a predatory activity by 'have-nots' against 'haves'. The 'haves' had responded by organising themselves for defence, after incurring heavy expense on fortification, and had gone over to the offensive, sometimes with success. The relentlessness of 'have-not' aggression, however, against peoples who had other calls on their time and energy – agriculture, city-building, commerce, the preoccupations of the mind, the spirit, the artistic impulse – was overbearing. Civilisation practised war when it had to, but could never bring itself to invest warmaking with supreme value. It had higher objects. At the end of the 15th century, what we can now recognise as the high point of 'have-not' success, however, material circumstances began to turn in civilisation's favour, in the West at least. Western man's material creativity quite suddenly resulted in the appearance of means of warmaking which negated the 'have-nots' advantages. Thitherto, from the beginning of history, warmaking had been a muscular activity. The horse was a muscular being; so, too, was man the warrior, even when, through the bow, he used mechanical means to enhance his muscular power in combat. Muscular energy is, nevertheless, a finite commodity, rapidly exhausted, particularly in the draining circumstances of battle. What civilised man put to use for warmaking purposes at the end of the 15th century was a source of energy, chemical energy, gun powder, which released man, the warrior, from dependence on his muscles in the struggle to win. Gunpowder reversed the balances between 'have-nots' and 'haves'. Gunpowder equipped the civilised 'haves' to be the victors over the savage 'have-nots'.

We must go back a step. In one corner of the world, the eastern Mediterranean, civilised peoples, even if only temporarily, had at an early stage evolved a way of making war which was quite at odds with the style of the horse-riding predators. The Greeks of the city states, the Romans who adopted their close-order method of fighting, conceived in the middle of the first millennium BC a revolutionary military ethic: battle to the death. Predation, though chronic, is parasitic, even symbiotic. The horse peoples were pitiless, but they sought either to incorporate the defeated into their own tribal systems or to preserve their economies for fiscal purposes. Nomads, as the Americans were to learn when they began to settle the Great Plains, are totally selfish. They despise the settled life while regarding it as a source of tribute. Nomads never, if they can, fight to the death. They believe in living to fight, and to loot, another day.

The Greeks, who invented so many other of the disciplines by which the modern world lives – the disciplines of philosophical logic, of scientific enquiry, of time, place and action in literary creation, of the democratic vote – also invented the discipline of decision on the battlefield, because they fought not to loot but to win. The object of winning was to preserve their means of livelihood and their liberties. Alexander, the half-Greek, the pupil of Aristotle, would pervert the idea of battlefield discipline and the ethic of victory to win an empire; but the spirit of his warmaking was not that of the Greek world. The true inheritors of the Greek military ethic were the Romans whose achievement was to create one vast city state whose citizens benefited from conquest, and not merely suffer by it, as the victims of nomad aggression everywhere did.

For 1,000 years after the fall of Rome the ethic of the battle to the death persisted in the West, but ineffectively. The barbarian successors, warlike though they were, remained too divided among themselves, too culturally inept to

achieve anything better than constant quarrelling among themselves and piecemeal resistance to nomadic assaults – by the horse peoples, by the sea raiders –
in what survived of western civilisation. The Christian church preserved the
vestiges of Roman pan-Europeanism, Charlemagne briefly re-energised it, the
Crusaders momentarily carried the battle to the enemy. At the end of 1,000
mediaeval years, however, nomadism was still in the military ascendant. If we
take 1454 as an index point, the Arabs still ruled Spain – there is much that
is good to be recognised in Islam, but autonomy of the intellect is not one of
its values – the Latin kingdoms of the east had been extinguished, Christian
civilisation in Russia was under Mongol domination, and Constantinople had
just fallen to the nomad Turks. The sun did not shine bright on the culture of
the West.

Then, suddenly, there was gunpowder. The Turks had gunpowder also; it was
with giant artillery that they battered down the Theodosian walls of Constantinople. What they did not have was the Greek and Roman idea of discipline,
then being rediscovered and repropagated in all its many forms in the renaissance kingdoms and city states of western Europe. Military discipline – drill,
mathematical fortification – was to prove as important a rediscovery as discipline of the intellect, the arts and the law. Gunpowder *plus* discipline quite
rapidly reversed the balance of advantage between the nomad and the settler
way of life. During the 16th and much of the 17th centuries the terrible Turks
remained a threat to the civilisation of the West, appearing twice outside Vienna,
the capital city of the Holy Roman Empire, driving Venice out of the eastern
Mediterranean, constantly threatening the frontiers of Christianity in Russia
and central Europe with reduction and annexation. Then, abruptly, at the end
of the 17th, the Turks were on the run. Defeated under the walls of Vienna,
they were rapidly forced to surrender territory, make treaties, concede that the
westerners had invented a way of making war, *la manière de combattre*, against
which their still semi-nomadic style could not prevail.

The 'haves' of the settled lands had achieved an ascendancy over the 'have-nots'
of the Eurasian interior – rich 'have-nots' though they had become – which
was to prevail thereafter, which persists to this day. It would eventuate in a
worldwide triumph of the 'haves'. In the meantime, however, the ascendancy
of the 'haves' resulted in an intensification of warfare within Europe, which
was to have dramatic consequences. Before gunpowder, warfare in Europe had
been a small-scale and short-range offensive. Wars between kingdoms were
often protracted – that between England and France over the rights of the

Angevin kings lasted 100 years – but rarely destructive. Warfare was a comparatively benign activity, an occupation for the landowning classes. After the christianisation and assimilation of the Norsemen, about 1000 AD, war rarely provoked crises in western European life. Gunpowder did. Gunpowder weapons were expensive. Only the greater rulers – those of England, Spain, above all France – could afford them in numbers. In 1494 Charles VIII of France set off into Italy with a great train of artillery, standardised bronze guns mounted on mobile field carriages, and subdued the peninsula in a single year of fighting. The powers would fight over Italy for the next century, but the pattern of future warfare had been set. During the 16th century the French kings would make themselves wasters of their own kingdom, crushing for good the capacity of local warlords to defy royal authority as they had so often done in the pre-gunpowder age. The English kings achieved the same ascendancy at the century's start, as the Spanish did by their victory over the Moors. By the end of the 16th century there were three great, centralised, gunpowder kingdoms in Europe, France, Spain, England, a diffuse but powerful Habsburg empire in central Europe and a number of smaller states – Sweden, The Netherlands – whose local power could not be ignored. They were all 'haves', efficient, taxing, agricultural, trading and potentially industrial states, with a high capacity for making war. Their history, over the next 300 years, was essentially to be that of warmaking against each other, in a struggle for position in the European heartland. 'Have' against 'have': this was the essence of the Thirty Years' War, the dynastic wars of the 18th century, the ideological wars of the Revolution and Napoleon, in which Russia for the first time showed itself to be a European player of significance, the nationalist and unificatory wars of the 19th century. These were wars in which the wealth of the greater 'haves' proved the decisive factor, since discipline was common to all. By 1914, repetitive competition in the expenditure of wealth and disciplined force had reduced the number of effective powers in Europe to five: Britain, France, Russia, the Habsburg Empire of Austria-Hungary, and recently united Germany. Recently united Italy was a marginal kingdom, once powerful Spain a has-been, once terrifying Turkey a shell. The pieces were in place for a climactic struggle of 'haves' against 'haves'. It resulted, in 1918, in an armistice of mutual exhaustion which left the least weakened combatants, France and Britain, nominally the victors. Austria-Hungary was dissolved by defeat, Turkey reduced by defeat from a decayed empire to a petty ethnic state, Russia consigned by defeat to backwardness through the victory of economic know-nothings in a civil war the greater war had provoked. At its reprise in 1939, the suicidal impulses of 'the haves' culminated six years later in their collective emasculation. There were no European victors of the war of 1939-45, only a collection of impoverished neighbours in a once great continent, which, not long before, had counted its mastery of the techniques of disciplined warfare among its greatest cultural achievements.

So, the warfare of 'haves' against 'haves' had ended in tragic nullity. While it had been running its course, however, some of the 'haves' had been exporting the lethal combination of gunpowder and discipline to the 'have-not' world. The Spanish and Portuguese had exported it to the southern Americas, a continent without writing or military metals. The French had exported it to the North America and Africa. The English had exported it to India. The Russians had exported it to Central Asia, heartland of the nomadic, predatory warfare of the 'have-nots'. All of them had taken bites at China and its zone of cultural influence, the Russians very big bites indeed. Between the arrival of Cortes in Mexico in 1518 and the Russian conquest of the central Asian emirate of Merv in 1885, virtually the whole of the non-European world had either passed to a European empire or been forced to acquiesce on European control of its government or economy; by 1945 the only states which had never accepted defeat at the hands of Europeans or control by them could be counted on the fingers of one hand: Thailand, Yemen, Saudi Arabia, Mongolia, perhaps Iran. Whenever confronted by what Professor Victor Hanson, the leading historian of the military history of the Greeks, has characterised as 'the Western Way of Warfare', the face-to-face, close-order, do-or-die contest for decision on a defined battlefield of mutual choice, the non-European world had always gone down to defeat by Europeans. There had been a handful of exceptions – Isandhlwana, the Zulu triumph, the Italian disaster and Adowa in Ethiopia, Anual, the Spanish defeat by the Moroccans, Custer's Last Stand – but they really were exceptions. Discipline and gunpowder, discipline more than gunpowder, had, in the non-European world, triumphed. Against that combination, numbers were an irrelevance – Clive, at Plassey, won the decisive battle against Moghul India when outnumbered fifteen to one in men and five to one in artillery pieces – and so, too, were the banshee wail, the death charge, the scalping impulse, the ghazi belief that death in holy war would open the gates of paradise. Relentlessly, step by step over the few centuries between the arrival of the conquistadors in the New World and the extinction of the last stronghold of nomad power in the Old, Europe, gunpowder and discipline conquered the world.

There was an exception. I have mentioned exceptions before. This is the most important of all. It is the exception of the United States. The United States was a society, European in origin, which, by discipline and gunpowder, escaped from European control, not merely into independence but into a near form of civilisation, philosophical not military in its basis. It was a civilisation, in Jefferson's words, which dedicated itself to 'peace, commerce and honest friendship with all nations, entangling alliances with none'. For nearly 150 years it succeeded in holding itself aloof from the world outside – with the assistance of the Royal Navy admittedly, but aloof nonetheless. In the course of the century and a half it fought a great war against itself but otherwise, with the most trifling of lapses, fought no wars at all. Then, through no entangling alliance, it decided its philosophy of state required it to foresake isolation and intervene in the warfare of the haves after all. Its intervention in 1917 tipped the scales of a very finely balanced European antagonism; its intervention in 1941 brought a decision not attainable without it. What was by then the greatest of the 'have' nations, dedicated to peace, imposed what we may suppose and hope will be the final peace between the old gunpowder nations.

So where are we now? The history of war in the world has been, I have suggested, a three-act drama. At the outset, war was an activity conducted by 'have-nots' against 'haves', greedy predatory, destructive. Its initiation may be dated to man's mastery of the horse 3500 years past and the act ran its course until the European peoples learnt how to put gunpowder to the service of their culture of discipline 500 years ago. In the second act, the European gunpowder-discipline culture resulted in the subjection of the war of the world, much of it once the victim of the predatory 'have-nots', to European control; in a parallel dramatic passage, European military culture turned disastrously in on itself, jutting gunpowder and discipline against gunpowder and discipline until the antagonists were exhausted and could be rescued from the sterile stalemate to which they had reduced themselves only by the mediation of the one exemplar of their culture which had held aloof from the contest. Its intervention proved decisive and, by its translation of western technical military dominance from a chemical to a nuclear physical basis, apparently, and we may hope actually, permanent.

Yet there is – we cannot ignore it or deny its reality – a fourth act. 'Have-nots' against 'haves', 'haves' against 'haves', 'haves' against 'have-nots'; that is war's history. Now our conscience is assailed by the pitiful and profitless phenomenon of war between 'have-nots' and 'have-nots'. War began as an attack by the poor on the rich, persisted as an exercise between the rich and the rich, resolved itself with a counter-attack by the rich against the poor. Now war is exclusively an occupation for the poor alone. There are, commentators tell us, 30 wars in progress in the world. They are taking place – where? In the world's remote, resourceless, unproductive places: in Bosnia, the poorest part of Europe, in the Caucasus, the poorest part of the old Soviet Union, in Cambodia, one of the poorest parts of Asia, in Angola, Mozambique, Somalia, Rwanda, some of the poorest parts of a continent by definition by poor. War, once a struggle over riches, or the proud vocation of peoples rich themselves, is now the calling of the wretched of the earth.

This is a pitiful conclusion to a human activity 5,000 years old, which at times may have been a necessary one and very often could not have been avoided. But war *is* now avoidable; war is no longer *necessary*. The poor may fight, but the rich rule. It is with their weapons that the mad ideologies of peasant countries tread the path of blood, that the child soldiers of tribal states massacre each other and each other's families. Without the weapons the rich world manufactures, sells, or gives for political profit, the 30 wars raging in the world today would rapidly fizzle into extinction. We are at the threshold of a new era in history, can we but seize the opportunity, on the threshold of a genuinely new world order. We can stop now if we only choose, by a simple economic decision of the governments of the rich states, not to make more arms than they need for their own purposes, and not to supply any surplus that remains to the poor, the 'have-nots'. That may sound a naïve and idealistic belief, but it is the conclusion I have come to after 40 years of thinking and writing about war. War has occupied my mind for a lifetime and, before I die, I hope and pray that I may see an end to it. The time has come.

13

THE PEACE-BRINGING POWERS OF WAR

Edward Luttwak

Bloch did not predict that war would or would not happen. He approached this issue like the engineer he was. He examined the capacity of societies to tolerate war.

First, he described future war in a scientific way. He studied weapons. He discussed the possibility of introducing 5mm high-velocity weapons. (At that time, weapons were 11mm, then later 7mm.) He was anticipating what we implemented in the 1970s.

Secondly, he examined future war as a process. Is this country, called the Russian Empire, strong enough to take this weight? His answer was 'no'. He was absolutely correct. It is interesting what a striking success was his prediction of the mechanics of war.

I would like to continue using this same engineer's methodology, but not at six volumes' length. What does war do as a process? War consumes. It consumes the resources needed to fight. To fight a war you need ammunition, fuel, food, troops. The more you fight, the less you have. War burns. It destroys resources. War also destroys hopes; hopes which drove somebody to start the war in the first place. You fight a war because you are hoping for a good result. The more you fight, the longer the war lasts, the less is this hope.

War, as a process, leads to peace. As war continues, it burns the will and the capacity to continue, so that, either by victory or by exhaustion, war brings peace. Every palace, every house that exists in Europe, every building, every road, every bridge, every factory, every school was created in peace time, when people stopped fighting. They stopped fighting because war achieved its purpose – its teleological purpose – which is to bring peace.

G. Prins and H. Tromp (eds.), The Future of War, 181-188.
© 2000 *Kluwer Law International. Printed in the Netherlands.*

That ancient logic has been interrupted. In recent times (in the last 50 years), the habit of interrupting other peoples' wars has grown. Instead of letting them fight their war, and burn the causes and means of war and bring them to peace, so they can also rebuild the roofs of the houses, the international community intervenes. During the Cold War, we had no choice (I say 'we', as a citizen of the USA). I could say 'we' as Americans and Russians, or citizens of the Soviet Union. Actually, I could say 'we' as everybody. We could not let war happen, because of the danger of an intervention by the Americans or the Russians to prevent their side losing. These interventions could become reciprocal interventions, which might escalate. Escalation could bring nuclear war. So, as soon as anybody started fighting, we went in with a cease fire, using the United Nations as a convenience. We – the Cold War antagonists and their allies – formalised great power relations, institutionalised habits, which had started at the Congress of Berlin. Remember what happened after the intervention of Disraeli and Bismarck; two Balkan wars and the conditions for further conflict.

What happens when you intervene with a ceasefire and nothing but a ceasefire? There is a war, which is exhausting the resources and the will to fight. Somebody comes along with a ceasefire. Fighting stops. The process of exhaustion stops. Automatically, there is a process of reconstitution, because new recruits enter the army; there is some in-flow of matériel. Exhaustion does not just stop. What may we conclude? That every ceasefire interrupts war and prolongs warfare: because of that ceasefire there will be more war, other things being equal, unless you do many other things.

The other way war was interrupted during the Cold War was in a more lasting fashion, by armistice. This is like a ceasefire, but not limited by time. A potential transformation by war was taking place and it is stopped. War is frozen, congealed. People do not rebuild their roofs because the war could start again at any time. Instead, resources are diverted into the competitive arms race, because an armistice is frozen war, not peace. It is not *proto* peace, not even *pre* peace: it is frozen war. The natural result of an armistice is not reconstruction, but an arms race.

In contrast, when war ends because one or the other side wins or because both sides are exhausted, the natural process leads to reconstruction, and reconstruction tends to lead to reconciliation. He is building a roof, you are building roof, you are going to help each other, buy roofing materials. At least you don't want to shoot against his roof because you know that he will shoot against yours. This logic was disrupted during the Cold War. Instead of war leading to peace, war led to ceasefires and armistices, so that it fostered a process whereby war begins but never ends. The Arab-Israeli conflict is an archetype; so too North-South Korea.

The Cold War required the sacrifice of the lesser powers. Keegan's 'have-nots', and some minor 'haves' all had to suffer so that we would not have escalation to nuclear war. We had to impose the war-prolonging effect of ceasefires, the war-freezing effect of armistices, because we could not afford the risk of nuclear war. However, the Cold War ended, and with it the risk of nuclear war ended. I do not see any great powers on the world scene which are behaving like great powers. The Russians are intervening all the time; we are intervening all the time; but we are not intervening reciprocally against each other. So the danger is no longer there. Yet, characteristically of human beings, we persist anachronistically with this bad habit of interfering to stop wars. It is like an addiction. We are continuing in the post-Cold War world to sabotage the process whereby war transforms itself into peace.

Those who have studied Clausewitz or Hegel or Lenin know that in conflict everything becomes its opposite. The further a victorious army advances, the weaker it becomes. The further the enemy retreats, the stronger it becomes. Victory in over-extended advance becomes defeat. This is called the coincidence of opposites.

By the same token, war becomes peace. War creates peace. The peace created by war, unlike the peace created by artificial treaties and other arrangements imposed by other countries, is a solid peace. That is how the confidence is created to build a building like the Marble Palace in St Petersburg, in all its ornate splendour. Nobody in Bosnia is going to risk building a building like this, because Dayton offers no peace. It is a fragile, temporary peace. As General Rose correctly pointed out, it is a peace in which the conflict was artificially frozen, where each country of the post-Federation countries is ruled by its war criminals.

Why do we have this problem? We have this problem because in war there is a place for everything; for intelligence and for stupidity; a place for flexibility and for stubbornness. All of this can help a country to achieve victory, or for the world to have peace. There is only one thing that war does not allow and that is disinterested behaviour. Selfish behaviour is permissible, but unselfish, *disinterested* behaviour has no place in conflict, because when disinterested behaviour enters, it randomises outcomes. Worse than that, it generalises this pattern. Let me give you some examples.

Immediately after the Second World War the United Nations Relief and Rehabilitation Agency (UNRRA) was created. In Europe UNRRA provided rudimentary, primitive camps, big camps in Central Europe, Germany and Italy. They were cold in winter and the refugees were fed with industrial slop food. The conditions were designed to encourage people to resettle locally or to emigrate as soon as possible. UNRRA was run on the basis that the standard of living was very low compared to the ambient, and that ambient was not California, but post-war Europe where people were hungry.

The arrangement seemed to work. Therefore, on the model of UNRRA, in 1948 near Palestine UNWRA was created, providing camps, regular food without back-breaking labour, medical care, schooling. In other words, a higher standard of living was provided than that of most of the Arab villagers who had come out from the area controlled by the Jews. Naturally, they stayed there because they were not UNRRA camps – a place that you want to leave. They became towns. Thus, a refugee nation was created. If every war in Europe had been followed by an UNWRA, instead of UNRRA, today Europe would still have giant camps for Gallo-Romans, Visigoths, Burgundians, sitting around, each of them preserved nations, with their revanchism preserved, their hatred preserved. It would be a mosaic of warring nations.

This is an example of what happens when there is disinterested action in conflict. The UNWRA model has been followed, not the UNRRA. So, in Africa, for example, in any refugee camp set up, however miserable its conditions, the standard of living, however low, will be higher than the surrounding average. By providing some kind of food, some kind of shelter and some kind of help, automatically a refugee nation is created. Wherever the UNWRA model – which is now the normal model of humanitarian relief – arrives, a refugee nation is created, sometimes big and aggressive, like the Hutus, sometimes smaller, less aggressive. In this way, the cohesion of the refugee group is maintained and prolonged. UNRRA in Europe broke up that cohesion. The Ukrainians, for example, were dispersed to different camps. Then they emigrated. Most of them went to Canada. There were not masses of Ukrainians or Poles sitting somewhere in Germany. In contrast, the UNWRA model concentrates these populations, thereby creating an automatic base for revanchist politics becoming normal politics. The Palestinians had many factions, but none was called 'peace now', 'integration now', or 'emigration now'. All of them were revanchist groups. Revanchism is normalised by maintaining the demographic cohesion. We did that too in northern and eastern Thailand by creating the camps for the Cambodians.

This disinterested intervention in the field of conflict has at best a random outcome, but Murphy's Law is usually worse than random. Staying at home, doing nothing, not intervening, not helping is usually the best thing you can do for humanity. (Of course, there are occasions when one can actually help, because it is a random process.) There are even worse phenomena.

So-called Non-Governmental Organisations (NGOs) collect money from people who do not think. They say 'we want to help'. Let me give you an example of how they help. The negative, counter-productive effects of NGO interventions in Africa go back so far that they are co-terminous with the colonial period, beginning with the Karamodja relief programmes east of Lake Tanganyika, which created parasitic dependence in a proud people, and ruined the economy of the Kikuyu farmers who used to buy their beef. This pattern of the counter-productive results of NGO intervention is established across Africa. Recently, in Rwanda, with the Hutus, it was so obvious and so massive that the NGOs were in fact supplying the logistics of the war. Africanists have been seeing this going on in Ethiopia. The government under Haile Mariam, in carrying out systematic population resettlement operations, actually relied on NGOs to bring food in to attract the populations.

NGOs have one dominant, absolute imperative and that is to exist. For this they have to collect money. For this they have to demonstrate activity in the light of the television cameras. Therefore, they arrive at conflicts like flies on sugar and their impact is overall highly negative. They feed conflicts indirectly. An NGO is not militarily strong. A militarily weak or unarmed defenceless group is introduced into a war. Therefore, it has to appease. It cannot separate the warriors from the non-warriors. Therefore, they feed the warriors. Bleeding hearts are no substitute for hard heads.

Returning to the question of what tips the balance from war to peace, the Americans intervened in the First World War on the slightly stronger side, and brought peace. Note that it was not done in a disinterested, impartial or even-handed way. The American arrival was one factor at least in bringing the First World War finally to an end. That was the good American intervention. They came in on one side, pursuing an American policy to make the strong stronger and the weak weaker, so that war would end sooner. I am in favour of all intervention on the side of the stronger in order to bring peace.

But then there was a second American intervention, the Wilsonian intervention. It was not a one-sided intervention. It was a disinterested intervention to give national rights to all kinds of populations, to prevent the French from achieving a Cartheginian peace. The French plan was to divide Germany: to say 'We love Germany so much that we want three of them' to 'pastoralise' its war-making industries. Clémenceau was blocked in that aim. The disinterested American intervention did many other things. It created state structures, bought Mr Masayrk's 'Czechoslovakia' package, for example. That was falsehood in the name of a country when actually there were more Germans than Slovaks in the territory. It should have been called 'Czechogermania'. This was the product of disinterested interventionism.

My final example is UN peacekeeping. I have made it plain that I believe that disinterested interventions have at best random outcomes. I further believe that when you interpose your country or group in a war and you are not willing to go and fight, you are forced into two roles; either appeasement of the stronger, or bombing: one of the two. These are the only options: there is no third way. Either you provide the kind or force that tends to make dictators stronger, or you appease them. Please understand that if you intervene in a situation, and you appease only the stronger side – let's say in the Bosnia case, if the UN intervention had helped the Serbs everywhere – then war would have ended immediately without years and years of suffering. Therefore, you prevent the emergence of a coherent outcome, of a winner and a loser. So the war never ends. Mark my words.

General Rose points out in his chapter that a UN peacekeeping force – or multilateral force of any sort (it could be anybody everybody is in this business, WEU, EU etc) wants to go to the war in a disinterested way without fighting. By so doing, not only do you prevent the emergence of outcomes that could bring a war to an end. You do something else. As General Rose points out, if you are not combat-oriented, not ready politically, physically, logistically equipped, you cannot protect civilians. But the mere fact that you have made a peacekeeping intervention is discouraging, dissuading, inhibiting civilians from doing the normal thing which is to run away. They don't run away because they have homes and illusions that they will be protected. The UN force does not come in and say 'wait a minute, we are peacekeeping, which is a very specialised activity and we will not protect you'. On the contrary, they get the impression that they will be protected. So, the population does not react in a normal way. Moreover, some countries will deny war refugee status. They say 'We don't give you war refugee status because there is no war, because the UN is there keeping the peace', even when it is not. The UN also is a victim of massive anachronism. 'Peacekeeping' belongs, with ceasefires and armistice, to a Cold War world that is gone.

Let us recall how UN peacekeeping started. It continued with much success during the Cold War. The Cold War the Russians and Americans would negotiate an end to a conflict. When the Russians and Americans had agreed 'no more shooting', then UN peacekeepers would come in, because the logic of war had already been suspended. At this point one could send in Colombians, standing to attention with smart uniforms and rifles. Nobody shoots at them and they don't shoot at anybody and this is called UN peacekeeping. In other words, UN peacekeeping works in a highly satisfactory way when the UN force does not need to be a force: when you can send in Colombians. (I farm in Bolivia and have the greatest respect for Colombians, and I observe that Colombians do not fight for money, and certainly not for the UN.)

What is the implication of the foregoing analysis? Uncomfortable, I hope. The practical end is that there is a challenge to state craft, a challenge for the policy makers, policy intellectuals, analysts and commentators to confront the plain and embarrassing fact that habits of mind appropriate to an earlier era have not been shed with its passing.

We have to be able to speak humanitarian language to humanitarian problems. We have to explain that the reason we do not want to intervene is not because we are disinterested, selfish and egoistic, but the very opposite: because we do not want to do harm. It is a challenge for journalists, historians, analysts, intellectuals to create the climate in which the presumption becomes one of non-intervention, except in highly specialised cases, and to reverse this wrong presumption which is an inheritance from the specialised conditions of the Cold War. During the Cold War we had to behave in that way, no matter the consequences, even though we were turning every war into an endless war. It is inexcusable to do this now. But to say this is not a solution. It is to define the problem; to reverse the expectation and the policy assumptions and presumptions so that we stop doing harm.

In that regard, needless to say, the most recent and noxious example is Bosnia. The Dayton Accord is an absent-minded piece of ill-reasoned diplomacy. It is a frozen armistice between obnoxious parties. I doubt that it will hold.

All around the world, wherever the blue flag of the UN is to be seen, conflict is being frozen, the fires of hatred stoked, revanchism preserved, and conflict-resolution mechanisms that work (as opposed to the soft-headed derivatives from inter-personal counselling) are being blocked.

Wherever you see those pretty baby blue helmets harm is being done. This paradox describes the new framework that we have to analyse and to limit. Of course, it has exceptions; there are always exceptions. This is not dogma or religion, this is an analytical process that may be uncomfortable and is certainly hard work. However, recollecting the lessons of Bloch's six volume engineer's assessment of future war, it is work of the kind that he teaches us to do.

14

THE INDISPENSABLE NUCLEAR BOMB

Martin van Creveld

John Keegan has presented us with an outline of the history of war. According to him, at first, it was a question of 'have-nots' fighting 'haves' and trying to take what they had away from them. Next, it changed into a conflict of 'haves' against 'haves'; then into a conflict of 'haves' against 'have-nots'; and finally, in our own day, to a struggle which is waged by some 'have-nots' against other 'have-nots'.

In a way, Keegan's talk sums up the tone of the St Petersburg discussions, which, I would argue, have been remarkably optimistic. War is now seen as something that is waged by 'have-nots' against 'have-nots'; hence it has nothing to do with the participants in the conference, all of whom, needless to say, are 'haves'. Some participants have even suggested that we are now entering, or at least capable of entering, a process of sustained development, whereby knowledge will be translated into prosperity and prosperity into indefinite peace. Others have argued that democracy and non-state actors, or international structures, or enforcement of international laws, are altering the world and are working towards a more peaceful world for us and our children.

On the whole, this is an optimistic line of thought, and had Jan Bloch been alive today, surely he would have agreed with it. For Bloch, too, was an optimist and a rationalist. By his analysis, war had become too terrible, too dangerous, too expensive to wage. If he could only convince people of this view, then logically war should have become impossible, to quote the short title of his work. I myself tend to agree that this optimism is well founded, at any rate as far as the 'developed' world is concerned; yet I believe that both Bloch (for reasons that he could not have foreseen) and his successors (with much less justification) have missed the real cause behind what peace the developed world enjoys today. I would argue that, to an overwhelming extent, that peace is due

G. Prins and H. Tromp (eds.), The Future of War, 189-193.
© 2000 *Kluwer Law International. Printed in the Netherlands.*

to fear of nuclear weapons; in other words, *not* to any of the remaining factors that have been mentioned in this conference.

Nuclear weapons are the real cause of whatever peace this planet of ours enjoys. Nuclear weapons grew out of the power of the state. In some ways they represent the culmination of the development of the modern state – the reason being that, so far, the only organisations that have been capable of developing and building and deploying them are states. Yet, at the same time as nuclear weapons provided states with an unprecedentedly powerful means of fighting each other, they also broke those states' power to make war against other states.

As one might expect, this paradoxical process did not affect all states at one time, at the same pace, or in the same manner. At first it was only the most powerful states of all, namely the United States and the Soviet Union, which were unable to fight each other. But then, by a process similar to a spreading stain of ink, it began to make its impact felt on other states as well. First, the Superpowers' 'close' allies on both sides of the Iron Curtain (and, after 1953, at both ends of the Eurasian continent) found themselves almost as secure against large-scale attack as were the Superpowers themselves. Then the process repeated itself between China and the Soviet Union, then between China and India, then between India and Pakistan, and finally – I hope and believe – in the Middle East too. This development did not result from spreading democracy, or of emerging international structures, or even of NGOs running about and spouting their messages. As Winston Churchill put it in the early 1950s, it was 'the sturdy child of terror'; to the extent that we do enjoy peace, this is still true today.

Yet one should not exaggerate the extent of the change. War existed long before nuclear weapons and long before states. War ultimately grows out of factors rooted very deeply in the human soul; one might almost say that the real reason why we have war is because men like war and women like warriors. The origins of war are to be found in fear and hope, and also in the desire to prove oneself, in the feeling of frustration that sometimes arises when one is unable to make a mark. It is not mainly, certainly not exclusively, an activity that people engage in to achieve this or that end. On the contrary, very often it is an activity that people engage in when their hopes of achieving this or that have failed; as John Frederick Fuller wrote very soon after the introduction and first use of nuclear weapons, one does not eradicate the causes of war by obliterating cities.

Given that war is rooted in the human heart, nuclear weapons for all their power have only had a limited effect on war since 1945. It is true they were able to eliminate war between the most powerful states; by the year 2000, any state capable of maintaining an armoured corps should also be able to build nuclear weapons. In this way, the restrictions which nuclear weapons placed on the warfighting abilities of the most powerful states slowly spread to second and third-rate states.

However, an important qualification needs to be made. By virtue of their very power, nuclear weapons are only useful against states. By states I mean that kind of political organisation that has sovereign control over a considerable stretch of territory. Even so, for nuclear weapons to be useful in war between states, one's enemy should be as far away from one's own territory as possible; the reason being that, if a nuclear bomb is dropped on an enemy who is close at hand, then the state which has done the dropping is going to feel at least some of the effects in the form of radiation, radioactive contamination etc.

While the use of nuclear weapons by one state against another is conditional on that state being as far away as possible, they are entirely useless against enemies who do not own large stretches of sovereign territory. As a result, their effect to date has been not so much to put an end to war as to force people to look for and find other forms of political organisation, in whose name they could fight. In such wars the enemy was not on the other side of the world, as during much of the Cold War; instead he might well be located, on the next mountain, the same mountain, in the next village, the same village, in the next street, in the same street, in the next house, in the same house, in the same room, as happened in Bosnia, for example. In this way, the power of nuclear weapons can be, and is being, undermined. By creating situations where friend and foe are locked together very closely, men can continue fighting to their hearts' contents.

It is true that, at the moment, almost all of the wars being waged by organisations that do not have large pieces of sovereign territory take place in what used to be called the Third World. Indeed, when Walter Laqueur published his book on the history of the guerrilla in 1977, he believed that this kind of war would soon come to an end, because, after all, there were no more places left to be decolonised. He could not have been more wrong. Starting from the Third World, this new kind of war – whose main characteristic is that it is being waged by organisations without solid territorial bases – has spread into the

Second World. We have all seen, or heard, or witnessed Georgia, Azerbaijan, Armenia, Chechnya: and Yugoslavia, of course. As the third millennium opens, nobody can tell whether this region of the European 'near abroad' will not see large-scale, non-state war on its territory in a few years.

As Keegan reminds us, so far the First World has been almost entirely immune to this and other types of war. However, let us not forget that this so-called First World only makes up approximately 15 per cent of humanity. In 85 per cent of the world, future war, meaning war waged overwhelmingly by and against organisations that are not states, has already triumphed. The First World is rather like a besieged castle, with the waves beating against the walls. They will certainly batter them down if we continue to have capitalism without equity and justice, as we increasingly have over the last few years. They will certainly breach the walls if we continue to have the retreat of welfare without a corresponding cut in taxation, as has happened over the last few years. They will certainly demolish our walls if we continue to have immigration without integration. Needless to say, the situation differs from one country to the next; yet probably none of our countries is so rich, so homogeneous, so just towards all its inhabitants and so wallowing in self-content as to be immune.

In face of this stark balance-sheet, too many people continue to talk, to write and, to some extent to prepare for things that are almost totally irrelevant. They talk about a 'system of systems', capable of knowing everything there is to know in a battlefield of 300 x 300 kms, at a time when there are very few, if any, such battlefields left on the face of the earth. They are talking about a 'revolution in military affairs' at a time when the absence of a threat is causing all militaries to cut back their forces. They are talking about 'cyber war' as a dominant trend, whereas war is tearing up societies where there are hardly any computers or other electronic devices, for that matter. They are talking about networks, referring to places where the only networks are networks of kin. Yet there are many countries, such as Somalia, where warriors have been able to prove their ability to operate below the sophistication threshold to defeat the electronic Goliath; even though the means at their disposal were very primitive indeed.

Future war will not be waged by or against super sophisticated armies, but by people wielding Kalashnikovs, anti-tank rockets, machine guns, maybe even literally knives, sticks and stones, as in the case of the Israeli-occupied territories. Before dismissing the stones and the sticks and the knives, let us not forget where the PLO was ten years ago and where it is now. By now, even Israelis who are rabid rightists realise that a Palestinian state is inevitable; an achievement gained by the Palestinians in the teeth of what the world's second most sophisticated manufacturer of software, Israel, could do. One only has to go to the Plain of Sharon, to the highway from Tel Aviv to Haifa, to see one shiny high-tech building after another: how useful were they when it came to fighting the sticks and stones?

To conclude, I am afraid I cannot share Bloch's optimistic views. Rather, I share Keegan's characterisation of the future of war and Luttwak's view of how it may best be fought to minimise suffering and maximise peace, assuming, that is, that we of the developed world choose to engage our energies; for, as Freedman reminds us, much of this chaotic violence needs only be entered by us, the fortunate 15 per cent, by choice.

War is not exclusively, maybe not even primarily, a question of gaining rational ends by rational means. If it had been, perhaps it would have come to an end ages and ages ago. Ultimately, war derives from the human soul, and I do not see that this human soul has changed. War has certainly not changed in the Third World. Even now it is threatening to engulf parts of the Second World, and one day it may even penetrate to the First. I believe that it is against this kind of war and for this kind of war that all of us need to prepare. The kind of low-tech war that has taken place in the Former Yugoslavia is not impossible in any state and is actually the future. It is for this and not for the highly sophisticated technological forms of warfare that all of us should prepare, and into which we should put our thoughts.

CHANGING POTENTIALS AND PURPOSES

15

BEYOND WAR AND TOTALITARIANISM: THE NEW DYNAMICS OF VIOLENCE

Pierre Hassner

To consider the transformations of violence is to think of St Petersburg. It is to think of the Petrograd Soviet, of the siege of Leningrad, of the mysterious 'Leningrad affair', of the assassination of Galina Starovoitova. What could illuminate better the main theme of this chapter than the dynamics which link revolution, war, totalitarianism and crime? In our *fin de siècle*, we may almost feel the pattern that underlines the great prophetic *fin de siècle* novel of Andrei Belyi, *Petersburg,* written after the revolution of 1905: 'A sphere, or circle, that widens and brings about disintegration and death'.[1]

What does this disintegration mean? Does it bring death or a new birth of peace? We don't know, because at this new turn of the century and of the millennium, the evolution of violence is highly contradictory: if, as I shall argue, violence undergoes a double process of diffusion and fragmentation, does that lead to its implosion or to its explosion, or to both, according to regions of the globe or to periods of the new century? I shall not attempt to predict, for I know one thing: that the events of the 21st century will be produced by trends and countertrends, whose relative strength and precise combinations can completely modify their meaning in one direction or another, and are by definition unpredictable. To take some of the trends observed and discussed at the present time: certainly the dimension of cultural and religious identity, of ethnic and family solidarity, takes on a new importance as consequence of the decline in the traditional political, economic and ideological cleavages, but that does not mean a clash of civilisations. It may just as well mean new combinations through mutual influences or culture conflicts within countries or regions, as between Hutus and Tutsis, or between advocates and opponents of President Clinton's

---

1   A. Belyi, *Petersburg.* Translator's introduction p. xxi. (Midland Books Edition, 1988).

G. Prins and H. Tromp (eds.), The Future of War, 197-211.
© 2000 Kluwer Law International. Printed in the Netherlands.

impeachment. Neither the degree of conflict or interpenetration nor their macro or micro level are predetermined.

Similarly, we can speak of a crisis of masculinity, but does that mean, as Frank Fukuyama believes,[2] that we are moving towards a world run by women and therefore more peaceful, or towards a violent reassertion of young males, within as well as across societies? We can speak of the decline of territory as a source of conflict, but we see a new salience of old geopolitical and geoeconomic stakes and vulnerabilities, concerning oil and gas pipelines from the Caspian to Turkey or China, water in the Middle East, oil and diamonds in Africa. But will these be superseded in the course of the next century by new findings, geological or technological? Will information technology ensure a stable superiority to the current leader, the United States, or make it more vulnerable? Or, to take the social and political dimension, on which I shall concentrate, will the rise of possessive or bourgeois individualism and the decline of the state lead to a bland, if prosaic, world, or to a renaissance of heroic, perhaps nihilistic, search for absolutes, or to an anarchy which, in turn, may produce a new authoritarianism or a new class struggle?

The late Ernst Gellner, in his last book, was proposing 'a new law of three stages: at first, violence was contingent and optional. In a second state violence became pervasive, mandatory and normative. Military skills became central to the dominant ethos. In the third stage, which we are at present entering: violence becomes once again optional, counter-productive and probably fatal.'[3] The crux of the argument is that agricultural societies were static and needed to be warlike to defend a fixed economic product, while, with prolonged economic growth, the balance went away from coercers towards producers and traders. But if growth stops, the coercers may return to power, and the evolution of technology may lead to their mutual neutralisation or, on the contrary, to an advantage for a nuclear first-strike or to an increased blackmailing or destructive power for more dispersed groups of more fanatical individuals.

---

2   F. Fukuyama, 'Women and the evolution of world politics', 77 *Foreign Affairs*, no. 5 (September-October, 1998).
3   E. Gellner, 'War and violence', in: *Anthropology and Politics* (Oxford: Basil Blackwell, 1995), p. 160.

Indeed, who can know whether the proliferation of nuclear and other weapons of mass destruction will lead to mutual deterrence or to a cycle of preventive offensive and retaliatory use, or whether China will be integrated in the capitalist system, or will disintegrate from within or make a bid for regional or global hegemony?

The name of the game is the unpredictable interplay of 'man, the state and war', to use Kenneth Waltz's triad, or, to complicate it even further, of the anthropological, the social, economic, technological, and political dimensions of the structure of the evolution of actors and of the system in a world where, as Brecht once said, the chess figures keep changing not only their rank but their shape and keep not only competing but interpenetrating.

The angle through which I would like to consider those complex interactions is the link between war and revolution. Three important French thinkers, Elie Halévy, in his Oxford lectures[4], Raymond Aron in *The Century of Total War*[5], and François Furet, in *Le Passé d'une Illusion*[6], have shown how the First World War produced the crumbling of empires, the rise of the total state and the barbarisation of social relations, which favoured the rise of totalitarian movements which, in turn, provoked the Second World War.

Today, after the end of the latter, through the defeat of nazism and the end of the Cold War through the defeat of communism, interstate wars and totalitarian revolutions seem equally inconceivable, at least in the part of the world dominated by mature capitalism. But is this also valid for the dynamics of violence of which they have been, in this century, the carriers or delivery vehicles? Anyone who has studied, as I have, the war in former Yugoslavia or the fate of refugees in the present world, must look beyond interstate war and totalitarian power to the collective passions and to the situation of modern man deprived of community and roots by the complexity of technological society or, at the other end of the scale, by the archaïc violence of fanaticism and banditry, to the subnational fights of civil wars and to the transnational movements of refugees and mafias.

---

4   E. Halevy, *L'Ere des tyrannies* (Paris, Gallimard, 1938), pp. 174-199.
5   R. Aron, *The Century of Total War* (Paris, Gallimard 1955).
6   F. Furet, *Le Passé d'une Illusion: Essai sur l'Idée communiste au XXme siècle* (Paris, R. Laffont, 1995).

Is one not led, then, to a distinction (which may indeed be too vague and facile) between modernity, which would be the domain both of national states, of totalitarian ideologies and of Clausewitzian wars, post-imperial pre-modernity (which we would find in parts of Africa, but also of the Balkans and of the former Soviet Union) and the post-modernity of the interdependence and interpenetration at the level of global society? It is difficult to escape this vocabulary when, in relation with our topic, we read more and more about 'post-modern terrorism'[7], 'post-modern war'[8], and 'The Post-modern State and World Order'.[9] Beyond the semantic issue, at any rate, the question with which we are dealing is indeed the hypothesis, put forward in particular by Hans Magnus Enzensberger in his essay on civil wars[10], of a violence which is both molecular (whether we call it pre-modern or not) and global (whether or not we call it post-modern), replacing the modern violence of interstate wars and totalitarian ideologies.

This hypothesis, however stimulating, is probably excessive, for it takes no account of the great diversity of regional conditions: certainly drug trafficking and urban violence, ethnic conflict and terrorism are present everywhere in our globalised world, but crime has declined in the United States, fragile multi-national countries like Canada or Belgium may break up, but are more likely to do so on the model of Czechoslovakia than on that of Yugoslavia, Tokyo is not Karachi, Los Angeles or Prague are not Tigali or Grozny. Nor do local conflicts – in spite of globalisation and transnational networks – spread as they did in the bipolar world of the Cold War or in that of the pre-1914 multipolar balance of power.

There are a few findings, however, which seem beyond dispute. Two are well-known and accepted by now: the great majority of wars, since 1945, are civil wars or at least have started as such, and the great majority of victims are civilians themselves. According to K.J. Holsti, 90 per cent of the victims of fighting died in civil wars, and 90 per cent of these dead were civilians.[11]

---

7   W. Laqueur, 'Postmodern terrorism', 75 *Foreign Affairs* no. 5 (September-October, 1996, p. 24-36).

8   C.H. Gray, *Postmodern War: the New Politics of Conflict* (London: Routledge, 1997).

9   R. Cooper, *The Post-Modern State and the World Order* (London: Demos, 1996).

10   H.M. Enzensberger, *Aussichten auf den Bürgerkrieg* (Frankfurt, Suhrkamp, 1994).

11   Cf. K.J. Holsti, *The State, War and the State of War* (Cambridge, Cambridge University Press, 1996).

But there is another statistic which is much less frequently mentioned and which made a deep impression on me when I first encountered it: the victims – whether civilian or not – of 20th century wars are much less numerous than those of genocidal and totalitarian massacres. According to Rudolph Rummel, among the victims of collective violence, around 150 million have been killed *by their own governments*, as compared with 35 million victims of wars, including the two world conflicts.[12]

If the 20th century was, according to Aron, the century of total war, then this war pitted governments against one part of the whole of their own people.[13] The slogan with which one could best sum up the history of the 20th century is probably the turning around, both by Lenin and by Ludendorf, of Clausewitz's famous formula ('War is the continuation of politics by other means') into 'Politics is the continuation of war by other means'.

The link, which we already mentioned, between wars in the 20th century and its totalitarian revolutions, consists not only in a historical sequence but also, and more deeply, in an intimate moral and political connection. It is best expressed by Carl Schmitt in the triad 'Total enemy, total war, total state'.[14] Military technology and ideological passions combine to erase the divisions between the domestic and the external, the rule of law and international anarchy, civilian populations and combattants which secular states and international law had instituted in order to limit and channel violence.

Today the question is whether the turn of the century marks a reversal of this evolution. If the 20th century was the century of violence, Could it be that the 21st should be that of peace? After the two world wars and the defeat of the two great totalitarian ideologies, this question is again before us.

Some philosophers think that the catastrophes of the 20th century were a huge parenthesis and that the march towards democracy and peace, in the name of commerce and science, of freedom and reason, is resuming, as it was envisaged by 18th and 19th century thinkers. The idea that prosperity brings democracy

---

12 Cf. R. Rummel, *Death by Government* (New Brunswick, Transaction, 1994).
13 See N. Werth, 'Un état contre son peuple', in: S. Courtois (ed.), *Le livre noir du communisme* (Paris, Seuil, 1997).
14 C. Schmitt, 'Totaler Feind, totaler Krieg, totaler Staat', in: Quaritsch *et al. Positionen und Begriffe* (Berlin, Duncker & Humblot, 1989).

and that democracy brings peace or, at any rate, that democracies don't fight each other, is central to the discussions of American political science. In the tradition of Norbert Elias, sociologists trace the process through which violence has been civilised or tamed under the influence of the evolution of manners, of institutions or of economics. For as Kant, who is being rediscovered, had predicted, pacifist optimism is, nowadays, based on interdependence and globalisation, which bring about the victory of society, *i.e.* of individualism and economics, over the state, *i.e.* over politics and warfare. After Clausewitz's formula, it is Charles Tilly's: 'War makes the state and the state makes war'[15] which is being confirmed by its very obsolescence. Not only the totalitarian state but the state as such seem to be linked to war and destined to wither away with it.

THE BOURGEOIS AND THE BARBARIAN

What is certain, at any rate, is that Carl Schmitt's triad mentioned above is not doing well. The union between a total ideology, claiming to be scientific and appealing to a hope, a devotion and a fanaticism of a religious nature, a boundless political power aiming at absorbing the whole of society, and finally a permanent war against a total, domestic or international enemy, exists only in a few relics like North Korea. But its different elements survive to varying degrees. The total state seems to be effectively deprived both of its impermeability and of its freedom of action by the progress of technology, particularly that of communications, and by economic interdependence. Does that mean that total war and total enemies are equally declining? This is where things get more complicated.

Great world wars, on the model of those of 1914-18 and 1939-45 which left such a mark on our century, and the great nuclear war, the fear of which has dominated the last decades, seem to be effectively excluded both through their suicidal character and through the fragmentation of the international system, of regional sub-systems, of blocs and alliances, of the dimensions of power,

---

15   C. Tilly, *Coercion, Capital & European States AD 990-1992* (Oxford, Basil Blackwell, 1993).

of state-ruled communities themselves. But do this fragmentation and multi-dimensionality guarantee the elimination of violence? This is highly debatable.

In the book already quoted – *The State, War and the State of War* – whose very title is an implicit reply to Kenneth Waltz's classic *Man, the State and War*, Holsti, after having reminded us that the vast majority of current violent conflicts are civil wars, goes on to show that their most frequent and fundamental cause is the weakness of the state. Of course, this explanation may seem to be tautological and to lead to highly debatable prescriptions like the one frequently heard in France, which recommends the universal freezing of the *status quo* and the rejection of self-determination, whereas, as Holsti knows well, violence often comes precisely from the effort of a state, which is losing its legitimacy, to hang on to power.

For him, the source of wars is to be sought primarily in the crumbling of colonial and communist empires, in the legitimacy deficit which is both the cause and the consequence of this crumbling, in the mixture of democracy and anarchy which characterises the disputed constitution of new units. Weak powers succeed other weak powers, for, according to him, the true force of state lies in its legitimacy. The absence of a legitimate state or of a recognised authority opens the door to a violence which is no longer that of interstate war but rather of anarchic or organised crime. Hence, a new formulation by Tilly, which completes the one quoted above and goes beyond it: 'Nowadays, the analogy between, on the one hand, making war and building the state and, in the other hand, practising organised crime becomes tragically apt.[16] The consequences one can draw from the tendency to the withering away of interstate war and of the state itself,[17] seem, then, to go in several directions. Looking back at Tilly's first formulation, one can replace 'the state' with 'society', and 'war' with 'criminality', and consider that *crime makes society and society makes crime.*

One may consider that, perhaps for a transitory period, linked both to the collapse of totalitarian dictatorships and of empires and to social modernisation,

---

16   C. Tilly, 'War making and state making as organized crime', in: Evans *et al.*, *Bringing the State Back In* (Cambridge, Cambridge University Press, 1985).
17   Cf. C. Fairbanks, 'The withering of the state (the lust for democracy in E. Europe)', *Uncaptive Minds*, New York (Summer, 1995).

the distinctions between state and society, between public and private, between international and domestic, tend to be erased or at least blurred, and that what tends to disappear is neither the state nor violence, but the monopoly of the former over the latter. One can, as do many empirical studies, show that the links we discussed between totalitarianism and war are being replicated in many complex and contradictory ways by their heirs.

In Russia and in South Africa, in Brazil and in Guatemala, the end of totalitarian, racist or military oppression is followed by an increase in crime and in the feelings of insecurity, and at the same time (at least initially) by a rejection of war and even of political violence, although to a lesser extent. An interesting study written in 1997 by a French sociologist, Anne Le Huérou, shows that in Russia violence appears where it was not expected and *vice-versa*. From totalitarian violence one goes to the crumbling of the regime practically (and astonishingly) without violence, then to a limited terrorist violence, to a rare and limited political violence. This latter is exemplified by the half-hearted character of the 1991 coup attempt. In one part it is explained by the memory of horrors of past war, civil, international and totalitarian terror, and in another by a pathological fear of insecurity, an organised and targeted private violence and above all an incredibly brutal violence embedded in institutions like the police and the army. All this leads, says Le Huérou, to 'a violence whose expressions are numerous but dispersed, disarticulated and without a political expression'.[18] Yet the war in Chechenya and the assassination of many journalists and of Galina Starovoïtova show that both brutality within the army and organised crime are not without political dimensions and consequences.

The same differentiation is shown in many other cases. A study on Columbia by the French specialist Daniel Pécaut concludes that in this country 'Violence leads to the erasing of the political dimension proper'.[19] With Michel Wieviorka commenting on these studies and others on the mystical violence of the 'Martyrs of Revolution' in Iran or of the Aum sect in Japan, one is tempted to speak, of 'a new paradigm of violence', which would be based on its becoming above all 'infrapolitical' and 'metapolitical'.[20]

---

18 A. Le Huerou, 'Russie: les paradoxes de la violence?', in: Wieviorka, 'Un nouveau paradigme de la violence', *Cultures et Conflits* (Spring-Summer 1998).

19 D. Pecaut, 'Réflexions sur la violence en Colombie', in: Héritier, *De la Violence* (Paris, Odile Jacob, 1997).

20 Wieviorka, *op.cit.*, pp. 45-52.

One could argue at least as well, however, that we are dealing, for the time being, less with a new paradigm than with the disintegration of *all* paradigms and with the (perhaps provisional) triumph of incoherence and fluidity. Perhaps it is precisely this that is meant by a 'post-modern paradigm'? One is tempted to think so and, without claiming to recover a lost rationality or globality, to sketch a few directions which would enable us to introduce a few dynamic elements into this paradigm. I shall try to propose two personal formulations and to put into perspective three broader but divergent interpretations, proposed by three important historians of war and violence, two elsewhere in this volume.

The first formulation, which is a kind of personal refrain of mine, is that of the dialectic of the bourgeois and the barbarian, tending to replace the Hegelian one of the master and the slave, or the duality, emphasised by Aron, of the diplomat and the soldier. The latter fitted with the Clausewitzian trinity of the government, army and people, and was fully valid for the relation between diplomacy and conventional war. It is being challenged on the political level by the decline of interstate war and of the state itself and, on the technological level, by the emergence of the nuclear and of the subconventional (from terrorism to 'low-intensity' warfare) dimensions.

Prolonging the nuclear revolution, we have today the American-promoted 'revolution in military affairs', which is typically the form of war of an essentially civil or bourgeois society which tries to be sparing with the life of its sons and tries to rely on technology in order to impose its superiority without having to fight. This is what Edward Luttwak calls 'post-heroic warfare'. Thanks to one's superiority in information capacity and to the progress of precision, the name of the game is to paralyse or blind the enemy rather than destroy him. This is obviously a way to maintain the superiority of the United States, but it is also a way to spare first of all American lives (in accordance with the axiom of 'zero deaths'), then those of civilian populations in general, and finally, those of enemy troops themselves. It is the form of war of a society which is averse to violence and risk and which is interested above all in economics and technology. As Lawrence Freedman argues in this book, there are strong reasons for scepticism.

At the other extreme, going further in the direction opened by terrorism, one finds forms of violence which, far from sparing civilian populations, are obviously targetting them: they are to be destroyed through genocide, humiliated or tortured by religious or totalitarian fanaticism, or, more prosaïcally, expelled by ethnic cleansing, or exploited by looting.

The specificity of the soldier fighting other soldiers disappears in favour of the technician or the bureaucrat, in one case, of the bandit or the militaria-men, the mafioso or the mercenary, the desperado or the warlord in the other.

In a sense, we are dealing with two separate worlds and in cases like Yugoslavia and, even more, Somalia and Rwanda, the problems of intervention have less to do with the rivalry between states than with the distance between societies.[21] But in another sense, the two worlds are in constant interaction and interpenetration, not only through the arms and drugs trades, or the networks of organised crime, or the flows of refugees, but also in a deeper sense through two competing processes. They can be seen as either alternative or complementary. These I have called the embourgeoisement of the barbarian and the barbarisation of the bourgeois.

From the technical point-of-view, the universe of the computer and of the laser on the one hand, and that of the Kalashnikov and of the machete on the other, may well converge. The democratisation and privatisation of violence can put the most sophisticated techniques into the most uncontrollable hands. The complexity of advanced societies can be turned against them, and they may themselves be driven to finance their own 'house barbarians' out of the illusion of controlling them, as happened with the United States' adventure with Islamic fundamentalists turned from anti-Soviet freedom fighters (in Afghanistan) into anti-American terrorists (at the New York Trade Center). The proliferation of nuclear and other weapons of mass destruction and the decrease in their cost[22] may in the long run challenge both the technological advance and the relative peace of developed societies.[23]

---

21 A distance which may sometimes be exaggerated as well as minimised. Cf. L. Freedman, 'The changing forms of military conflict', 40 *Survival*, no. 4 (Winter, 1998-99), pp. 46-48.

22 See the calculations of M. Shubik, 'Terrorism, technology and the socio-economics of death, *Comparative Strategy*, 16 (1997).

23 See C. Ikle, The second coming of the Nuclear Age, *Foreign Affairs* (January-February, 1996): 'The next Lenin', *The National Interest* (Spring, 1997).

From the point-of-view of the evolution of societies, the two processes we mentioned are at work, and can even more easily be combined and either compensate or reinforce each other. On the one hand, the *embourgeoisement* of the barbarian is at work in post-totalitarian and post-warlike societies: from Russia and China to South Africa and Mozambique, and even in Mr Milosevic's and Mrs Plavsic's two Serbias, the attraction of western capital has seemed at times to trump that of ideology and of arms. What is certain is that the 'creative destruction' of capitalism seems to transform social relations even more deeply than the latter. But it remains to be seen whether capitalism replaces violence or whether it gives rise, with it, to new and possibly monstrous combinations. General privatisation, including that of the army and of justice, is as inimical to the idea of the rule of law as totalitarian general politicisation. The child of their marriage may be a form of society where the mafia sense of 'contract' is as important as the legal one.

One may of course hope that this represents a first phase of wild capitalism (today's gangster is tomorrow's businessman) and that present *mafiosi* will learn the advantages of fair competition and of legal guarantees like their predecessors in western societies. But precisely the latter have already experienced barbarisation through fascism. They are not immune to new authoritarian or xenophobic temptations if their economic and social crisis gets deeper. If, nowadays, the threat perceived is less that of foreign armies than that of immigration, terrorism and domestic insecurity, a drift towards the search for scapegoats or towards a police state cannot fully be excluded.

My other remark concerns the ambiguity of the term 'police' and the different directions in which it can lead. Once, contrary to the classical model, international violence penetrates within, in particular through terrorism, and, conversely, external interventions seem more often destined to re-establish or keep order and peace in troubled parts of the world than to fight states or conquer territories, the distinction between army and police tends to be blurred or to become counter-productive. The discussions on the respective roles of NATO and of the international civil police force in Bosnia are a case in point. But the idea of a 'constabulary ethos', as opposed to the traditional professional military ethos, or the new figure of the 'guardian-soldier',[24] is more and more revived in connection with peace-keeping operations.

Paradoxically, at the very moment when there are reasons to fear a domestic police state, there are reasons to call for an 'international police force'. The paradox can easily be brushed aside if one remarks that in one case when we talk of police we mean 'repression' and in the other we think rather of 'protection', and that there are few abuses to fear from an international authority which, precisely, is not a state. But it comes back very rapidly if one is reminded that, in the name of a problematic 'international community', it is states which are called to exercise a kind of protectorate and, hence, their armies may fall back into the roles and reactions of colonial armies, with all their historical ambiguities. Suffice it to think of American and Canadian troops in Somalia.

The best way I can think of to throw light on these ambiguities, as well as on many others connected with possible comparisons between the present situation and those which have preceded it or may succeed it, is to confront the diverging diagnoses of three great historians, namely Pierre Chaunu, John Keegan and Martin van Creveld.

THREE INTERPRETATIONS ON THE FUTURE OF VIOLENCE

Let us start first, however, with the hypothesis of Robert Cooper, whom I have already quoted on the theme of the post-modern state. Perhaps, he says, it is the strong modern state which represents an historical anomaly, and the post-modern state will go back to the weakness of the pre-modern one.[25] The thought of Pierre Chaunu seems to move in the same direction, but he goes back much further in time and his conclusions are much more dramatic. According to him, over a period of 5 to 10,000 years, the institutionalisation of war between polities, or political units, has reduced murderous violence. During this period, he claims that the percentage of the population which was a victim

---

24 Cf. G. Daniker, 'The guardian-soldier: on the nature and use of future armed forces, UNIDIR *Research Paper* 56 (1995).

25 R. Cooper, 'Gibt es eine neue Weltordnung', in: Senghas (ed.), *Frieden machen* (Frankfurt, Suhrkamp, 1997), p. 119.

of violent death has decreased from 10 per cent to 1 per cent. While he admits that modern nuclear weapons are an exception, he maintains that the progress of armaments has represented a progress for peace, in the long term, and that the decline of war, coupled with that of the state, can only mean the return to a much more murderous social violence.[26]

John Keegan seems to adopt the opposite position. For him, far from representing a universal progress, war is a cultural invention, and its Clausewitzian version as a continuation of politics – with a tendency to escalate to the extremes and a preference for direct confrontation – constitutes a highly destructive contribution of Western culture. Today, a cultural transformation is on the way, partly because of nuclear weapons and partly because war is no longer considered a normal, legitimate or productive institution. However, Keegan does not go as far as optimistic abolitionists like John Mueller.[27] He argues that, while war can and must be abolished, violence will continue to exist and that 'a world without armies – disciplined, obedient and law-abiding armies – would be uninhabitable'.[28] 'The world community needs more than it has ever done, skillful and disciplined warriors, who are ready to put themselves at the service of its authority. They must fight for civilisation – against ethnic bigots, regional warlords, ideological intransigents, common pillagers and organised international criminals'.[29] But for that they must unlearn the western way of war and learn again the ritualisation, the negotiation and the restraint of oriental and primitive war.

Both visions raise as many problems as they solve. Chaunu is a little too quick to reject the murderous consequences of organised warfare and modern technology, and to announce an apocalyptic rise of social violence, produced by the decline of insterstate war. As for Keegan, his prophetic concluding paragraphs seem astonishingly optimistic in at least four respects.

First, where could his international armies acquire their disciplined and law-abiding character, given the decline of the state and the permissive character

---

26 P. Chaunu, 'Violence, guerre et paix', *Politique Etrangère* 4 (Winter, 1996-97), 887-898.

27 J. Mueller, *Retreat from Doomsday. On the obsolescence of major war* (London, Harper Collins/Basic, 1990).

28 J. Keegan, *A History of Warfare* (London, Hutchinson, 1993), p. 384.

29 *Ibid.*, p. 391-392.

of modern society? Can one have the virtues of the regiment without its dangers, which Keegan criticises when speaking of Clausewitz? Secondly, whence would that elusive entity, the 'international community' draw its authority and its ability to act? Thirdly, if it must cross swords with the list of enemies he describes, this means a permanent and not necessarily victorious fight against very diverse and powerful forces. Finally, why would these pillagers, these bigots and these criminals conform to the style, the restraint and the ritualisation which characterise the primitive and the oriental way of war and, if they don't, how could the forces of the international community hold to it unilaterally? In other words, can someone like Keegan who puts cultural factors above political ones, take it for granted that the conflict, which would pit a UN-type bureaucratic-bourgeois culture against a criminal, macho and mafioso one, will adopt a style which is normally alien to both?

At first sight, van Creveld's vision seems more plausible than either Chaunu's apocalyptic and nostalgic pessimism or Keegan's globalist-culturalist optimism.

Like his two colleagues, van Creveld announces the decline of Clausewitzian interstate war. In his view, it is because of the decline of the state itself. Like Keegan and most English-speaking authors, he accuses the Clausewitzian vision of being both rationalistic and brutal. Like Keegan, he underlines the cultural and religious dimension of war. But his conclusion is very different. He thinks the decline of the state, as well as the evolution of technology, brings about the obsolescence of armies, in particular of conventional forces, whether national or international. He argues in this volume, as elsewhere, that nuclear weapons make the great war impossible, including between Israel and the Arabs or between India and Pakistan. The order of the day belongs to 'low-intensity' conflicts, ranging from Intifada to guerrilla warfare *via* terrorism. They bring about a kind of return to the Middle Ages and express the anthropological features – from the festive to the sacred, from sacrifice to violence – which have always produced the revival of wars. But the proliferation of persistent, small-scale threats promises to be less deadly than the great modern wars.[30]

One would be tempted to adopt this relative optimism based on the vision of a moderate anarchy if , on the one hand, as some of Van Creveld's critics have

---

30   M. van Creveld, *The Transformation of War* (New York, Free Press, 1991).

pointed out,[31] events like the Gulf War did not show that there still are states, armies and wars, and if, on the other hand, the new economics of violence did not promise small groups, or even individuals, the nuclear, chemical or above all biological power which once belonged only to superpowers or at least to states.[32] We are back with the Aum sect, and with the possible alliance between modern technologies and the destructive religions or ideological madness which characterised totalitarianism. Can't one imagine (following Jack London quoted by Laqueur) at the level of individuals the 'Unit Veto System' (envisaged by Morton Kaplan[33] at the level of states) implying the possession of a 'Doomsday Machine' and the possibility for each of destroying the planet? Of course no technological progress which can be reasonably foreseen would go so far and it would be more than misleading to let this thought guide our fears and our policies. It is always a mistake to neglect the normal case in favour of the apocalyptic or extreme one. But the experience of our century should teach us that the extreme case may unexpectedly become the normal one. This possibility should be kept at the back of our minds. It may be useful to meditate on the extreme case, precisely because reality, as far as one can guess, is likely to be dominated by the multiplicity of actors and alliances, of organisations and governmental or non-governmental networks and, through these, by many different forms of violence. Precisely because fluidity and complexity are the order of the day after the decline of the great wars and the great totalitarianisms, it may be useful to remind ourselves that the dream of unity and the contrasting nightmares of anarchy, of total domination and of total destruction, will stay with us during the next century and into the next millennium.[34]

---

31   G. Saunders, *The New World Strategy* (New York, Free Press, 1991).

32   R. Betts, 'The new threat of mass destruction', 77 *Foreign Affairs*, No. 1 (January-February, 1998). See also M. Shubik, *loc. cit.* and W. Laqueur, 'The new face of terrorism', *The Washington Quarterly* (Autumn, 1998).

33   M. Kaplan, *System and Process in International Politics* (New York, John Wiley, 1957).

34   I have drawn freely on an article published in French, in *Histoire et Anthropologie* 16 (January-June, 1998), and reproduced in *Esprit* (December, 1998).

16

CIVIL AND UNCIVIL WAR

Gwyn Prins

The traveller leaving the small Belgian town of Binche soon finds himself on a long, straight road that undulates up and down gentle hills in the direction of Mons. At the crest of a hill not far from Mons, he reaches a crossroads. Today, a yellow flashing light marks this spot; and flash it might: for, as the traveller passes across that intersection, unmarked, he passes the threshold into the European experience of war in the 20th century.

On 20 August 1914, an advance party of German reconnaissance cavalry arrived, by train, at the station in Binche. They detrained and camped for the night and the next morning set off in the direction of Mons along that same road. They were spied by British observers on top of the mine dumps, who relayed the news to the British Expeditionary Force in Mons. A contingent of British reconnaissance bicyclists was sent out to investigate further. Meanwhile, the German cavalry having reached a gentle slope moved from a walk to a trot and arrived across the brow of the hill sooner than the British bicyclists had expected. An exchange of fire took place and L/14196 Private Parr, of the Middlesex Regiment, became the first British soldier to lose his life in the First World War. He did so at about the place where now the yellow light flashes at the road intersection. Each party returned to report and the following day German forces began a two-pronged advance upon Mons.[1]

The main thrust was towards the Mons-Condé canal, to the right. On 23 August at the Obourg cement works, during those first hours of the First World War, fierce fighting occurred. In the end, the Middlesex regiment could no longer

---

1 I am grateful to Christopher Donnelly for this information, and for walking the ground with me. For the context of the Mons campaign, see J. Keegan, *The First World War* (London, Hutchinson, 1998), pp. 107-110.

G. Prins and H. Tromp (eds.), The Future of War, 213-225.
© 2000 *Kluwer Law International. Printed in the Netherlands.*

hold its position and was forced to retreat. Lieutenant Maurice Dease, of the Royal Fusiliers, kept his machine-gun section in action until he and all the gunners were dead, bar one. Private Sid Godley continued to fire until he ran out of ammunition. Dease and Godley were awarded the first Victoria Crosses for valour of the war. In recognition of the courage with which the Middlesex regiment had fought, in the graveyard at St Symphorien where British soldiers were buried by German hands, was also erected a granite column on which their German enemies inscribed a recognition of the courage of the 'Royal' Middlesex Regiment. The Middlesex regiment was not a royal regiment; but so bravely had the soldiers fought that their German adversaries assumed that it was.

Such chivalrous – such civil – conduct continued to splutter in sporadic episodes, such as the celebrated Christmas truce and football matches; but it did not, could not, last long in the face of the brutalising juggernaut of war by gas, by shell and by machine gun – an experience so terrible and so alien that, in the eyes of British war poets like Wilfred Owen, it took on a demonic life of its own, consuming lives and any fragile principles of humanity indiscriminately.

That wild and wanton power of war, making itself its own end whatever may have been the initial impetus in political disagreement, has been the rising characteristic of war-making in Europe's long century of violence. At the other end from the gentlemanly tragedy of St Symphorien we find Dame Anne Warburton's report on the employment of systematic rape in the wars of the former Yugoslavia. Copious and dreadful evidence exists of the manner in which the rape of Muslim women was used by Bosnian Serbs as one among the other available means to break the will and to annihilate the identity of Bosnian Muslims. Women of all ages were gathered together and subjected to continuous and random assault; certain women were taken aside and subjected to systematic rape with the explicit intention of making them pregnant so that, by carrying Serbian children, they would expiate the sin of being born Muslim, as their tormentors told them. Such violation of body and mind led to suicides and to profound mental disturbance. It offers an unusually precise illustration of the manner in which uncivil behaviour has become the norm rather than the exception in civil wars. As Martin van Creveld argues, it is a lasting consequence of the way in which the Nazi offensives of the Second World War flagrantly and deliberately added terrorising and killing civilians to war by soldiers against soldiers.[2] A countervailing force arose also: the explicit *protection* of civilians under the expanded Geneva protocols.

The campaign of systematic rape in the former Yugoslavia is illuminating of the same fundamental proposition about the nature of war as the Geneva protocols. For both implicitly recognised that war is an exceptional activity. It is the licensed trespass to cross normally prohibited boundaries. To mark those boundaries, there is a need to 'exceptionalise' such acts: soldiers wear uniforms, are subject to discipline, they tread a narrow path between action and inaction in combat (a point well made in John Keegan's justly famous book, which explains, with harrowing, but in some sense reassuring, clarity how often commanders have experienced difficulty in motivating their troops to risk their lives and to take the lives of others, when all human instinct cries out that the sane thing to do is to flee).[3] There is a narrow path to be trodden between sanity and insanity also.

In 1899 the participants in the Hague conference gathered under the paradox that modern 19th century ways of making war – the application of industrial process to killing that had first been seen on the battlefields of the American civil war – might make war simultaneously morally intolerable and politically useless. In 1999, the same question persists, but in an adapted form. By the transformation of war in the 20th century, we have been forced to enlarge our scope so that we consider not only uncivil behaviour in wars, but uncivil wars also.

There are distinguishable ways in which the word 'civil' is employed. One recognises value in the enemy. That value may be perhaps at the lowest level, only financial: it makes better sense to hold the unseated knight for ransom rather than to cut his throat. But, in the later 19th century, war widened its grasp upon a society facilitated by the powers of industry. Simultaneously, there occurred formalisations, codifications of the fundamental humanity of enemies. It was as if, recognising the increasing strength of the military/technical momentum towards indiscriminate destruction, a countervailing tendency arose, which

---

2   M. van Creveld, 'Postmodern war' in (ed.) C. Townsend, *Oxford Illustrated History of Warfare* (Oxford University Press, 1997).

3   J. Keegan, *The Face of Battle* (London, Jonathan Cape, 1976).

attempted to assert what had hitherto been implicitly assumed. There were two strands to this.

The first was a continuing reaction to the proliferating ingenuity of the means of destruction, of which the St Petersburg Convention of 1868 on the use of expanding ('dumdum') bullets, was the first attempt to outlaw inhumane weapons. It stated plainly that 'the only legitimate object which states should endeavour to accomplish during war is to weaken the *military forces* (emphasis added) of the enemy', and that anything which sought to do more than disable soldiers by inflicting unnecessary pain or injury was in violation of the principles of humanity. It led to a succession of such arms control measures. The promiscuous use of poison gas in the First World War propelled initiatives to outlaw weapons of mass destruction. This has led in 1997 to the US-sponsored effort to ban chemical weapons. There has been a continuing effort to extend this ambit, recently recurring in the World Court ruling of 1996, that the use of nuclear weapons, by virtue of their indiscriminate effects, fell under that prohibition. Similarly, attempts to proscribe the use of plastic shrapnel (used to make fragments in a victim's body invisible to X-ray) or blinding lasers have continued to make the St Petersburg point that clean and unclean ways of giving death to the legitimate enemy exist; whereas the campaign against land mines expresses the rising public demand that the means of waging war should not place non-combatants at risk in the way that, classically and most numerously in the world's arsenals, land mines do.

The second strand in the countervailing tendency was first spun in the St Petersburg and The Hague conferences of 1899 and 1907 and the Conventions of 1907 on the proper conduct of soldiers in war, with regard to civilians and non-combatants, and in the handling of prisoners of war. From this came a set of principles which, honoured in the breach, still have considerable power to shock international public opinion. Both strands express, in modern form, the principles of Just War. The first of these, that one should have justification in going to war (*ius ad bellum*), has been reaffirmed each time in the 20th century that a dictator has hastened to offer the justification of self-defence for an act of aggression. It has been the second principle, that wars should be conducted cleanly – that there should be *ius in bello* –, that violence should be discriminate as between combatants and non-combatants and proportionate to the degree of violence and injury offered, that has created increasing difficulty. Yet it has been principally by these means that in the 20th century international opinion has sought to outlaw 'uncivil' behaviour in wars. Now, as we approach the turn of the millennium, it becomes plain that another meaning of the word 'civil' is more important.

'Civil' distinguishes between war and crime. It refers to two circumstances which are quite different and only in part reconcilable, although both spring from the manner in which civil society is related to state power.

The first of these new senses was defined rapidly and strongly at the end of the Second World War, as a consequence of the behaviour of the Third Reich. It addresses the problem of uncivil behaviour in wars by a rogue state, whose leadership, supported by large parts of its population, subscribed to a doctrine obnoxious to civilised behaviour. Whether one bases judgment upon the contentious Hossbach Memorandum of the Wannzee Conference, upon Hitler's own writings about Jews, or upon the evidence of conduct in the war against the Jews (as Lucy Dawidowicz has named the entire period of genocidal action from 1932 to 1945), the fact was that this aspect in particular of the Third Reich faced the international community with a new problem.[4] The way that it was resolved at Nuremberg was to establish the principle of individual responsibility and with it the concept of 'war crime'. By extension, Nuremberg gave prominence to a key question and a key concept that has framed the approach to uncivil war ever since; the question is that of who sets the norms. The Nuremberg answer, of course, was that it was the victors; but, as the Nuremberg principle was extended through instruments like the Helsinki process, that historically specific consequence became broadened and softened. The concept is that of 'human rights' – a great new 20th century invention which led in 1948 to promulgation of the Genocide Convention, one of the most widely subscribed of all the international legal instruments of the post-Second World War period. This led in turn to the foundation of the present pressure for enforceable human rights.

Until the early 1990s, it was generally thought that the European continent would not see such acts as led to Nuremberg again, fifty years after the fiery collapse of the Third Reich and five years after the quiet collapse of the Soviet Union. The death of Yugoslavia proved that to be wrong. Within the evolution of that tangled conflict there came a decisive development. For, whereas the

---

4   L. Dawidowicz, *The War against the Jews 1933-45* (Harmondsworth, Penguin, 1975).

international motivation for intervention over Bosnia in 1991 was for *raison d'état*, that in 1999 in Kosovo is fundamentally different. The drama plays as the centenary conference convenes; but what is already evident is that the motivation is expressed in a mandate for enforceable human rights, given priority over unqualified sovereignty. It stands beside the other notable example of the same trend – the endeavour to extradite General Pinochet from Britain to Spain to answer for acts committed in Chile. This drama, too, plays as the conference convenes. In Lord Steyn's opinion, given at the first House of Lords' appeal hearing of the case, he took his reason for upholding extradition back to Nuremberg. He argued that if Pinochet were permitted the defence of blanket immunity as a former head of state, then so too could Hitler and his colleagues have been in respect of the holocaust; and, by implication, Nuremberg would have been a mis-trial.[5] The cases of Kosovo and Pinochet show how sharp has become the 1999 restatement of the 1899 St Petersburg paradox.

For better or worse (and largely not entirely for worse) this inheritance is the one deployed to face another sense in which uncivil war is encountered. This is in the context of civil war and intra-state violence. In Israel, in the former Yugoslavia, in Rwanda, in Zaïre, a lengthening list of regions at the faultlines of international politics is scarred with what John Keane has called 'uncivil wars ... [which] ... ransack the legal monopoly of armed force long claimed by states. They put an end to the distinction between war and crime'.[6]

Intra-state violence in these inflamed and increasingly common contexts shares six features. First, they tend to occur in post-colonial territories or in regions where previously an imposed imperial solution enforced the legal monopoly of force; secondly, they are frequently, indeed usually, circumstances where differences are expressed in terms of ethnic differentiation. This second feature imparts particular venom to the rest. Thirdly, given that the language of conflict is ethnic, different groups deploy mutually-exclusive invented histories of themselves and their enemies; fourthly, about these histories no argument is tolerated other than with bullets; for – the fifth characteristic – such riven communities are disfigured by a lust for simplification, a denial of complexity, a preference

---

5   House of Lords Judgment-Regina *v* Bartle and the Commissioner of Police for the Metropolis and Others, *ex parte* Pinochet, 25 November 1998, opinion of Lord Justice Steyn.
6   J. Keane, *Reflections on Violence* (London, Verso, 1996), p. 141.

for (in John Keane's elegant phrase) 'a chosen ignorance'.[7] He explains: it is 'not the ignorance of innocence. It thereby has a tendency to crash into the world, crushing or throttling everything that crosses its path.' And all this gives peculiar impulsion to the sixth feature which is that, in circumstances so defined and so described, the ends are easily seen by combatants to justify the means. Hence, the chilling combination of cruelty and familiarity between persecutors and victims that was so prominent a feature of the wars during the death of Yugoslavia in the early 1990s.[8]

In all these circumstances, the 'international community' – meaning, in so far as it exists, those flashes of self-conscious community of value and purpose expressed commonly and simultaneously in the streets, newspapers, parliaments or chancelleries of different countries – has felt increasingly obliged to intervene and do something. That is a laudable consequence of the post-Nuremberg inheritance; but that same inheritance creates the problem, which the international community has wrestled with since the end of the Soviet Union, namely that of applying institutions and mechanisms, devised under and for the circumstances of dealing with uncivil behaviour in wars by rogue states, to circumstances of uncivil wars.

In the United Nations era, the first device for responding to pressures to intervene was 'peacekeeping'. Peacekeeping was the deployment of symbolic force based on the consent of all parties and in circumstances where all parties believed that they had more to lose than they had to gain by defying the international community, embodied in the blue-helmeted troops of the United Nations contingents. Those troops, in turn, protected themselves by remaining entirely disengaged from the actual conflict; they were both impartial and neutral; they made no moral judgment as to the rights and wrongs of the combatant parties, but sought by their presence only to separate, to shame through observation of hostilities and atrocities, and thereby to calm circumstances. Their own protection was their conspicuous vulnerability and, thus made explicit, moral authority.

---

7   *Ibid.*, p. 126.
8   For powerful reflections upon this theme, see E. Vulliamy, 'Bosnia: the secret war' reports, *The Guardian*, 1996; M. Ignatieff, *The Warrior's Honour: Ethnic War and the Modern Conscience* (London, Vintage, 1997).

That post-1945 device formed the leading concept with which the international community has entered almost all its interventions, recently and most notably so in the case of the former Yugoslavia. It was in that war that the turning point occurred. It led to a sharper reorientation towards enforceable human rights.

The turning point was in July 1995. The place was the Muslim enclave of Srebrenica and the occasion was the forced evacuation of the enclave by the Dutch battalion of the United Nations Protection Force. The Dutch soldiers were forced to leave without equipment and powerless to protect the civilian inhabitants of the enclave from what followed. This was the planned and premeditated execution of around 6,000 Muslim men. All the elements of Auschwitz were suddenly again apparent in Europe: the forced separation of men from women; transport of the men to a killing ground; the victims ordered to undress before being killed in order to impede the identification of bodies at any future stage. A Dutch soldier being evacuated from Srebrenica in a bus reported seeing neat rows of shoes lined up beside the road in the area of which, later that month, in the United Nations, American Ambassador Madeleine Albright waved spy satellite photographs showing the disturbed earth of mass graves. Subsequently, through the investigations of *Der Spiegel*, it transpired that American spy satellites had earlier photographed lines of bodies after execution and awaiting burial. So, as Prof. Tromp argued in his analysis of the Srebrenica episode, a conspicuous contrast between this and the Nazi final solution was the speed with which incontrovertible confirmation of the atrocity reached the public domain. In the case of the German death camps, the public only became aware when Allied troops reached Belsen (although there is persuasive evidence that the Allied higher command knew the purpose of the camp much earlier). In the case of Srebrenica it was a matter of days. This evidence, combined with the memory of the position taken in Srebrenica during the first crisis in March 1993 when Gen. Philippe Morillon had announced from the town post office to crowds of Muslim women and children 'you are now under the protection of the UN forces ... I will never abandon you.' Yet abandoned they were. The evidence of Srebrenica led first to the passing of the United Nations Security Council Resolution 819 on Safe Areas, and soon thereafter to the implementation of NATO airstrikes, including the use of cruise missiles to attack Bosnian Serb military installations around Banja Luka.

The Srebrenica enclave became the focus point in the summer of 1995 because the strategies and ambitions of major players in the Bosnian crisis had come to pivot upon it. General Radko Mladic wanted the Bosnian civilians out, naturally, in order to incorporate the enclave into the Bosnian Serb republic. He also wanted to humiliate the international community in general and the Dutch in particular for interfering in the region. Revealingly, in an interview in March 1996, he was quoted as saying,

> 'There is no greater shame for us Serbs than to be bombed by some Dutchman. I have no idea whom Holland could bomb on its own. Not even Denmark, but they simply dared to bomb Serbs. Their miserable Van den Broek committed great atrocities and made a great contribution to the collapse of the former Yugoslavia.'[9]

The Bosnian Muslims equally strongly wished to keep civilians in the pocket, for only in this way could they keep the United Nations present and tied down, and only if the UN was present could the enclave be preserved, not in the expectation that it would be permanently held, but as a chip to be bargained against land in a forthcoming settlement.

For its part, the international community wanted to take a principled stand. This was especially true in The Netherlands, where Dutch public opinion strongly supported a more robust line: and The Netherlands alone had offered the Secretary-General of the United Nations a promise of forces. In the event, Dutch deployment and its surrounding diplomacy were clumsily handled. Too many troops were sent, with poor logistics, without any agreement for a helicopter resupply corridor and incoherently armed – a mixture of 'peacekeeping' symbolism and a military mission to be sent into hostile territory. This was not helped by the fact that the enclave was not demilitarised, so there was some force in the Bosnian Serb accusation that the United Nations was partial because it was acting as a military shield for Bosnian Muslim soldiers.

Secondly, Dutch diplomacy was inept. Opposition to withdrawal was maintained beyond the point at which military advice thought it prudent, and with veiled talk on the diplomatic circuit about the need to find a nation to replace The Netherlands in a *roulement* in Srebrenica. All this told the Bosnian Serbs that, put under pressure, the Dutch were likely to crack.

---

9   H. Tromp, 'A clash of paradigms: the fall of Srebrenica and its aftermath', mss. I am grateful to Prof. Tromp for bringing Mladic's quoted remark to my attention.

What finally precipitated the Dutch withdrawal was failure to secure air support in July 1995. As Honig and Both argue convincingly in their definitive account of the Srebrenica episode, Generals Janvier and Smith both sought to deploy an escalation package in support of DutchBat but were overruled by the United Nations representative, Mr Akashi, on the one hand and by the Dutch government on the other, which was fearful that military escalation would place the Dutch soldiers' lives at risk.[10]

But axiomatic to the crisis of Srebrenica was the fact that no-one really believed that the Bosnian Serbs would press their defiance on the United Nations in the way in which Mladic did. After Srebrenica, American diplomacy in particular began to pay closer attention. The successful deployment of air power, the provision of the Rapid Reaction Force with heavy artillery to open the Mount Igman road into Sarajevo were overtures for the rough diplomatic handling which the region's combatants experienced at American hands at Dayton. After Dayton, with the change from UNPROFOR to IFOR, not only did the colour of the vehicles change from white to khaki, but the nature of communication with General Mladic changed also. One IFOR commander has described how, early during his term, he met with the Bosnian Serb military authorities for a one-sided conversation in which he informed them that they would either comply with the Dayton terms or he would hit them with all the military force at his command.

What are the remedies for this type of situation, of which, it appears we may expect to see more? The most immediate, while vivid, are nonetheless only palliatives. After Bosnia, 'peace enforcement' became the rule rather than the exception. With the Bosnian fiasco we have probably seen the end of the curious career of 'conflict resolution' – presented as some sort of clever alternative between diplomacy and force. The problem, perhaps best exemplified by the so-called Oslo 'peace process' for the Middle East, is that it ascribes to the process of negotiation some special power, which plainly it does not possess in the harsh world of *Realpolitik*. Concentrated force rapidly opened the road to Sarajevo which, in turn, led to the banging together of Balkan heads in Dayton by Richard Holbrooke and the Americans, which in turn led to the deployment of a khaki – not white painted – implementation force in the region.

---

10   J.W. Honig & N. Both, *Srebrenica: Record of a War Crime* (Harmondsworth, Penguin, 1996).

This is a developing trend (as Operation Alba showed, just down the coast in Albania).[11] It is doubtful whether ever again NATO forces will be allowed to go symbolically clad or symbolically armed in harm's way.

The lesson may be being learned only slowly, and late. It may be too late to exploit fully the golden moment, which followed the implosion of the Soviet Union. Certainly, Charles William Maynes believes so. The point he makes is that the political leverage from late 20th century military force is switching away from the mid-century idiom of deterrence, back to a more straightforward, late 19th century emphasis upon 'compellence'. '... The uses of force have changed in much of the world', he writes. '... Throughout the Cold War, force was needed to deter the other side from doing bad things outside its borders. Today force is needed to compel the other side to do good things inside its borders.'[12] Modern forces and the prevailing philosophy underpinning them are ill suited to this task.

This change of emphasis has important implications, not least for the way in which Article 2(1) of the United Nations Charter, which states the principle of the sovereign equality of all members, is interpreted. Patently, this is not and will not in the future any longer be uncontroversially the defining case. The possibility exists of reactivating the trusteeship clauses of the Charter (Ch. XII), now not in the context of decolonisation but of the collapse of soft and post-colonial states. However, this will have to be treated with great care because there is danger of falling into the unhelpful 'chosen ignorance' exemplified by such writers as Robert Kaplan and Samuel Huntington.

The second remedy is intellectual rather than practical. It is to resist the Balkanisation of the mind. This is a new coining of the old term Balkanisation applying now not so much to the splitting up of territory as to the atomising of identities. In this regard, five areas of applied research are urgently needed.

---

11 UNA-USA, International Task Force on the Enforcement of U.N. Security Council Resolutions (Chairman, Lord Carrington), *Words to Deeds: Strengthening the U.N.'s Enforcement Capabilities*, Final Report (UNA-USA, New York, 1997); E. Greco, *Delegating Peace Operations: Improvision and Innovation in Georgia and Albania*, UNA-USA International Dialogue on the Enforcement of Security Council Resolutions, No. 7 (UNA-USA, New York, 1998).

12 C.W. Maynes, 'Squandering Triumph: the West botched the Post-Cold War World', 78 *Foreign Affairs* no.1, 1999, 21.

Research on the comparative history of the abuse of history is an unfairly neglected aspect of historical research, but essential for contextualising and the
detoxification of this particularly poisonous trend. Secondly, there would be
virtue in setting uncivil war in its international context. In the Balkans fires
have been stoked beneath a bubbling pot into which has been stirred a brew
of broken totalitarianism with ethnic nationalism, with international action and
an ample supply of weapons. Thirdly – and this is part of a much wider international need – research on stereotyping and the way in which it happens and
in which it is used is urgent and important. Fourth and fifth are practical tasks
which follow from palliative actions already in place. A regime of enforceable
extended human rights is becoming central to the international political agenda
for the next decade.[13] So too is the development of practical and working early
warning systems (as distinct from the failed early warning systems of current
international diplomacy).

On 11 November 1918, at a quarter to eleven in the morning, a German observation post on top of a mine dump near Mons, close to the site of the death of
Private Parr in August 1914, inflicted the last casualties of the First World War,
including one, L/12643 Private Ellison of the 5th Lancers. In consequence, both
Parr and Ellison, the first and the last British soldiers to die in that great
disaster, lie buried in the same graveyard at St Symphorien and not many yards
apart. Their poignant, permanent juxtaposition mutely and sadly poses the central question of that war. What was the result of the millions of deaths that are
jammed between the bookends of those two, facing gravestones? Wilfred Owen,
the British poet who lost his life only seven days before Private Ellison, predicted acidly within the conversations which he and his companions had with
Death. They joked with him; they laughed with him, 'knowing that better men
would come and greater wars'.

The fulfilment of the second part of Owen's prediction has been the whole 20th
century experience of civil and uncivil war. The emergence of the new regime
of human rights suggests that his faith in human nature was not wholly in vain.
All that is now history.

---

13   G. Prins, 'Why adhere to international law?', paper given at the Roeling Com-
     memoration Conference, University of Groningen, The Netherlands, 16 June 1999.

Peering into the new millennium, we might do worse than to consider again Wilfred Owen's prediction from the beginning of this century and ask whether we see grounds upon which we might, with any confidence, base a rebuttal of the second clause and a reinforcement of the first.

IMPLICATIONS FOR PRACTICE

17

REVOLUTIONS IN MILITARY AFFAIRS

Lawrence Freedman

Considerations of future war can easily tend to technological determinism. The latest scientific breakthroughs are noted, their practical applications identified and then their relevance to the standard military tasks of the time considered. Sometimes it becomes apparent that new technologies are so significant that these standard tasks have been rendered either obsolescent or elevated to a quite new status. Operations that would once have been routine become hazardous, while others that could only be imagined suddenly move into the realm of possibility. For those inclined to hyperbole, such step changes in military affairs are defined as revolutionary.

The term revolution in military affairs (RMA) re-entered the vernacular in the 1990s as a result of the Gulf War and the stunning performance of American sensors and precision guidance weapons, and the prospect of this becoming even more stunning when their integration become complete. Forward projections now in the US services concentrate on the impact of information technology on military performance, and I will do the same. However, a few observations on the notion of revolutions in military affairs may be in order beforehand.

The term itself came into vogue in the 1950s largely through Russian commentary on the military consequences of nuclear energy. Historians have used the term to consider the great transformations in the past that changed the whole character of warfare. RMAs for the 20th century would look at the impact of submarines, aircraft carriers on sea warfare and then long-range artillery and tanks on land warfare, and then the implications of air power, the most significant of all developments up to nuclear weapons. Even nuclear weapons would have lost some of their significance had there not been available means to deliver them. It is hard looking back to say that any one of these developments by itself has completely revolutionised warfare, and they can neutralise

G. Prins and H. Tromp (eds.), The Future of War, 229-240.
© 2000 *Kluwer Law International. Printed in the Netherlands.*

each other in their effects, but in various combinations they have progressively transformed its character.

In all of this we can see three basic trends over the past century. First, the reach of military power has been steadily extended. The pattern has been that the most forward units or systems have first been used to scout or spy, because they could not be substantial enough to pack a formidable punch. Then it has proved possible to pack a crude punch and eventually there is a capability to pack a more precise punch. The second trend follows logically from this. As the range has been extended so all aspects of civil society have become steadily more vulnerable to attack. Quite recently, at least in western countries, this has been contradicted, however, by a third trend according to which the degree of dependence upon society as a whole seems to be declining when it comes to waging war. Manpower has become less important, economic mobilisation less relevant, and accumulations of raw power unnecessary as precision takes over from brute force. Most of the West's armed forces have shrunk in size, but become much more professional and better equipped.

The RMA reflects this by offering political leaders an extraordinary attractive option. You can have war without tears. Targets can be attacked with great accuracy over great distances with fewer and fewer troops put in harm's way. The right targets can be chosen because sensors can overcome the obstacles of distance, terrain and climate. This means that not only can casualties on your own side be kept down, but no unnecessary suffering need be caused to the civil society of your opponent. This is war that fits modern values as well as modern methods. It is unfortunately also a war that is unlikely to be fought. To qualify that last sentence there is a fortunate reason why such a war is unlikely to be fought. It provides a formidable deterrent to waging classical warfare against the West. Because such a strategy fits in so well with American predilections and capabilities, and those of its allies, it is now recognised to be a sub-optimal strategy for its opponents.

Up to 1991, American military history gave support to those who claimed it was a flawed and clumsy giant, prone to stumbling. It turned out to be a rather efficient and ruthless giant. From the Gulf War on, gamblers could calculate the odds more realistically and avoid combat of this nature. They may be prepared to take on their neighbours or some interfering regional power, but they will think long and hard before taking on the United States in a full-blown conventional war. This is a game that no-one else can play. The nuclear RMA neutralised itself in other ways, because the capabilities were distributed between two ideological enemies, but the effect was the same. Extensive and expensive preparations were made for a war that could not sensibly be fought.

This means that classical, Clausewitzian wars if they occur at all will probably be those in which the US has scant interest. This is also of course probably true now for nuclear wars. For the moment at least, a critical factor in future wars is to distinguish between those in which the United States will be involved and those in which it will not.

This raises my fundamental objection to the concept of an RMA. The impact of technological developments depends, as I indicated earlier, on the character of the standard military tasks of the time. This depends on what governments (and other political entities) expect to achieve through the development and deployment of armed forces and the interaction of these forces with those of their enemies. The image of deadlock and bitter attrition from the First World War reflected an inability to overcome prevailing military technology, but also the fact that the two forces were evenly matched. The sweeping victory of the Gulf reflected the fact that Iraq was completely outclassed in every department. The Iraqis had, however, just finished a war with Iran which bore some resemblance to the First World War (and went on longer).

It is therefore extremely difficult to consider the future of warfare without taking account of the changing nature of contemporary political affairs. It has, of course, been argued that the same advances in information technology that shape the RMAs are also revolutionising economic and political affairs. After the events of 1998 we might take more care when it comes to glib discussions of the creation of global markets as a result of the extraordinary capacity of traders to communicate with each other without regard to space or time. The financial crisis brought to the fore questions with regard to the redistribution of power resulting from the easy traffic in financial assets across continents, and the determination of those states who feel victimised by this process to regain some control over their currencies. Economies recently celebrated for their emerging status were suddenly in danger of submerging. The results of this power struggle are still uncertain. Nonetheless, these are struggles in which the military instrument itself is irrelevant, while it remains the case that the growing interdependence among the advanced capitalist states renders it less likely than ever that they will contemplate war against each other.

On the other hand, the political fall-out from this crisis indicates the extent to which contemporary conflict is a function of social cohesion. Social cohesion is always sorely tested by economic failure and the incompetent and illegitimate political structures this often revealed. All this suggests that the military question for western states is no longer one of how they might confront an ideological competitor of equivalent capacity, let alone each other, but how they cope with turmoil in and around weak states. The proliferation of weak states reflects the long-term effects of decolonisation combined with the short-term effects of the end of the Cold War. They have already generated a succession of prolonged low-intensity conflicts in and around societies with compound economic, social and political fractures.

Elsewhere I have talked of a revolution in strategic affairs rather than military affairs. This offers no reliable model of future war. The range of potential belligerents covers everything from fanatical terrorists to disaffected great powers, while they might employ a spectrum of means from the improvised explosive device in a shopping mall to guerrilla ambushes to traditional battle to nuclear exchanges. Terrorists might gain access to weapons of mass destruction, while renegade states might insert bombs into public places.

The strategies that the weak have consistently adopted against the strong often involve targeting the enemy's domestic political base as much as his forward military capabilities. Essentially, they involve inflicting pain over time without suffering unbearable retaliation. They often rely on the opponent's intolerance of casualties. This intolerance is more likely if it can be assumed that the stronger force has a weaker stake in the resolution of the conflict. Thus, it did not take many casualties to encourage the US to cut its losses in Somalia. These strategies can also play on the reluctance in the West to cause civilian suffering. Both the Iraqis and the Bosnian Serbs located some of their most important assets close to schools or architectural monuments or in the middle of highly populated areas. In short, whereas stronger military powers have a natural preference for decisive battlefield victories, the weaker are more ready to draw the civilian sphere into the conflict while avoiding open battle.

So the favoured model for western military operations points to their initiation before those of the opponents, a sharp distinction maintained between combatants and non-combatants, and the role of ground forces limited by reliance on stand-off weapons rather than organic firepower, and, in consequence, reduced dependence on logistics. It presumes a conflict that can be decided quickly and unequivocally. In practice, contemporary conflicts have tended to require tortuous and time-consuming coalition building, with negotiations over objectives, rules of engagement and burden sharing. Operations appear likely to be conducted some distance from home, and so are expeditionary in character, relying on whatever forces are available, and putting a great stress on logistics. If they involve sustaining a military presence over an extended area for a long time then an appropriate local logistical network will have to be constructed. Politicians dislike putting troops into exposed settings that they may need to occupy for some time. It is also a task upon which new technologies may have little impact. Yet large numbers and raw military power can be valuable precisely because they are conspicuous. Strength on the ground matters. When conflicts are about the ownership of land, then 'presence' remains a high priority for armed forces.

Furthermore, by their nature these conflicts tend to involve complex interactions with the civil societies of all participants. This will work against attempts to maintain a sharp differentiation between combatants and non-combatants. They tend to irregular war – either at the high end of environmental carnage and mass destruction or the low end of intra-state conflicts and terrorism. These can arise out of conflicts of all shapes and sizes. They point to areas where size measured in terms of input (commitments of regular armed forces) may have little relation to that of the output (social impact).

Future wars may be fought in the desert, as was the case in 1991, providing an effective backdrop for sensors and making it possible to stay clear of populated areas. As likely they will be fought in jungles, forests and cities. Urban combat remains manpower intensive and imposes complicated requirements on targeting and manoeuvring, given the nature of the infrastructure which supports cities and the likely political and symbolic importance of many of the buildings they contain. Consider, for example, the implications of a situation in February 1991 if, instead of retreating in a hurry from Kuwait City, Iraqi forces had decided to make a stand and fight.

One consequence of improved sensors is that aggression should be rendered more difficult as preparations for a major offensive unavoidably become much more transparent and the systems required individually much more vulnerable. However, the problem is less that intelligence agencies will fail to notice a force being prepared to move against a neighbour but that it will not then act. There was no shortage of indicators that Iraq was in a position to attack Kuwait. The reason that so little was done to warn Iraq off was not a lack of information but a complacent assessment of the information and a policy decision about what the US could do in this situation. The result was a need to react to a *fait accompli*, which meant that dislodging Iraq from Kuwait would involve taking the offensive. Domestic opinion, and also allies, required some persuading that this was at all a wise thing to do. Through the wars of the Yugoslav dissolution, the next stage has been advertised well in advance. There has been no reason to be surprised. The preparations and the policy response were still lamentable. With Kosovo there were even promises that the same mistake would not be made again. It was. So, whatever the possibilities for 'real-time' military decision and action, policy formulation and political persuasion tend to take time. The demands of coalition formation mean that the initiative may be difficult to seize from a local aggressor.

Force still has to be despatched. The speed of mobilisation was always recognised to be NATO's basic difficulty in responding in a timely fashion to indicators of imminent Warsaw Pact aggression, leading in the 1970s to fears of being caught by a 'standing start' attack. Not only are 'real-time logistics' impossible, but the advances in the movement of personnel and matériel into battle have not been anything like as substantial as those in mounting operations once they have arrived. The more stand-off weapons can be used the more it may be possible to rely on the far greater ranges of missiles and aircraft from home bases or naval task forces.

The West's interest now lies in the progressive marginalisation of nuclear weapons and other weapons of mass destruction as factors in international politics and even their elimination, in part because of the limits on its freedom of manoeuvre they represent. For a country fearing that it might otherwise be on the receiving end of American military power, the deterrent effect of a nuclear capacity retains a certain attraction. The prospect of a developing Russian inferiority in the most advanced conventional capabilities led to anxiety in Moscow long before the collapse of communism. It has now stimulated a greater readiness in Russia to rely on its nuclear arsenal as the ultimate source of security. The US still has alliance obligations that involve the provision of some form of nuclear guarantee, and it risks its allies and clients following their own programmes if this guarantee is withdrawn.

Even when belligerents start with the intention of confining hostilities to combatants, it is very difficult to prevent a conflict spilling over into civil society.

Attacks on power supplies, communication nodes and the transportation system can all be justified by the need to disable enemy armed forces. Few advancing armies have the time or the inclination to skirt round civilian obstacles in their path. Most seriously, when a country is in desperate straits, and facing defeat in conventional war, attacking the enemy's society can appear as the only option left. All these reasons help to explain why the history of the 20th century war is so discouraging to those who believe that armed force can be used decisively while contained in its effects.

Does information technology offer any ways out of this conundrum? The military issues raised by information are quite different from those associated with other commodities of both an agricultural and industrial nature – fuel, food, spare parts and ammunition. These are finite resources that can only be moved to where they are most needed by specific forms of transportation. There is normally a deficit. Without these commodities an otherwise well-equipped army will become desperate and immobile. This puts a premium on successful interdiction. The interdiction of information is much more problematic. Here we are dealing with the provision of services rather than goods. Information does not directly energise, destroy, shelter or move, but a lack of it can hamper effective operations by disorienting units and their weapons.

The sort of information that previous commanders might have dreamt about receiving in good time will be available almost immediately. The problem is to know what can be known, for this information has to be identified out of all that is being received and stored. It is the familiar intelligence problem of 'noise' magnified many times. It can lead to information dependence, whereby it is assumed that the next bit will provide the final clue and make a difficult decision easier. Intuition and hunch become more suspect for there appears to be less excuse for ignorance. Yet in high tempo war there will be reluctance to wait for even more information and few opportunities for considered reflection of the information as received, or to address the ambiguity that it will inevitably contain. Information overload means that the apparently efficient means of communication will become suspect.

Information is becoming less and less of a privileged resource as more people have more means of tapping into more forms. At times of peace, military-relevant information can be obtained through the civilian sphere and can be shared by friend and foe. Commercial receivers for the NAVSTAR global positioning satellites now far exceed military receivers, and while their accuracy is not as great it is still good. The immediate dissemination of data of a high intelligence value on CNN and other news channels has now come to be taken for granted. Clever legal and technical minds are, of course, attempting to work out how to limit access to these services or deny them at time of war. Such efforts, however, may well be thwarted by the intensity of the commercial imperatives, which will include demands for contractual guarantees, and also the development of competition. The need for commercial outfits to provide an uninterrupted service, unimpeded by considerations of national policy, has limited all efforts at restrictions. If American satellite images come with too many restrictions then it is possible to turn to France, Russia and India. Commercial launches exceeded governmental launches of satellites in 1996 for the first time in history. At the end of 1997 a Colorado company launched the world's first civilian spy satellite atop a Russian rocket. It is claimed to offer military quality resolution.

A September 1997 wargame organised by the US Army featured an enemy with no organic military space capability, but which was able to use commercially available communication and navigational satellites. This highlighted the problems of denying systems to an enemy and not to everyone else: the enemy was able to develop an impressive communications network using cellular phones, which could not be singled out for jamming. Satellite imagery still poses special problems of collection and interpretation, but GPS will go the way of radios, mobile phones and personal computers and become portable and widely available. There are now some 150 million computers existing world-wide while 25 years ago there were barely 50,000. The power of some of the smallest is equivalent to types that not that long ago were subject to the most stringent export licensing controls. We must now be approaching 100 million people on the Internet.

The quality of civilian information systems tends to be so substantial that even military organisations tend to consider buying off-the-shelf. Commanders are also tempted to turn to the BBC rather than wait for crucial information to pass through the military hierarchy and arrive with them in a filtered form. The Pentagon now relies on commercial telecommunication for 95% of its information traffic.

One claim is that the power of modern sensors is such that there is said to be no need to be confused by a fog of war. It might even be possible to answer the problem of 'friction', which Clausewitz identified as one of the most persistent and perplexing features of war. Proponents of the RMA stress the ability to operate with ever more timely and pertinent information and communicate directly, constantly and instantaneously with colleagues and subordinates. This all seems to be overstated. Information flows create their own potential for friction, as too much of the wrong sort of information, or too little of the right sort, is received. The possibilities for misunderstanding and mistakes remain, and the growing dependence upon the management of information means that the impact of any errors may well be magnified. If unreal expectations are created for the conduct of war, commanders and their units will become disoriented not so much because they are at a real tactical disadvantage but because the reality is so different from the 'cyberworld' of simulations and wargaming.

Another problem is that opponents will be attempting to interfere with information systems, either stemming the data flow or substituting inaccurate material. The sophistication and ingenuity of hackers and the inventors of viruses are notoriously impressive. This may well be a growth area for military organisations. Disabling air defence systems, sending missiles off-course, leaving local commanders in the dark and senior commanders confused by interfering with software or causing catastrophic hardware malfunctions have obvious appeal. The fear that this might be done to you is also a powerful motivating force.

There are two reasons for caution here. The first is the unavoidable degree of uncertainty surrounding any attempt to interfere with another's information networks. Have the right systems been targeted? How dependent is the enemy upon them? Might interference become apparent before the critical moment and any damage rectified? Is it possible to become the victim of a double bluff? For these reasons, there will be a reluctance to rely solely on information warfare operations, no matter how brilliant in conception and successful in implementation. Faced with the task of disabling a critical facility, clever and subtle forms of electronic warfare may well seem unnecessarily risky when compared with something cruder, simpler and probably more violent. In short, the multiplication of channels through which information can pass both reduces dependence upon a single channel but also the opportunities to control the flow. There are few information 'choke points', no 'command of info-power' easily obtained, no 'centre of gravity' to be targeted.

Some of the more excitable analysts, noting the importance of complex information systems to all aspects of modern society, have imagined the consequences of their sudden absence, and concluded from this that they have identified a natural target for an inventive and resourceful belligerent. Hence, the great interest in information warfare. Even if there was a serious prospect of designing and mounting a successful strategic information campaign, there could be no guarantee that a victim would respond in kind, but rather with whatever means are available. The countries most at risk are probably those becoming increasingly dependent upon information technology yet still behind in indigenous capabilities. Not surprisingly, given past sensitivities to this issue, Russian generals are particularly concerned about the vulnerability of their country to this sort of attack, and so warn of the risk of a 'strategic' response of a different sort.

This is not to say that attacks on information systems do not now pose serious problems. There are serious difficulties – but they are as likely to stem from the disgruntled employee, or the fraudtser and extortionist, or even the mischievous hacker, than a hostile power or even a terrorist.

The current focus on the capacity to deny information or interfere in some way with information systems risks missing the point. It is obviously appropriate for those responsible for the integrity of these systems to worry about such things, but, in strategic terms, the key issues now revolve around the increasing openness of information and access to information systems. Even before the Internet, new forms of communication were giving rise to new forms of subversive action, as part of the search to disseminate political messages and avoid censorship. Thus, audio tapes were employed during the 1978 overthrow of the Shah of Iran, and videotapes in the mid-1980s Philippine Revolution. More recently, when the Mexican government moved against the Zapatistas, the rebels used laptops to issue commands and the Internet to publicise allegations of government atrocities to gain support from international organisations. In national politics, e-mail campaigns of harassment have been devised and these can be extended internationally. The possibilities grow with the ease of transmission of video and audio material through the Internet.

Information wars tend to be – as much as anything – public relations battles to either gain – or lose – western attention. Precisely because military engagements have become much more discretionary for western countries, belligerents must work hard to persuade them to either get in or stay out. Governments must pay close attention to the quality of rationales for both intervention and non-intervention. If battle is joined, then operations will be judged against political criteria relating to casualties and collateral damage, justice and fairness.

At this point the information age may start to let political leaders down. The high-speed, analytical systems at their disposal may drive them towards certain kinds of decision, but they will always need to take account of aspects which may not be readily quantifiable, such as the morale of forces, the demands of allies, the mood in the United Nations, the state of domestic opinion, the economic implications of resources being expended at a particular rate, and so on. Francis Bacon observed centuries ago that knowledge is power, but information is not knowledge, let alone wisdom or judgment.

The marketing of modern conflicts reflects the extent to which war for western countries is a discretionary activity. For the moment at least they can choose their enemies and are not obliged to fight on anybody else's terms. Yet the terms in which fighting does take place in the modern world is removed from sort of cool, calculating, commercial activity, based on the accumulation and manipulation of information, that modern military managers appear to want to emulate. Even the money manager can be prone to sudden bursts of panic and exaggerated response, relying suddenly on an untutored intuition as much as a knowledge bank and sophisticated mathematical models of risk that should facilitate quick and accurate judgment.

The money managers like the military managers find themselves struggling to comprehend political entities that are fearful, desperate, vengeful and angry, that are struggling to maintain a sense of proportion and clarity of objective. Both may wish to stay clear of the risks such entities pose, yet the more they fly from risk the more the risk keeps on catching up with them. They wish to operate in conditions of restraint yet these conditions can break down in circumstances of political turmoil. The money managers may, in their irrational exuberance, have started to believe in a virtual economy, detached from the real worlds of work and consumption, where the key factors were those they could track on a screen. The military managers should avoid making the same mistake. War is also not a virtual thing, played out on screens, but intensely physical. That is why it tends to violence and destruction.

While the technology of armed force and its forms of organisation may change, its use or invocation still excites emotions and passions that are timeless. Its influence on political events still depends on an actual or demonstrable capacity to damage life and property. There would be reasons for relief if belligerents only targeted information flows. Unfortunately, they will as likely turn to any methods of causing hurt, in an effort to encourage a sense of disproportion in the population and unhinge multilateral coalitions. The revolution in military affairs does not offer the prospect of a virtual war, detached from the things people fight about – territory, prosperity, identity, order, values. It is not the case that in the information age only information matters.

18

THE ART OF MILITARY INTERVENTION

Michael Rose

On 16 December 1998 the US and the UK, in an act of war, struck violently
at Iraq, with the declared intention of degrading and diminishing Iraq's capability to wage a war of mass destruction. It was also hoped that, by such action,
Saddam Hussein might be compelled to abandon his weapons of mass destruction. This limited war aim has, of course, been pursued by the West since the
end of the Gulf War, so far without any successful result. It is my view that
repeated military actions of this sort that we see currently taking place almost
daily in Iraq are the results of confused strategic thinking, for it is pointless
to attempt to obtain goals through limited war means that are properly only
obtained by waging absolute war. There is a risk that such attacks will produce
progressively negative political consequences in the surrounding region, and
that they will also end up by alienating our own public at home. For the continual images on our TV screens of the West's high technology weapons causing
death and destruction to civilians in the Third World, who have already been
reduced to the borders of survival by the imposition of sanctions are not ones
which will be forever contemplated by a civilised people. There is another, and
I believe more far-reaching danger created by these actions, which is that by
firing missiles at Afghanistan, Sudan, Iraq, threatening recently to do so yet
again in Kosovo, we are actually creating a universal culture of violence based
on the false believe that intractable political problems can only be solved by
military force. As Liddell Hart once wrote 'The more I reflect on the experience
of history, the more I come to see the instability of solutions achieved by force'.
Of course, cultures, as any doctor will tell you, have a nasty habit of spreading.
The increasing use of terrorism as a political instrument in the world today
serves to act as a clear warning to those who indulge carelessly in the use of
force.

Since the end of the Cold War, it has been clear that the nature of conflict is
in the process of considerable change. The prospect of major power conflict,

G. Prins and H. Tromp (eds.), The Future of War, 241-249.
© 2000 *Kluwer Law International. Printed in the Netherlands.*

which so dominated our strategic thinking for the past 50 years now seems remote, while regional conflict, possibly including the use of weapons of mass destruction have become more likely. Of course, at the lower end of the spectrum of conflict intercommunal struggle continues to destruct large parts of the globe today. According to the latest figures from the International Institute for Strategic Studies, of the 35 major conflicts taking place in the world today, excluding terrorism, 29 are civil wars. The consequences of these civil wars make chilling reading indeed. There are some 36 million displaced people or refugees, some quarter of a million people are killed in these conflicts each year, of whom half are thought to be children. What is more sinister is the fact that half of them are apparently being killed by other children. There are 55 million Kalashnikovs on the loose in the world today, and a Kalashnikov, unlike a mine, can be used time and time again to kill or maim. Some 2,000 killed or maimed by mines each month, and since 1945 it is estimated that some 22 million people have been killed. All this is happening in a world where there are some 4.5 billion people, and yet within a century the world population will be more like 10 billion. Yet the West already seems incapable of meeting the sorts of challenges to peace and security that we are facing today. We certainly cannot afford to stand aside and hope that political and humanitarian disasters on this scale can be resolved without our involvement. However, it seems less obvious to those who say something must be done that dealing with such complex situations involves rather sustaining the condition of the mankind on this planet through the applications of principles of democracy, freedom and justice than looking for solutions in the belly of an aircraft or from the barrel of a gun. It is quite clear to me, however, that in the future military force will continue to play a very significant part in attempts to bring peace and security to the world. But that military force can only be applied within a credible and achievable political and social framework.

As we come to the end of the 20th century, armies everywhere are in the process of defining their strategies, so that they are better able to respond to the changing nature of conflict. In reviewing these defence strategies, the principal purpose of our armed forces – the defence of our nations – should not be forgotten. It is vitally important that armed forces should always continue to be able to fight at the high-tech, intensive end of the spectrum of conflict, prepare for general war, and then downshift for operations short of war. Wider peacekeeping demands anyway all the discipline, psychologies and technologies of war fighting. But too much emphasis on peacekeeping is surely bad for your military health.

Since 1992 NATO has somewhat belatedly come to realise that its future lies as much in peace support operations as it does in deterring general war. It is a tragedy for the people of the Balkans that NATO remained trapped for so long in the logic of the Cold War, after the Berlin Wall. For it would have been far better in 1992 for NATO to have been deployed as peacekeepers to Croatia and Bosnia, rather than UN forces, which will always be something of a come-as-you-are party. If this had happened, I believe that the war in Bosnia might never have taken place. The UN would anyway have been better suited than NATO, in my opinion, to have implemented the Dayton Peace Accord under Chapter VI arrangements.

As we analyse the changed operational circumstances, which face peacekeepers at the beginning of the next century, and as we define new doctrines and concepts for peacekeeping operations, I believe it is important that we understand the legal and moral basis on which nations have the right to intervene in another nation's affairs. The principle of non-intervention, under Art.2 of the UN Charter, which clearly establishes the equal sovereignty of all nations, remains central to international law. Yet today the international community seems increasingly willing to opt for a policy of political and military intervention, often under Art.39, on the grounds that where nation states no longer exist, where civil wars are in danger of spreading, where there is a dire need for humanitarian aid or where there are gross violations of human rights, then the UN does have a duty to intervene. These are ill-defined criteria and I am not at all sure where they fit into the justification for military intervention in Kosovo.

Many moral questions are also posed by such military interventions. To which crises should the international community respond, and which ones should we ignore? For we cannot act as the policeman of the world everywhere, nor indeed it is appropriate to intervene in all crises. I don't suppose the British army would have been particularly pleased to have seen blue helmets flooding down the Falls Road in Belfast in 1969 at the start of our drawn-out campaign in Northern Ireland, and being told to move over and being regarded as just one more warring party. Nor should we allow the media to make international policy.

The BBC once referred to there being 16 members of the Security Council, the 15 national permanent and rotating members and CNN. Is the international community only to react to those conflicts where the media moguls send their most capable teams and whose slick sound bites and clever camera angles have attracted the concern of the viewer, and therefore hijack the international debate?

The peacekeeping mission in Bosnia was the largest that the world has ever seen. Some 23,500 peacekeepers were deployed in an operation that cost billions of US$, but when General Dallaire asked for 3,000 soldiers to go to Rwanda to stop what was a genuine genocide taking place there, where over one million people were killed, there was no response from the international community. What is the moral basis for such inequality? If we do decide on military intervention, how much can we work towards preventing such terrible situations occurring in the first place – preventative action? Surely we should learn something from the considerable successes of the United States and Scandanavian troops that were deployed into Macedonia in 1993, and who undoubtedly have stopped the war in Bosnia from spreading there. Finally, once we have deployed on the ground, how far should we allow peacekeepers to be caught up in peace enforcement operations, and where do those operations end and war fighting begin?

Last year marked the 50th anniversary of the Universal Declaration of Human Rights, and the Secretary-General of the UN wrote to the Security Council as early as 1993 about Angola, saying that respect for human rights constitutes a vital, indeed a critical component amongst methods to resolve on a long-term basis conflicts of this nature.

It is clear that the international community must develop a more reasoned, morally-based decision-making process and one that is beyond that of narrow self-interest. The emotional response that we must do something, driven by television images, does not provide not a sufficient mission statement for a commander in the field.

Liddell Hart once wrote that 'strategy was the art of distributing and applying military means to fulfil the ends of policy', but in the confused and brutal circumstances prevailing in so much of the world today it is often impossible to define clearly what are the ends of policy. In any military intervention, whether absolute or limited war, the prime requirement is obvious, which is that there must be a clear and unequivocal mandate, which is continuously backed by adequate resources and the political will of the community. It is less clear that in operations short of war that mandate must also define the limitations of the operation as well as the aspirations of the international community. This will prevent confused aims, for example in which the UN Protection Force, an ill-named mission in Bosnia, was often asked to deliver war fighting goals, something which a peacekeeping mission clearly cannot do. A clear mandate is something that military men will always ask for, but which is rarely forth-coming, even less so in an organisation such as the UN, where there are so many nations pursuing their own national agenda. It is, therefore, probably that military men will have to draw their own mandate from what will often be a confusing number of UN Security Council resolutions. In my case, they ranged from 740 to the high 900s, and indeed my predecessor resigned because he could not get a clear mission statement from his political masters. I chose to pluck my own mission statement from these often conflicting resolutions. In my view, the mission of the UNPROFOR in Bosnia was primarily to sustain the people of Bosnia in the midst of a three-sided, drawn out civil war. Secondly, it was to try to bring about the conditions in which there could be a peaceful settlement of that war. Finally, it was to contain the conflict to Bosnia. It is my contention that the UN mission in Bosnia, if judged against these specific tasks, was indeed accomplished in a most heroic way by the 23,500 young men and women who volunteered to go there as peacekeepers, so that others may live better or may live at all. Many of those young peacekeepers – Frenchmen, Englishmen, Dutchmen, Russians – failed to come home at the end of the mission. The opportunities for peace, ignored by the political leaders of Bosnia, can scarcely be blamed on the UN. As we are all only too aware, it is the same political leaders who so often block progress in terms of reconciliation and the introduction of the institutions of democracy and justice in that part of the world today. The suicide rate in Sarajevo is now higher than it was during the war. Nevertheless, the UNPROFOR in Bosnia during its mission did successfully sustain the lives of some 2.7 million people. Over 2,000 metric tonnes of food and fuel and shelter were delivered each day to people who would have died had they not had that aid. This aid had to be delivered across a countryside where all the roads, bridges, tunnels had largely been destroyed. The airlift into Sarajevo, which sustained the lives of the 350,000 inhabitants for two years, was the biggest airlift in history, carried out often under fire, which the Berlin airlift was not.

The second part of the mission, which was also achieved in my view, was the creation of conditions in which there could be some peaceful settlement of the conflict, first by lowering the level of violence. The casualty rate in the war dropped from 130,000 – mainly civilians – in 1992, prior to the arrival of UNPROFOR in 1993. The mission aim was mainly to deliver humanitarian aid, but just by their very presence in 1993 the casualty rate fell to 30,000. By 1994, the year I was there, the figure was 3,000, mainly soldiers caught up in the fighting. Far from presiding over genocide, as many propagandists would have us believe, or perpetuating the suffering of the people, it was the presence of UNPROFOR which stopped that genocide dead in its tracks. It was UNPROFOR that had to implement the Washington Accord, the first necessary step towards the end of that war – by halting the fighting between the Muslims and the Croats. The UN had to implement the Accord in exactly the same way that NATO subsequently had to implement the Dayton Peace Accord, except the UN had to do it in the midst of an ongoing war, with all its civilian responsibilities in the delivery of humanitarian aid, and with half the number of troops. If they had not done it, it would not have been possible to bring about the subsequent conditions for the Dayton Peace Accord. Finally, the conflict was actually limited to Bosnia.

The lesson from all this is that the mandate must be clear, unequivocal and express the limitations of the capabilities of the mission. This will reduce the room for manoeuvre by propagandists and will eliminate the chance of mission creep. It will also allow sensible lessons, rather than false lessons to be drawn from the experience.

In order to achieve the successful outcome of a peacekeeping mission in the new conditions of world disorder, any peacekeeping force will have to be extremely robust in its use of military force. In the circumstances in which they find themselves, peacekeepers today cannot afford to be pacifists. UNPROFOR was no exception. Millions of rounds of small arms, tank armament, artillery and mortars were used, as were air strikes by NATO aircraft. Indeed, the Dutch tank unit, which destroyed five Serb tanks in enforcing the passage of a convoy of aid urgently north-east of Tuzla in the early summer of 1994, fired more rounds and destroyed more enemy tanks than they did in the Second World War. And they were peacekeepers. When the tank commander was asked why he had fired 76 rounds of tank anti-armour shells, he said that was all the ammunition he had. What is certain is that the aid continued in that part of the region for quite a long time afterwards.

However, in any peacekeeping, humanitarian-based mission there will always be limits on the use of force. Indeed, this is what distinguishes it from war fighting. For every time force is used there will be an inevitable halt for the flow of aid, and people at risk will start to die. It is a consideration which all military commanders will have to bear in mind, where the consent for the presence of peacekeepers is patchy or indeed exists at all. The difficult question therefore to answer is how much force can a peacekeeping mission use, even a force like NATO, without crossing the line into war fighting. The answer I believe is less determined by the level of force used than by how it is used, for whenever military force is used it must clearly obey the principles governing the use of force by a peacekeeping mission, something which is not widely understood. In Bosnia, when I called for NATO close air support I was often accused of using pin pricks against the Serbs. This, of course, would have been true if I had been at war. It would have been crazy to use aircraft to take out single tanks in amongst buildings. But I was not at war, I was a peacekeeper whose prime mission was the delivery of humanitarian aid.

In a peacekeeping operation force must be proportional to the aims of the mission. It must be used at a minimum level to achieve a specific aim. It must be used impartially and with due warning. It must never be used in pursuit of war fighting objectives. Force cannot be used to punish an aggressor, to deliver military solutions, such as defending or protecting a civilian population, stopping ethnic cleansing, defending a safe area. Those are war fighting goals. It can merely create the conditions in which there can be a peaceful resolution of the conflict, and it can help the people of that country to survive. At the end of the day, you do not go to war in white-painted vehicles, unless of course you are up here north of the Arctic Circle.

One of the most incorrect and dangerous lessons that is still being drawn from the painful experience of the UN in Bosnia is the assertion that NATO delivered the Dayton Peace Accord by bombing the Serbs into submission in the late summer of 1995. The inference, of course, is that bombing will therefore work in Iraq, Afghanistan, Kosovo etc. Nothing could be further from the truth. Dayton was not merely delivered by NATO bombing. It was delivered over a protracted period of time through a combination of political and military activities, in which of course NATO played a major part. It was of course the UN which sustained the people of that country, and indeed preserved the existence of the state for the period of the civil war. People forget that the Serbs, the dominant military force until 1995, were within 100m of the presidency, controlled 70 per cent of the territory and all the high ground and key terrain in that country. It was the UN that created the necessary conditions by their actions for the final delivery of the Dayton Accord. If we are looking for a decisive military blow being struck against the Serbs, which delivered Dayton, it was of course the attack by the Croatian army through the Krajinas in the summer of 1995, which took much of the land which the Serbs hoped to trade for peace on their terms. Of course, the NATO bombing raids had some impact psychologically on the

Bosnian Serb leadership, but we should not forget the effect of the Rapid Reaction Force's artillery and mortar firing down from the top of Mount Igmon directly onto Serb targets around Sarajevo. The simple read-across of NATO's presumed actions in Bosnia to Kosovo risk bringing about the same sort of disastrous consequences that would have occurred in Bosnia had the UN given way to the Americans over lift and strike in the early years of the Bosnian war. Would the bombing of the Serbs in Kosovo in the autumn of last year, for example, have stopped Milosevic's terrible policy of ethnic cleansing the Albanians from that province? Of course not, he would merely have changed his tactics. Would the bombing have helped the 250,000 refugees, who in the autumn of last year, with the onset of winter, were living on the mountainsides under plastic sheeting? Quite the reverse, because the aid organisations would have had to withdraw prior to that bombing. Would the bombing have had a beneficial effect on the political situation in Bosnia or in Macedonia? We already saw that the sabre-rattling by NATO caused a hardening of the Serb position in the elections in Bosnia in September 1998. Of course, it would ultimately have had a negative consequence on our relations with Russia.

What is clear from everything that I have said so far is that the role of regional organisations, such as NATO, in support of peacekeeping is likely to become more important in the future than it has been in the past. But it is always going to be essential that where are two organisations, such as the UN and NATO, are operating in the same theatre, they pursue the same goals and share the same mandate. We should never allow two organisations to pursue two different mandates, as happened in Bosnia – the UN the peaceful resolution of the problem, NATO a desire to resolve the problem by force of arms. The partiality of NATO, in the way it applied force, I believe was ultimately responsible for the collapse of the peacekeeping mission, and certainly helped to prolong the war.

Thuycidides once commented that it was never sensible to believe the first messenger who arrived with reports of a battle, for it was inevitably that person who had run away from the battle first and would therefore have a highly coloured view of what had happened. In the same way, it is unwise for politicians to believe everything they see on television, or to believe the reports from the battlefield. The internal commission to enquire into the causes and conduct of the Balkan wars of 1912 and 1913 declared that 'the real culprits in the long list of executions, assassinations, drownings, burnings, massacres and atrocities are those who mislead public opinion and take advantage of people's ignorance.' Today, nothing much has changed. The war in Bosnia has been described as a war of information and misinformation, a war for the sympathies of the world, in which the media itself all too often became manipulated by the propaganda machines of the protagonists. One of the greatest failures of the UN in Bosnia was its inability to win the information battle. In any future military intervention, this will be one of the critical areas.

In conclusion, I would make a plea. We should place as much emphasis as possible on pre-emption and prevention in the future when considering military intervention, for it is far better to try to stop these situations in their early days than to have to cope with disasters which occur later on. I also believe that it is important that we do not, as we have done so frequently in the past and have done in Bosnia, put money for reconstruction into a country in the post-conflict phase before we put in the institutions, which will guarantee justice and democracy. If you throw money at a problem without ensuring that it is going to be properly spent or that there is proper accountability and that the people themselves have a say in what is happening, then of course you are merely going to institutionalise corruption.

The road to peace is long and difficult. It is also very expensive. As President Truman once said, 'If you are not prepared to pay the price of peace, then you'd better be prepared to pay the price of war.'

PRACTICALITY, IN SUPPORT OF PRINCIPLES

Klaus-Peter Klaiber

This collection addresses the legacy of a great thinker – Jan Bloch. Therefore, it reflects on the *future* of war. Today, we would call it how to build peace. The contributions in this book range over many aspects of the subject. Let me, if I may, offer some comments.

In Section III one finds some very different approaches to this question. Professor van Creveld dismisses optimism, and leaves us with a hint of pessimism. Dr Luttwak proposes realism – to let wars be fought and won, in the interest of long-term stability. I would like to suggest a middle road – practicality, in support of principles. Let me explain.

Calls to build peace in a variety of ways have been made: through total nuclear disarmament; through a total halt on arms sales to the developing world; by exporting the EU model of integration to the rest of the world; through an invigorated, fully-funded United Nations. These are laudable goals. But even as we are optimistic, let us also be practical. Let us look, for a moment, at the history of this century. In no other century has war been more severely banned. In these past one hundred years, more arms control treaties have been signed, more international organisations created, and more peace groups founded than ever before. It is a cruel irony that the century has also seen more brutal wars, more people killed and more human rights violated than ever before.

A more practical approach suggests, therefore, that, in the future, we will need to be prepared for conflict. We need to understand it; we must build mechanisms to prevent it; and we must be ready and able to manage conflict, when we have no other choice.

How do we understand the future of conflict, if I may be permitted to adjust the title of the collection a little? We are all familiar with the principal changes

G. Prins and H. Tromp (eds.), The Future of War, 251-255.
© 2000 *Kluwer Law International. Printed in the Netherlands.*

that have taken place in the international system over the last decade, so mention here will be brief.

First, more and more conflicts are internal to states, rather than between them. Secondly, civilian populations are suffering from these conflicts more than ever. Thirdly, the political and legal protection that sovereignty offers to a state seem to be eroding. Fourthly, international law is putting new obligations on states to protect their own citizens. And finally, the ubiquitous media – the 16th member of the Security Council – is bringing images of human rights violations to our citizens, and they are demanding action.

So, in a nutshell, this is the *new* problem: today, 350 years after the Westphalia Treaty, we face a dilemma – how to prevent or end crises that cause humanitarian emergencies, while observing the custom of non-interference in the internal affairs of sovereign states? Let me offer a few thoughts.

First, let me address Luttwak's main thesis head on. Indeed, peace is important, wars should end quickly, and the international community shouldn't contribute to extending conflict. If that means not interfering, fine. *But* we cannot stand aside in the face of genocide – even if standing aside brings the war to an end more quickly. We cannot sit on our hands in the face of ethnic cleansing, of mass executions and rapes, of mass terror, of gross violations of human rights. Peace is important – *but peace must come with justice*. It means a messier international system – but it is a system, which follows at least some ethical guidelines. This is the heart of the United Nations system, and we cannot discard that.

My second point flows from this. When we *are* faced with a conflict that requires outside intervention, we simply cannot wait for all the legal and political wrinkles of our *new* system to be ironed out before we take action. When people are dying, where massive human rights violations are taking place, we need to act to stop it, even as we work out the theoretical framework. Theory must not be allowed to prevent necessary action.

In taking action, we *can* effect change for the better. NATO and the rest of the international community acted in Bosnia and Kosovo because it had to, and, in doing so, we charted new political territory. Today, we can see the benefits. We are developing our way politically, legally and militarily, guided by the values of democracy, human rights and the rule of law, which are the basis of NATO's Washington Treaty.

Some people assume that this is a veiled way of giving NATO a role as 'global policeman'. Let me be clear – there will be no 'global NATO'. NATO will always act in the spirit of the United Nations Charter. In Kosovo, for example, the Alliance determined that UN Security Council Resolutions 1199 and 1203, and the likelihood of a humanitarian catastrophe, provided sufficient legal authority for it to act.

Thirdly, as an international community, we need to work much harder to prevent conflicts before they begin. Everybody knew for many years that Kosovo was a powder keg, but the international community did not develop an effective policy to prevent the situation from exploding. We simply must do better.

The European Union has been cited as an example of how economic and political integration can create the conditions for a lasting peace, and thereby prevent conflict. We have to be a little careful of using the EU as a model or as a prototype for export of stability or peace. First, the EU was created in unique circumstances, with an overwhelming threat preventing any internal conflict in western Europe, and with an external superpower ready to provide security.

In fact, the *military* integration and security provided by NATO by 1949 helped to make economic and political integration possible. Put simply, the countries in the Alliance trusted each other totally on the most fundamental issue – national security. This confidence was an indispensable foundation for political and economic integration.

On the other hand, there is no better political and economic model for stability available at this moment. We should therefore explore the EU model to see what characteristics can encourage peace and stability in other parts of the world.

After the end of the Cold War, both NATO and the OSCE have been taking steps to build this kind of military integration and trust right across Europe. The OSCE plays a leading role in the arms control process in Europe, and helps to develop confidence-building measures in potentially tense areas. NATO, too, has been trying to build military cooperation and security across the wider Europe. Through enlargement, for example, we bring three more countries, and some 60 million more people, into a zone in which conflict is now inconceivable.

The Alliance has also set up structures for military cooperation with countries outside the Alliance. The Partnership for Peace Programme now includes 27 countries from central and eastern Europe, including Russia and Ukraine, and even non-aligned nations. Together with the Euro-Atlantic Partnership Council, these structures create a framework within which every country in Europe can come together to discuss security issues, *and* cooperate in solving them. This is historically unprecedented on this continent. And the value of this programme can be seen where it matters most – on the ground. Today, NATO, Russia and 19 other Partner countries are keeping the peace in S-FOR in Bosnia, and a similar formula has been achieved for Kosovo with K-FOR. Again, practical solutions to new problems.

Clearly, NATO's relationship with Russia is vitally important, which brings me to my fourth point, particularly Euro-centric unfortunately. Simply, NATO and Russia must work together to manage conflict. Cooperation between the Alliance and Russia brings enormous resources to bear in solving almost any security challenge, be it crisis management, peacekeeping or proliferation. The progress made together in Bosnia is testament to that potential.

The corollary to this, of course, is that when NATO and Russia work at cross-purposes, it is very difficult to find solutions. Crises can worsen; perhaps even more importantly, crises have the potential to poison the new strategic relationship between NATO and Russia. It is simply *practical* for this relationship to work, and to deepen. It serves the interests of Russia; it serves the interests of NATO; and it serves the interest of peace in the Euro-Atlantic area.

Fifthly, we must build peace by fostering democracy. Many conflicts in Europe and beyond can be traced directly to the absence of democracy and openness. The absence of the pressure valve of democracy can lead societies to explode into violence. Democracies remain far better equipped to deal peacefully with the challenges of modernisation and globalisation, because they provide checks and balances. Open societies are better geared towards change and creative problem-solving – the keys to survival for the next century. Open and free media are the best insurance against the replacement of historical fact with self-serving myths. And it remains a fact that open, multi-cultural societies are the best insurance against excesses of the kind we have seen in Bosnia.

Finally, we have to overcome the old 'zero-sum' perception of the international system, where a political gain for Russia is seen as a loss to the West, and *vice versa*. In today's world, that is simply not the case. The sooner we overcome any mutual suspicions, the sooner we will do what we need to do – work together to solve problems. Of course, overcoming the mutual mistrust between Russia and the West will take time – not least because it dates back far before the Cold War. At the Congress of Vienna in 1815, a messenger approached the famous Austrian statesman, Count Metternich. He said, 'Count Metternich, a tragedy has just occurred! The Russian Ambassador has just died!' Metternich replied, 'I wonder what he meant by that?'

In conclusion, we must fundamentally re-examine the concepts around which our security has been structured for decades. Wherever they remain sound, we must retain them. Wherever they have become dogma, or a shield behind which perpetrators of violence hide, they must be re-examined. Let us build *practical* solutions – that is the best way to justify optimism. In doing so, let us always remember that a security policy that does not take as its point of reference human values and the needs of *people* is worth nothing.

EPILOGUE

What might Jan Bloch make of this? In this book, those who have re-examined his questions on his centenary have come to two broad conclusions about them. One is that – somehow or other – we may have learned from the great and ghastly experiment which Bloch feared and that Europeans have now endured. War, in the massive sense of total war between post-modern states, has now become impossible. But how? And why? The reasons for this are interpreted entirely differently among the contributors, and the differences are instructive, for they map the fault-lines in the 20th century treatment of the social contract; fault-lines whose cracking has defined the promontory upon which we are obliged to stand, facing the millennium.

Three forms of argument are advanced: Some authors see *positive reasons* for transcendence of that stage of modern history in which states, within an international system of states, resolve differences by fighting. In short, the end of the so-called 'Westphalian system' is also the end of major war. War makes the state and the state makes war: so the transcendence of the one leads necessarily to the obsolescence of the other. 'Post-modern' states have – happily – moved closer to the Kantian ideal of perpetual peace. They may fight over quotas for bananas, or the safety of beef, or the role of biotechnology in agriculture, but not by force of arms. That would be just plain silly.

Secondly, and linked, is another sort of reason. Huge military/technological inventiveness has become strategically self-defeating. The means of making major war have exceeded their culminating point of efficiency (a central tenet within the paradoxical logic of war and peace, brilliantly illuminated by Edward

Luttwak in an earlier work).[1] It was already to be seen in Bloch's war. No-one could win; everyone could destroy. It took an external intervention to push matters to a conclusion. Even more so in the Second World War. The nuclear age, coinciding with further technological advance in civil society, making it both more flexible and more fragile, meant that paralysis could be produced in addition to, or as well as massive destruction, as an effect of major war. But to what end? The second case is less a positive argument than *an argument of irrelevance.*

Thirdly, the case of *fear as the spur* was reasserted: the view that the apocalyptic destruction promised by nuclear weapons spreads pervasive political paralysis which is the surest foundation of security in post-war Europe.

Yet war being extruded from within post-modern Europe (for whatever reason) is only party of the story. All authors also agree that it has not shrivelled away. Political violence appears in two forms. One is familiar from other times of great transformation. Frequently the edges of eras are crazed with the violence of irredentism and of dispute over the division of the inheritance from the previous regime. So it is now in continuing wars of identity (as Mary Kaldor has aptly named the recent wars in the Balkans).[2] But beyond the borderlands of the rich world, war is alive and predatory in the killing fields of the poor world; for, secondly, in the 21st century we may, with some unhappy confidence, expect to see more 'frontier brawls or punative operations ... on the frontiers of your extended empire', as Bloch expressed it to Stead during their conversation in 1899.

The boundaries of the late 20th century empire are sharply etched, and war is its starkest cursor. Ours is a world where zones of historically unprecedented peace abut heaving zones of uncivil war. Faced with this, contributors seem broadly to support the view that it is correct for the strong, who are able to do so, to take action to being peace and justice in a realm of war. They also endorse the need to ensure that action is taken in ways which are militarily and institutionally effective and, therefore, if necessary, robust. Motivation for this sentiment is fired by energy welling up from deeper fissures. The titanic

---

1   E. Luttwak, *Strategy: the Logic of War and Peace* (Cambridge MA, Belknap/Harvard, 1987).

2   M. Kaldor, *New and Old Wars*, (Cambridge, Polity Press, 1999).

eruption of creativity which became possible when reason was applied to nature in the late 18th century – creativity which gave us the weapons for Bloch's War and more, as well as the means to construct the comfortable fabric and secular beliefs of modern Europe – has left us obliged to live at the end of the 20th century in a world hauntingly described by Philip Allott '... half-filled with brilliant light and half-filled with terrible darkness ... an age of the Unreason of Reason.'[3] Both light and dark, he argues, are products of the way in which reason was released into common understanding 200 years ago, which is not an argument to pursue in detail here; but noteworthy is the consequence, that the dialectic has, at century's end, left us a legacy whose inner contradictions mirror itself.

The threat to global security from the continuation of uncivil wars, where political violence merges with crime, is seen to be intolerable. The century which was shaped by the war that Bloch so accurately predicted in form and likelihood has, at its end, seen a reassertion of the principles of the Rights of Man at the moment of the downfall of totalitarianism within Europe. What splendid synergy! The horror of total war was the source of energy and motive for the great mid-century efforts which gave us both the UN and the Nuremberg Principles. These, especially the latter, have become the underpinning for the attack on war in the poor world beginning to be mounted from the strongholds of the cosmopolitan-minded at its end.

However, there are two different sorts of action, which can be taken in respect of wars between 'have-nots' and 'have-nots'. One is to intervene and, having intervened, to take more or less strenuous action to cause the fighting to stop. The authors recognise that the scope of United Nations peacekeeping in blue helmets is much constrained in post-Cold War circumstances. Broadly, they subscribe to the belief that vigorous action based on firm political decision is sensible. But, equally, the palliative qualities of any form of military intervention are recognised. Therefore, the choice to intervene pre-emptively and non-militarily – to change the economic and social context of conflict – is widely signalled. We shall see whether this rediscovered commitment to cosmopolitanism could form the grounds for global confrontation with Asian states and societies (notably China) that do not share either the philosophy or acceptance

---

3   P. Allott, 'Eutopia: a Revolution in the Mind'. Mss. p. 172 (forthcoming).

of the rights of humanitarian intervention world-wide by those who do espouse them.

In John Keegan's *tour d'horizon*, the conclusion is reached that another form of intervention, less likely to trigger a new set of geo-political confrontations, is especially prescribed, namely abolition of the international arms trade. His view has considerable contemporary resonance with the general public. Public opinion was instrumental in propelling governments into agreeing the Ottawa Convention which restricts to some degree the manufacture, stockpiling and use of landmines. Equally, a rising crescendo is to be heard, demanding restriction in the manufacture and relatively unhindered sale of so-called 'light arms'. The term sounds almost innocuous: 'light' is surely of lesser threat than 'heavy'? Yet these are the type of weapon – Kalashnikov assault rifles, pistols and other hand-guns whose only use is the killing of people – which in their robust, even rusty millions, kill directly more people in the world today than exotic planes and missiles ever do.[4]

Therefore a current trend in American courts is noteworthy. Attempts are proliferating to follow the success of pinning upon tobacco companies the costs for the consequences of the use of their products. As a result, in Detroit, the District Attorney is pursuing hand-gun manufacturers to pay for the costs of the use of their products. The citizens of an American city with a high rate of hand-gun murder and wounding may, perhaps, look across the lake to Canada, a state where citizens do not run the risks forced upon inhabitants of Detroit. In 1999 the original mass-producer of guns, the Colt Company, decided to withdraw from the civilian market for hand-guns, referring to fear of such litigation as its reason. Such domestic precedents are interesting indicators of international moves towards probibition.

Keegan's suggestion raises the wider question of the degree to which the 21st century is likely to be one in which a political agenda of abolition is either possible or appropriate. The Cold War era carries within it the Pugwash declaration of Russell and Einstein in 1956. It is emblematic of opposition to its deepest tendencies and it found partial expression in the Partial Test Ban Treaty.

---

4   J. Boutwell and M. Klare, *Light Weapons and Civil Conflict: Controlling the Tools of Violence* (Carnegie Commission on Preventing Deadly Conflict Series, AAAS, 1999).

Einstein and Russell believed that there was no moral or practical way in which humanity could trust itself to live with nuclear weapons. We are too monotonously creatures of anachronism, who cannot usually summon up the mental force to make ourselves think in time in new ways for new circumstances. The normal condition of humanity is to barge into the future facing backwards, which, they thought, might easily become fatal. In the event, we survived, but only by a whisker. While public consciousness registers the Cuban missile crisis as having been the most dangerous moment, it has recently become evident that the Able Archer episode, in November 1983, at the depth of the second Cold War, brought us much closer to the brink.[5]

---

5   'Able Archer' is the code name of a regularly repeated command post exercise to rehearse nuclear release procedures. From 1981 to 1984, under Operation RYAN, initiated by its then Chief, Yuri Andropov, the KGB had instructed operatives to keep special watch for signs of western mobilisation. It was top priority in 1982. Now General Secretary, Andropov's anxieties were further inflamed in 1983 by the combination of Reagan's Orlando speech about the Evil Empire on 8 March, his 'Star Wars' announcement on 23 March, and, on 1 September, the shooting down of the Korean airliner KAL-007 trespassing over a Soviet missile submarine bastion. RYAN was given further increased priority. The failing Andropov took a morbidly apocalyptic view. In November 1983, US bases were already on heightened alert following the bombing of the marine barracks in Lebanon. Russia expectation (conveyed in documents leaked by Oleg Gordievsky) was that a pre-emptive nuclear attack would most likely be initiated under cover of a military exercise. 'Able Archer' took place from 2-11 November 1983 in a context of high Soviet anxiety about American intentions. In response, major elements of Soviet forces in the GSFG and elsewhere, including nuclear forces, went onto alert. On 14 November, the first of the Cruise and Pershing II missile deployments to Europe arrived in the UK. Robert Gates (later Director of the CIA) reports all this and a British intelligence assessment, reviewing information supplied by its source, Oleg Gordievsky, that 'Able Archer' gave rise to exceptional anxiety within the Warsaw Pact and that they were not crying wolf. Yet at the time, US intelligence failed to grasp that fact. See R. Gates, *From the Shadows* (New York, Simon & Schuster, 1996), p. 270-77; C. Andrew and O. Gordievsky, *KGB: the Inside Story of its Foreign Operations from Lenin to Gorbachev* (London, Hodder & Stoughton, 1990), pp. 499-501; C. Andrew, *For the President's Eyes Only: Secret Intelligence and the American Presidency from Washington to Bush* (London, Harper Collins, 1995), pp. 475-77. 'Able Archer' *plus* RYAN *plus* US ignorance of the former's effect on Soviet paranoia made 1983 the most dangerous year, in Mr Gates's opinion. We are grateful to Christopher Andrew and Robert Gates for conversations on this subject and to Mary Bone and Paul Rogers for further assistance. For further discussion, see G. Prins, 'The four-stroke cycle in security studies', 74 *International Affairs* no.4, pp. 781-

Forty years after the Einstein/Russell Declaration, the International Court of Justice ruled that the use or threat to use nuclear weapons was illegal. It was a land-mark judgement and in 1999 it was used successfully in another land-mark case. The jury in a Scottish court, under direction from the Sheriff, acquitted Angie Zelter, an anti-nuclear campaigner accused of criminal damage to test facilities relating to nuclear ballistic missile carrying submarines. While freely admitting her act of criminal damage, Ms Zelter's successful defence was that she honestly believed herself and others to be at risk of crime. Her own crime should be excused on the ground that it was committed in order to draw attention to (and thereby help to prevent) commission of a greater crime.

On 5 December 1996, General Lee Butler, formerly Commander of the Strategic Command of the USAF and sixty other retired officers issued a Declaration which endorsed the finding of the Canberra Commission which had called for nuclear abolition. They stated the political case towards the same end as Ms Zelter with her hammer in a Scottish loch. Plainly there is an accelerating tendency to put legal distance between humanity and the nuclear age.

The choice of practical and reasoned idealism (the very label that Bloch affixed to himself in his conversation with Stead) seemed to be between abolition and death. The moral choice seemed to be the same, with the proviso, argued eloquently and, unknowingly at that darkest time, by Jonathan Schell that moral atrophy, and eventual death, would come from continuing possession of nuclear weapons, without their use, as reliably as their use would give the planet back to the grasslands and the insects.[6]

With respect to chemical and biological weapons, the end of the century has witnessed, likewise, but on a less immediately apocalyptic scale, proposals for abolition. Therefore, if one assumes that there will continue to be a positive attraction in continuing to have such arsenals – and this is a large assumption – the choice in the 21st century will likely be the same as that with which we are now familiar: between generalised competition, expressed as localised arms races which result in general patterns of regionally specific deterrence or an attempt to produce *ex cathedra* regimes of control, and abolition.

808.
6   J. Schell, *The Fate of the Earth* (London, Jonathan Cape, 1982).

To do this, as during the 20th century, begs the question of agency: *quis custodiet custodies*? Hitherto, the Athenian view, delivered coldly to the Melians before they annihilated them, has provided the answer: 'the strong do what they have the power to do and the weak accept what they have to accept ... our knowledge of men leads us to conclude that it is a general and necessary law of nature to rule wherever we can.'[7] Should one still agree with Stanley Hoffmann's statement in 1981 that 'the drama of international politics is that there is, as of now, no generally accepted alternative to Machiavellian state-craft'?[8]

A common ground of evidence adduced to suggest that the Melians' concern with fair-play and justice has advanced against the machiavellian Athenians is the creation of the UN. Yet it is not evident that the UN is likely or able to adopt the role of overseer without fundamental reconstruction. The authors have noted in several places that only the shock of major war galvanises major effort to find or make alternatives. The Cold War ended without such a shock, mercifully; yet one ironic penalty of this manner of survival has been that we must soldier on into the new century with a UN forged and shaped to the needs of the end of the war before last. Its Charter is plainly an anachronism today. It awkwardly juggles an evident desire to promote human rights, expressed in the cosmopolitan sense, with the realities of state-centred power politics in the 1940s. So, both by merely existing, and by enunciating those human rights, it has some continuing value. But, equally plainly, we cannot change it in substance without risking its general collapse. Our international institutions are egg shell strong. That we live with this dilemma and this anachronism and these security problems is simply the price of our escape from Bloch's century. Compared with what might have been, it is not much to endure. At least – at priceless, very least – we may raise a cautious and salutary toast to Bloch's centenary in the knowledge that we have been given a chance to try again not given to the 200 million victims of 'democide' –the killing of its own citizens by authoritarian governments – since he wrote.[9]

At Bloch's centenary, the dilemma over what to do with the UN is one illustrative aspect of a larger hiatus. The international system – meaning the West-

---

7   Thuycidides, *The Peleponnesian War,* Bk V, translated by Rex Warner (Harmondsworth, Penguin Books, 1954), pp. 360, 363.
8   S. Hoffmann, *Duties beyond Borders* (Syracuse, Syracuse University Press, 1981), p. 24.
9   R. Rummel, *Death by Government* (New Brunswick, Transaction, 1994), pp. 31-43.

phalian international system of nation states – plainly neither has nor can have again that absolute sway which shaped Bloch's century; but the future global civil society the flickering first sparks of whose fires are to be seen in the 1999 Kosovo-Pinochet nexus, does not yet burn brightly enough to drive away the cold and dark. Such a nascent global society has, as its orienting distinguishing feature the fact that it takes the individual as its point of reference. It may seem to be new, but in fact it is rather old; for there has been an earlier systematic attempt 'to institutionalise the means of violence in such a way that the unaccountable quality of state violence and the bellicose anarchy among states typical of the Westphalian model are overcome.'[10] It was the Philadephian system upon which Tom Paine, with his sharp pen, described the ideal and with his compatriot rebels, grounded the reality of the American republic. Its pivot, ironically and now bitterly for the beleaguered citizens of gun-infested Detroit, was the Second Amendment: ' A well-regulated Militia, being necessary to the security of a free state...' The National Rifle Association may have chosen to forget or to ignore the vital first clause which conditions the right of citizens to bear arms, but it reminds us at the end of Bloch's Century that the United States which is now among the oldest of states with continuously applied constitutions and that the Philadelphian premise of America chimes loudly with the axiom of emergent global civil society.

What is to be done, as Lenin might have asked at this revolutionary hour, and as Professor Susan Strange did in her last, posthumously published essay?

The UN is a mid-century child of its time, and could not be other than primarily responsive to the demands of state power. To be sure, the drafters of the Charter have included references to higher priorities: they are there in the Preamble, where the reaffirmation of faith in fundamental human rights comes immediately after the aspiration to save succeeding generations from the scourge of war and before acknowledgement of equal rights of nations large and small. It is also present in sleeping chapters, notably Chapters XII that set up the international trusteeship system. While we may expect and hope for creative reinterpretations, which will align the UN Charter and organisation with the emerging enforceable

---

10 J. Keane, *Reflections on Violence* (London, Verso, 1996), pp. 45-6. See also, D.H. Deudney, 'The Philadelphian system: sovereignty, arms control, and the balance of power in the American states-union, circa 1787-1861' *International Organization*, 49, 2, (Spring, 1995), pp. 191-228.

human rights agenda, there should be no illusion that such moves are in any sense acts of fundamental reform. They are stop-gap measures: desirable, necessary but stop-gap, nonetheless. They are also part of the failure of the Westphalian system to protect in any powerful way the interests of two-thirds of humanity (two-thirds at least, depending on where you draw boundary lines) who live at risk of the continuing scourge of war in the ways foreseen and agreed among the authors in this collection, and grimly documented in Rummel's catalogues of 'democide'.

Of what is this an instance? Strange believes that the state-centered system is misnamed; not Westphalia; rather Westfailure.[11] It has failed to protect people from war, and failure is also its record in two other fundamental dimensions of global society.

The Westphalian system has fallen short of the mark when asked to deliver a regime for the effective management of the global financial system. Global Keynesianism has proved to be too hard to do. On the 20th century record, the degree of management which Keynesianism alone possessed, might have given the world financial system positive strategic direction, or buffering under stress and instability. Instead, as Charles Kindleberger famously observed in his account of the inter-war depression, it was '... so wide, so deep and so long because the international economic system was rendered unstable by British inability and American unwillingness to assume responsibility for stabilizing it ...'[12] *Laissez faire* was *laissez pourrir*. Strange sees no evidence that things are anything other than worse at century's end, because the intermingling of the financial and information systems mean that there are not even competently empowered, identifiable actors capable of taking decisive action as was the case in 1929.

Nor has the Westphalian system served the planetary interest well. The size of the Antarctic ozone hole; the melting of polar sea-ice; die-back of coral reefs; the rates of global temperature increase; the decline in the five major pelagic fisheries are key indicators of global environmental stress. All are worsening.

---

11   S. Strange, 'The Westfailure System', 25 *Review of International Studies* 3, 1999, pp. 345-54.
12   C. Kindleberger, *The World in Depression 1929-1939* (London, Allan Lane, 1973), p. 292.

The ozone diplomacy of the 1980s was welcomed as the herald of a new sort of international politics tuned to these new sorts of global problem. It was followed by major environmental set-piece conferences. But they have been long on words and short on effective actions. Clever devices for reduction in the emission of ozone-destroying gases, or for the trading of carbon emissions, have been thought up; but the Westphalian system has not proved capable of generating the political will to put them into effect.[13]

Thus, the net result of much-vaunted ozone diplomacy, culminating in the Toronto Protocol, has been far less than hoped for: global rates of emission of CFCs continue to rise, and CFCs are, after narcotics, by value, the second ranking smuggled commodity entering Florida. The Rio Earth Summit in 1992 was windy, but burned gallons of jet-fuel to allow heads of state that opportunity to blow off. The hard, simple issues, such as agreeing an Earth Charter, were avoided. A western diplomat was heard to say before going that 'we are not going down there to be held up by a bunch of highwaymen'. No hand-outs of conscience money. The Kyoto review meeting was fractious and inconclusive. It was only when, at the Buenos Aires meeting in November 1998, several of the major multinational energy companies – the non-state powers too long invisible to the simple black-and-white Westphalian way of thinking – changed sides and saw their own best interests in the promotion of greenhouse gas emission control that anything much at all began to happen. Little and late.

Little has been done to address fundamental future threats to security in the 21st century in any of these three areas; 'From a globalist, humanitarian and true political economy perspective, the system known as Westphalian has been an abject failure', writes Strange, nor does she see any likely signs of either political will or reforming capacity to be present within the system. Yet even were that will present, the structural contradictions within the 'Westphalian' system strain against successful reform.

In 1758, Emer de Vattel described a bargain that seemed wholly reasonable when western Europeans felt closer to the personal insecurities of a state of

---

13 An attempt to force attention to be paid to environmental stress by extending the well familiar concept of national interest into planetary interest, seeking to capture the triggering ability of the Westphalian lesser for the benefit of the planetary larger is made in (ed.) K. Graham, *The Planetary Interest* (London, UCL Press, 1999).

nature. 'Nations or States are political bodies, societies of men who have united together and combined their forces, *in order to procure their mutual advantage and security* (*'leur salut et leur avantage, à forces réunies'* emphasis added).' The resultant composite creation became animated with their energy: 'it thus becomes a moral person which has understanding and will, and is competent to undertake obligations and to hold rights.' From these proceed the laws of nations ('...Law being nothing other than the ability to do what is morally possible, that is to say what is good, that which conforms to Duty (*Devoir*)'.) The consequence of that bargain has proven to be fateful since 1789, because, this ambitious analysis all being agreed, '... it becomes necessary to establish a public authority to order and guide what each person should do relative to the objectives of the union. That Political Authority is *Sovereignty*.' Its impact is inescapable: '... by the act of civil or political association, *each citizen submits himself to the authority of the whole body*' (emphasis added).[14]

It is a fine bargain, so long as those men continue with a shared commitment to and vision of their creature, the Nation or State; for, in those circumstances, the union can be maintained which bonds internal rights of national self-determination (upon which the international legitimacy of the state ultimately depends) to what Stanley Hoffmann terms 'cosmopolitan concerns that transcend states' rights.'[15] But in the 20th century, as Rummel's statistics show, the connective tissue linking these two has been systematically torn apart; and, as the authors in this collection seem generally to fear, the 21st century will experience much more such injury. Human rights have become the *fin de siècle* issue for 'the collision between man as a citizen of his national community and what could be called an incipient cosmopolitanism'.[16]

What is to be done, indeed? The practical choice now is no different from that a century ago. Either the future threats to security will be pre-empted by powerful actions driven by determined political will, or the crises will be dealt with reactively, as has usually been the case in the past. Bloch's predictions and

---

14 E. de Vattel, *Le Droit des Gens. Ou principes de la loi naturelle appliqués à la conduite et aux affaires des Nations et des Souverains* (1758), Preliminaires ¶ 1,2; Liv I, Ch 1 ¶ 1,2 Facsimile of original reproduced in Vol. I, Carnegie Institution of Washington, 1916; author's translations.
15 Hoffmann, *loc.cit.*, pp. 69-70.
16 Hoffmann, *loc.cit.*, p. 95.

Bloch's century should therefore remind us of the dreadful costs attached to that latter choice.

In order to begin to map out a strategy for security in 21st century circumstances of revised, post-Westfailure power relationships, the first thing to establish is that the inherited contradiction is not pre-ordained. The dismal and tiring zig-zag in the dialectic can be deflected. Under conditions not yet prevailing, but suddenly, and maybe for the first time, not inconceivable, the rupture between states' rights and human rights – so deep and bloody in this century – can be healed with transformation of both and without the diminishment of either. With effort, we can perceive grounds in practical reason and describe them in practical theory, upon which we may build a practical political alternative – a Philadelphian alternative – to Machiavellian state-craft, and on the way, surprisingly, discover another answer to Hoffmann's 1981 question.[17]

The nub of the issue is whether the internalised legitimation of patterns of social power in Vattel's bargain is self-willed or imposed. There really is a world of difference – Athenian to Melian in distance – between a moral imperialism thrust upon resentful serfs by philosopher-kings and the construction of a shared, cosmopolitan standard of global civil society. The basis of both national self-determination and of cosmopolitanism is the same: a sense of community shared to a degree which implies *obligation*. Obligation is a projected moral force and action that describes social space by inclusion and which stands in contrast to a social order whose boundaries are etched under the countervailing pressures of opposing claims of rights.

What distinguishes the national and the cosmopolitan is simply scale – two sibilant words that span the dark terrain at the end of the Westphalian system.

The Old Testament view was that where there is no vision (meaning shared, collective vision), the people perish. In Ireland, the Balkans, the Middle East, North-East, West, West-Central and East Africa, in Kashmir, Korea, Sri Lanka or Burma, in implosive, internecine and uncivil civil wars among peoples with colliding micro-visions of incompatible identities, the later 20th century has

---

17 Practical theory is the theory of willed action: the definition is further explained in Philip Allott's earlier book, *Eunomia: New Order for a New World* (Oxford, Oxford University Press, 1990), ¶ 2.52, pp. 32-33.

provided ample, jagged illustration of the proposition that scale matters. If enough of humanity could only reimagine the level of highest personal political and social relevance in a manner that is congruent with cosmopolitan needs, the warring microvisions could be over-ridden. But we are still far from that utopia.

Enlightenment thought, well expressed and publicised in Vattel's book, held the view of there being two worlds, one internal, the other external; one private, the other public. The worst of human behaviour, including the pervasive cruelties of uncivil war, brews within and wells up from the fissures between the two: barbaric and uncontrolled behaviour appearing from an un-policed no-mans-land, like the gas-clouds must have seemed to uncomprehending and ill-protected soldiers when first they appeared in the Ypres Salient during Bloch's War.

The tension in the handling of human rights in the UN Charter, juggling across the private and public realms already mentioned above, serves as clear illustration of the provisional, the stop-gap and ultimately only partially successful manner in which the 20th century has confronted the consequence of this dualism in its world-view. Yet, at century's end, forced by revulsion at what the television pictures of massacre and misery show, this is the chosen ground on which we are trying to force a transformation. How may it be handled?

The starkness in the choices has been illustrated in the divergent approaches taken among the authors in this collection. Certainly, one could try to push out further across no-mans-land, and refurbish, and string with lights and beacons, a bridge of international law to which hapless, helpless victims might try to stagger for sanctuary. That is what we have done since the St Petersburg conventions of 1868 first sought to ameliorate the cruelty of war by banning expanding bullets. But a bridge-building approach to human rights, by its very nature, has no effect on the terrain that it spans; in a way it reinforces the dualism by being an exception to it.

Authors in the collection are sensitive to there being new material sources of power which may be plugged into this task. The dualism within the Westfailure system's world-view made us oddly unable to recognise three new features of the post-Cold War world. The first was the arrival of the new globally active threats: they concerned individuals deeply but privately and did not respond well to national security analysis or action. The second was the arrival of non-state actors in profusion – from multi-national corporations to new and strangely powerful pressure groups, often focussed upon those threats. The third was their power source. The democracy movement among the students in Tienanmen Square used fax machines to breach the walls of silence with which the communist authorities sought to stifle them. The Chiapas rebel movement in Mexico moved up a level as technology permitted and used the Internet to find supporters and to organise actions, as well as to broadcast information. The same explosion of computing power and of 'connectivity' underpins the creation of global financial markets which behave with a rollicking disregard for the leaden-footed, geographically rooted formal supervisory agencies, as Susan Strange has described in her later work.

On the one hand, the frenzied trading of Internet stocks in the summer of 1999 has an eery resonance with the frenzy of trading RCA (Radio Corp of America) stocks in the summer of 1929.[18] It has been estimated that information technology activities account for about 30% of the growth in the United States' longest bull market since the Great Crash of 1929. But, in contrast to a radio corporation, IT is an embedded aspect of most areas of the contemporary world economy: there is a real economic value buried somewhere there. Nor is it by any means fully developed. To date, only about one-third of humanity has yet made a telephone call; so the potential for this truly unprecedented phenomenon of global connectivity to be harnessed to an articulated global consciousness cannot yet be gauged precisely, but may be confidently expected on the evidence of the last five decades in the western world; and it will be there whenever and however the stock-market 'adjusts' itself for the new century.

Thus, facing the new millennium, humanity has a future potential form of being as an inter-active and self-conscious community: the ideal of a community which is not riven by the internal/external dualism of the last two centuries can be conceived by practical theory and can be created, This ideal is one within which the bargain of the social contract between the individual and the group can be restruck in a manner that obviates the need for Vattel's detour into subordination

---

18 J.K. Galbraith, *The Great Crash 1929* (1954) (Harmondsworth, Penguin, 1977), p. 40. On the occasion of the award of an honorary degree at the LSE in 1999, Professor Galbraith remarked that whenever there was anxiety about the stock market, sales of his book about the Great Crash rose; and that latterly they had soared, calling for a reprint. See also, D. Hughes, 'Galbraith warns on markets "insanity"', *Sunday Business*, 29 August 1999.

of individual freedom to state sovereignty. In practice, the constraints of sovereignty have become irrelevant for those among the richest, luckiest third of humanity who, in Anthony Gidden's memorable phrase, 'ride the juggernaut' and whose intimate lives are already lived in a fashion which defies – actually ignores – time and space.[19] A central challenge of the next century is to ensure that by 2099, at Bloch's bicentenary, the war-extruding powers of the recent past in Europe, which as this collection attests, appear to have broken and banished the forces which drove Bloch's century of war, have become uncontroversially universal.

Bloch's tragedy was that of any unheeded messenger. He did not live to experience the full frustration of the failure of the Hague Conferences to derail the Schlieffen Plan, nor the bitterness in fulfilment of his expectation, hinted in his conversation with Stead, that humanity would only come to his point of view, finding it to be true, after wading through the morass that he predicted.

Constitution of a new social contract between individuals and superordinate power is exactly what we see occurring in the vibrant development of customary international law at century's end. One may suspect that Bloch also, were he alive today, would find such indicators – first flickerings of new light – to be significant. Our challenge, as his successors, is to find the moral courage, generosity of vision and philosophical self-confidence to translate that intellectual conviction into practical action. If we can make the most of the global revolution in communication, we can belt our vision of global civil society into a sturdier vehicle than was ever available before. That is indeed unique. It need not be the fire (again) next time.

---

19   A. Giddens, *Consequences of Modernity* (Cambridge, Polity Press, 1990).

INDEX

prepared by Zuzana Olšová

NIJHOFF LAW SPECIALS

NIJHOFF LAW SPECIALS